China's Economic Engagement in Africa

Sezgi Cemiloğlu

China's Economic Engagement in Africa

A Case Study of Angola

PL ACADEMIC RESEARCH

Bibliographic Information published by the Deutsche Nationalbibliothek
The Deutsche Nationalbibliothek lists this publication in the Deutsche Nationalbibliografie; detailed bibliographic data is available in the internet at http://dnb.d-nb.de.

Zugl.: Bonn, Univ., Diss., 2015

Library of Congress Cataloging-in-Publication Data
Names: Cemiloğlu, Sezgi, 1982- author.
Title: China's economic engagement in Africa : a case study of Angola / Sezgi Cemiloğlu.
Description: New York : Peter Lang, 2015. | Includes bibliographical references.
Identifiers: LCCN 2015042613 | ISBN 9783631670354
Subjects: LCSH: Economic development--Angola. | Angola–Relations–China. | China–Relations–Angola. | Angola–Economic conditions–21st century.
Classification: LCC HC950.Z9 .E442 2015 | DDC 338.9673–dc23 LC record available at http://lccn.loc.gov/2015042613

D 5

ISBN 978-3-631-67035-4 (Print)
E-ISBN 978-3-653-06244-1 (E-Book)
DOI 10.3726/978-3-653-06244-1

PL Academic Research is an Imprint of Peter Lang GmbH.

Peter Lang – Frankfurt am Main · Bern · Bruxelles · New York · Oxford · Warszawa · Wien

This publication has been peer reviewed.

www.peterlang.com

to my parents and my sister

Table of Contents

List of Figures

List of Maps

List of Tables

List of Abbreviations

ADPA	African Diamond Producers Association
AFDB	African Development Bank
AGOA	African Growth and Opportunity Act
ANIP	*Agência Nacional de Investimento Privado*
ASB	*Alcatel Shanghai Bell*
BFA	*Banco de Fomento Angola*
BP	British Petroleum
BPI	*Banco Português de Investimento*
CACEM	China Association of Construction Enterprise Management
CAMCE	China CAMC Engineering Co. Ltd
CAN2010	*Coupe d'Afrique des Nations de Football 2010*
CATIC	China National Aero-Technology Import and Export Corporation
CATTF	China Africa Think Tank Forum
CCB	China Construction Bank
CCCC	China Communication Construction Company
CCTV	China Central Television
CEIEC	China National Electronics Import and Export Corporation
CFB	*Caminho de Ferro de Benguela*
CFHC	Chung Fong Holding Company
CFM	*Caminho de Ferro de Moçâmedes*
CIF	China International Fund
CITCC	China International Telecommunication Construction Corporation
CITIC	China International Trust and Investment Corporation
CMIC	China Machine-Building International Corporation
CMEC	China Machinery Engineering Corporation
CNOOC	China National Overseas Oil Company
CNPC	China National Petroleum Corporation
COVEC	China Overseas Engineering Group
CR20	China Ferrovia
CRBC	China Road and Bridge Corporation

CRCC	China Railway Construction Corporation
CRI	China Radio International
CRSC	China Railway Signal and Communication Corporation
CSIH	China Sonangol International Holding Ltd.
DRC	Democratic Republic of Congo
EDEL	*Empresa de Distribuição de Electricidade*
EIA	Energy Information Administration
EITI	Extractive Industries Transparency Initative
Endiama	*Empresa Nacional de Diamantes*
Exim Bank	Export-Import Bank of China
FAO	Food and Agriculture Organization of the United Nations
FILDA	*Feira Internacional de Luanda*
FNLA	*Frente Nacional de Libertação de Angola*
FOCAC	Forum on China-Africa Cooperation
GAT	*Gabinet de Apoio Técnico*
GDP	Gross Domestic Product
GOCC	Guangdong Overseas Construction Corporation
GSA	Global Mobile Suppliers Association
IGA	*Instituto Geológico de Angola*
IMF	International Money Fund
INE	*Instituto Nacional de Estatística Angola*
IR	International Relations
ITEL	*Instituto Nacional de Telecomunicações em Angola*
KBR	Kellogg Brown & Root
LIBOR	London Inter-bank Lending Rate
LNG	Liquefied Natural Gas
LTE	Long Term Evolution
MPLA	*Movimento Popular de Libertação de Angola*
MPS	Ministry of Public Safety
NGN	Next Generation Network
OECD	Organization for Economic Co-operation and Development
ODA	Official Development Assistance
ONGC	Oil and Natural Gas Corporation
OPEC	Organization for Petroleum Exporting Countries
PIB	Program for Public Investment
PPP	Power Parity Per Capita

PRC	People's Republic of China
SADC	Southern African Development Community
SAIC	South African Indian Congress
SAP	Structural Adjustment Programme
SCG	Shanghai Urban Construction Group
SINOMACH	China National Machinery Equipment Import and Export Corporation
Sinopec	China Petroleum & Chemical Corporation
Sodiam	*Sociedade de Comercialização de Diamantes de Angola*
Sonangol	*Sociedade Nacional de Combustíveis de Angola*
SOOG	Sinopec Overseas Oil and Gas
SSEC	Sinopec Shanghai Engineering Company
SSI	Sinopec Sonangol International
TPA	Angolan Public Television
UAE	United Arab Emirates
UK	United Kingdom
UN	United Nations
UNITA	*União Nacional para a Independência Total de Angola*
UNDP	United Nations Development Programme
US	United States
VoIP	Voice over IP
WiMAX	Worldwide Interoperability for Microwave Access
WTO	World Trade Organization
ZEE	*Zona Económica Especial*

Deutsche Zusammenfassung Das Wirtschaftliche Engagement Chinas in Afrika: Am Beispiel Angola

Afrika hat sich, entgegen der Prognosen westlicher Staaten, zu einem strategisch wichtigen Kontinent mit vielen unentdeckten Ressourcen und Möglichkeiten entwickelt. Insbesondere viele Schwellenländer haben kürzlich ihre Aktivitäten in Afrika verstärkt. China, aufgrund der eigenen rapiden wirtschaftlichen Entwicklung, ist zu einem wichtigen Akteur auf dem afrikanischen Kontinenten geworden: „In den letzten 60 Jahren hat kein Land einen so großen Einfluss auf die politische, ökonomische und soziale Struktur Afrikas ausgeübt wie China seit Beginn des neuen Jahrtausends.“[‡]

Der Einfluss, den China in Afrika gewonnen hat, stellt die zentrale Frage der vorliegenden Dissertation dar: Wie und inwiefern hat die Volksrepublik Einfluss auf die wirtschaftliche Entwicklung Afrikas genommen? Die Forschungsfrage soll am Beispiel Angola untersucht werden, da es ein wichtiges Land ist um die interdependente Struktur der Beziehung zwischen China und Angola sowie Chinas Erfolg und Einfluss in Angola analysieren zu können. Für den Wiederaufbau und die wirtschaftliche und soziale Reintegration in der Postkonfliktphase benötigte Angola finanzielle Hilfe. Zur gleichen Zeit suchte China nach neuen Zugängen zu Rohstoffen, um ihre Produktion bei steigender Nachfrage zu gewährleisten und das weitere Wirtschaftswachstum abzusichern. Die Beziehung zwischen China und Angola wird allerdings nicht nur durch Rohstoffe und übliche Entwicklungshilfe geprägt. Mit anderen Worten hat sich Angola zu mehr als nur einem zentralen Umschlagplatz für Energie entwickelt. Zusammenfassend lässt sich sagen, dass der jahrzehntelange Bürgerkrieg die Infrastruktur des Landes zerstörte, das Wirtschaftswachstum zum Halten brachte und jeden sozialen Fortschritt verhinderte. Die insbesondere finanzielle Bedürftigkeit Angolas im Hinblick auf den Wiederaufbau des Landes und der Wirtschaft, brachte China dazu, seine Interessen in Angola zu diversifizieren.

‡ Dambisa Moyo, *Dead Aid: Warum Entwicklungshilfe nicht funktioniert und was Afrika besser machen kann.* (Berlin: Haffmans&Tolkemitt, 2011) 145.

Die Hypothesen dieser Dissertation sind dreierlei: Zuerst beabsichtigt sie zu prüfen, ob die Beziehung zwischen China und Angola auf gegenseitiger politischer und wirtschaftlicher Abhängigkeit basiert. An zweiter Stelle wird versucht, eine Untersuchung zu den Auswirkungen von Chinas Präsenz auf die Präferenzen der angolanischen Regierung anzustellen. Zuletzt sollen die zwei Hauptkonzepte, der Angola-Mode und der Grundsatz der Nichteinmischung in innere Angelegenheiten souveräner Staaten, auf das Beispiel Angola angewendet werden um herauszufinden, ob sich China gegenüber Angolas traditionellen Partnern, wie den USA, Wettbewerbsvorteil erkämpfte.

Es wird beabsichtigt, dass diese drei Hypothesen in Zusammenhang mit Andrew Moravciks Kommerziellem Liberalismus verifiziert werden. Daher beginnt die Arbeit mit einer Darstellung des Neoliberalismus nach Moravcsik. Der Fokus wird auf den kommerziellen Liberalismus gelegt:

> „Je größer die Gewinne des transnationalen Austausches für die Akteure, desto intensiver setzen sie bei den Regierungen Druck ein um geschäftliche Transaktionen zu erleichtern; je größer die Kosten durch eine adjustierte Öffnung der Märkte, desto mehr Wiederstand entsteht.“[§]

Um die wirtschaftliche Beziehung zwischen China und Angola aus Sicht des kommerziellen Liberalismus analysieren zu können, werden zunächst die angolanische Interessengruppe im Rahmen der Wirtschaftsbeziehungen und deren Einfluss auf die Entscheidungsfindung der angolanischen Regierung untersucht. Die Kernfrage der Arbeit ist daher nicht nur, wie die Volksrepublik China wirtschaftlichen Einfluss auf Angola genommen hat, sondern auch, wie groß dieser Einfluss ist und inwiefern China und Angola sich gegenseitig unterstützen.

Diese Dissertation stellt die Behauptung auf dass der wirtschaftliche Einfluss, den die Volksrepublik China auf Angola genommen hat, mit zwei Instrumenten, die China einsetzt, erklärt werden kann. Diese sind: i) Der Tausch von Infrastruktur gegen Ölaufträge, der sogenannte Angola-Mode. ii) Der Grundsatz der Nichteinmischung in die inneren Angelegenheiten souveräner Staaten. Das Tauschgeschäft oder der sogenannte „Angola-Mode“ ist einer der wichtigsten Indikatoren dieser interdependenten Beziehungsstruktur.

§ Andrew Moravcsik, “Taking Preferences Seriously: A Liberal Theory of International Politics,” *International Organization*, 51:4 (1997): 528.

Während China die Energieversorgung sichert und die natürlichen Ressourcen für die Wirtschaft als Voraussetzung für Wachstum, Wohlstand und Beschäftigung gestalten will, genießt Angola eine Periode der Stabilität mit zahlreichen Projekten, die darauf abzielen, die Infrastruktur und die Wirtschaft des Landes zu verbessern. Gleichzeitig bietet dies China die Möglichkeit, seine Popularität in Angola zu erhöhen und erleichtert sein Engagement. Angola wird als Marktchance mit beträchtlichem Geschäftspotenzial angesehen: Nicht zur Ausbeutung, sondern für eine Handelspartnerschaft auf Augenhöhe. Seitdem China sich für den angolanischen Markt interessiert, hat Angola beachtliche Fortschritte im wirtschaftlichen Bereich gezeigt.

Die Arbeit ist in fünf Kapitel gegliedert; sie beginnt im ersten Kapitel mit einer allgemeinen Einführung und endet in Kapitel fünf mit dem Fazit. Die folgenden Abschnitte bieten einen kurzen Einblick in die Kapitel der vorliegenden Dissertation.

Kapitel 1: Einleitung

Kapitel eins stellt das Thema der Dissertation einleitend vor. Abschnitt 1.1 liefert einen kurzen Einblick in den Hintergrund der Beziehung zwischen China und Afrika, beginnend mit der ersten Kontaktanbahnungen zwischen China und Afrika zu Zeiten der Tang Dynastie. Der Reisende Du Huan (杜环) beschreibt in seinen ‚Notes on Travel' eine Reise in ein Land, das von schwarzen Menschen mit rauhen Sitten bevölkert ist. Dies ist einer der wichtigsten Hinweise mit Bezug auf eine Verbindung zwischen China und Afrika, die bis ins 7–10. Jahrhundert zurückgeht. Auch aus der Yuan Dynastie gibt es Anzeichen darauf, dass China seine Kenntnisse der Region Afrika vertiefte. So entwickelte beispielsweise der chinesische Kartographier Zhu Sibens（朱思本）eine dreieckige, südlich erweiterte Karte. Die bedeutendste Entdeckung des afrikanischen Kontinents allerdings fand durch den chinesischen Muslimen Admiral Zheng He（郑和）zu Zeiten der Ming-Dynastie. Zheng Hes Reise spielt eine große Rolle in der Fortentwicklung der gegenseitigen Beziehungen. Tatsächlich gibt es heute noch Dörfer in Somalia und Kenia, die nach ihm benannt worden sind. Nach der für diese Untersuchung wichtigen Erklärung der ersten Kontaktanbahnungen, zeigt der Abschnitt die Entwicklung der bilateralen Beziehung bis in die Neuzeit.

Aufbauend auf der geschichtlichen Übersicht der chinesisch-afrikanischen Beziehung, werden die außenpolitischen Instrumente Chinas in Afrika, das diplomatische Engagement, die Austausch- und Kulturprogramme, die Darstellung des Engagements in Medien und Werbung sowie die ausländische Hilfe mit chinesischen Merkmalen erläutert. In Abschnitt 1.2 wird der Fokus auf das Länderbeispiel (Angola) mit einem historischen Abriss der Beziehung zwischen China und Angola gelegt. Hier wird auch die wechselseitige Bedeutung der Länder erläutert. In Abschnitt 1.3 wird die wesentliche Forschungsliteratur vorgestellt, die sowohl die negative Perspektive („China als neo-koloniale Macht") als auch die positive Perspektive („Auswirkungen Chinas auf die Entwicklung und das Wirtschaftswachstum in Afrika") einschließt. Abschließend erläutert Abschnitt 1.4 die zentrale Frage der Dissertation (Wie und inwiefern hat die Volksrepublik China Einfluss auf die wirtschaftliche Entwicklung Angolas genommen?) sowie die drei Forschungshypothesen im Rahmen der Theorie Andrew Moravciks zum Kommerziellen Liberalismus.

Kapitel 2: Angola-Mode als ein Indikator für die gegenseitige wirtschaftliche Abhängigkeit und Erleichterungsfaktoren für den Zugang zu Handel, Öl und Infrastrukturaufträgen

Kapitel zwei stellt die interdependente Struktur der finanziellen Unterstützung Chinas für Angola durch den Begriff „Angola-Mode", der sich auf die Art und Weise bezieht, in der die natürlichen Ressourcen der Empfängerländer durch zinsgünstige Kredite und essentiellen Infrastrukturprojekten gesichert werden. In diesem Kapitel wird die Behauptung aufgestellt, dass im Rahmen des Angola-Modes zinsgünstige chinesische Kredite eine große Rolle spielen. Als wichtige Faktoren erleichtern sie den Zugang Chinas zu Handel, Öl und Infrastrukturaufträgen. Chinas Zugang zu diesen drei Bereichen wird in drei verschiedenen Abschnitten erläutert. An erster Stelle stehen chinesische Kredite, die eng verknüpft sind mit dem Erdölhandel, weil die chinesischen Kredite nur dann vergeben werden, wenn sie durch ein konkretes, langfristiges Handelsabkommen sichergestellt werden. Es kann also eine hohe Korrelation zwischen chinesischen Krediten und expandierenden Handelsbeziehungen festgestellt werden. Seit dem Jahr 2007 hat China die Vereinigte Staaten, die seit den 1970er größter Abnehmer angolanischen Öls waren, überholt. Chinesische Kredite sorgen zweitens auch für einen erleichterten Zugang zum angolanischen Erdöl. Chinas Exim Bank, deren erste Kredite durch Erdölexporte zurückgezahlt werden, konnte allmählich ihre Stellung im angolanischen Ölmarkt stärken, seit sie verschiedene Joint Ventures mit dem staatlichen Ölkonzern Sonangol in Angola eingegangen ist. Als nächstes wird der Zusammenhang zwischen chinesischen Krediten und einem erleichterten Zugang zu Infrastrukturaufträgen analysiert. Wie bereits dargelegt, ist der Schwerpunkt der Angola-Mode, dass die dringenden Infrastrukturprobleme in Angola durch die Kredite der chinesischen Regierung gelöst werden. Dabei spielt die Tatsache, dass die Kredite der China Exim Bank unter der Bedienung vergeben werden, dass 70 % der öffentlichen Aufträge an chinesische Unternehmen vergeben werden müssen, eine bedeutende Rolle. In diesem Kapitel wird die Erläuterung der verschiedenen Projekte chinesischer Unternehmen folgendermaßen unterteilt: Wiederaufbau der Bahnstrecken, Straßen und Brücken; Aufbau der Telekommunikationseinrichtungen; Aufbau der Städte und Aufbau der Kraftwerke. Außerdem werden in diesem Kapitel drei Folgen der Angola-Mode untersucht. Die erste Konsequenz der Angola-Mode stellt fest, dass beide Konzepte, der Angola-Mode (Tausch von Infrastruktur gegen natürliche Ressourcen) und der Grundsatz der Nichteinmischung in die inneren Angelegenheiten souveräner Staaten, Möglichkeiten für chinesische Unternehmen bieten, um eine globalere Ausrichtungen zu erreichen und auf dem internationalen Markt konkurrieren zu können.

Die zweite Konsequenz führt an, dass beim Angola-Mode bemerkenswert schnelle Entscheidungen in Bezug auf Vereinbarungen getroffen werden können. Weil die Öl-gestützten Kredite teilweise nur unter oben genannten Bedingungen zu Stande kommen, wie beispielsweise dass 70 % der öffentlichen Aufträge an chinesische Unternehmen vergeben werden müssen oder dass mindestens 50 % der Materialbeschaffung aus China geliefert werden muss, kann die Volksrepublik China oft finanzielle Mittel und Arbeitskräfte und Experten schneller als konkurrierende Länder liefern. Die dritte Konsequenz stellt fest, dass die massive Präsenz chinesischer Bauunternehmen und ihr Erfolg bei Großaufträgen regional Auswirkungen mit sich brachten. Unter anderem führte dies zu sinkenden Preisen bei Baustoffen, sodass sich der lokalen Bevölkerung die Möglichkeit erschloss, ihre eigenen Häuser kostengünstig renovieren zu können.

Kapitel 3: Unternehmenskooperationen zwischen China und Angola

Kapitel drei beleuchtet die wachsende geschäftliche Beziehung zwischen China und dem Krieg-zerrissenen Angola. Der rasante Anstieg des Handelsvolumens und chinesischer Investitionen in Angola haben die bilateralen Beziehungen verstärkt und gleichzeitig die Verbesserung der Rahmenbedingungen in Angola ermöglicht. Im Rahmen dessen, versucht dieses Kapital Chinas Rolle in der Diversifizierung von Angolas Öl dominierter Wirtschaft zu analysieren. In Abschnitt 3.1 wird die Unternehmenskooperation in den Sektoren Öl und Diamanten ausgewertet. Die Verbindung des staatlichen angolanischen Ölkonzerns Sonangols mit der staatlichen Ölgesellschaft Sinopec Chinas und mit einer in Hong Kong ansässigen Institution, Dayuan International Development, die 99 % der Anteile an China International Fund (CIF) hält, wird als Schwerpunkt dieses Abschnitts veranschaulicht. Die Erdöl Joint Ventures Sonangol Sinopec International (SSI) und China Sonangol International Holding Ltd. (CSIH), zusammen mit anderen Joint Venture im Diamanten-Sektor, Endiama China International Holding Ltd. (中安鑽石國際控股有限公), sind sehr gute Beispiele um Chinas expandierende Einfluss in Angolas Geschäftsfeld illustrieren zu können. Abschnitt 3.2 konzentriert sich auf die Unternehmenskooperation im Automobilesektor. Eine signifikante Entwicklung in diesem Bereich erfolgte im Jahr 2007 mit der Gründung der ersten Automobilfabrik in Angolas, gegründet als Joint Venture „CSG Automovel-Zhengzhou Nissan“ durch das angolanische Unternehmen Automovel, dem zweitgrößten Automobilhersteller Chinas, Dongfeng (东风汽车股份有限公司), und dem japanischen Nissan. Dem Abkommen zufolge, finanzierte der China International Fund (CIF) das Joint-Venture, das Autos auf der Basis japanischer Nissan-Modelle herstellen sollte. In Abschnitt 3.3 werden die Aktivitäten Chinas in den Sektoren Landwirtschaft und Fischerei einer Untersuchung unterzogen. Expandierende chinesische Investitionen in die angolanische Landwirtschaft fördern nicht nur die Diversifizierung der öldominierten Wirtschaft Angolas. Auch für China, das durch zunehmende Wasserknappheit und Umweltschäden auf der Suche nach fruchtbaren Landstrichen und reichen Fischgründen ist, bietet eine Kooperation die Möglichkeit zu Wohlstandssicherung. Dieser Abschnitt analysiert somit die Möglichkeit und Chancen beider Länder, sich durch gemeinsame Vereinbarungen und Kooperationen weiterentwickeln zu können.

Kapitel 4: Die Auswirkungen der bilateralen Wirtschaftsbeziehungen auf Angolas Präferenzen

Kapitel vier wertet den Einfluss Chinas auf angolanische Präferenzen aus. Es wird argumentiert, dass sich China an dem Grundsatz der Nichteinmischung in die inneren Angelegenheiten souveräner Staaten orientiert und sich somit aus den internen Problemen der afrikanischen Länder heraushält. Stattdessen werden eher Begriffe wie gemeinsame Entwicklung, Kooperation und gegenseitiger Nutzen betont. Durch dieses Vorgehen konnte China den Einfluss auf die Prozesse der Entscheidungsfindung der angolanischen Regierung erhöhen.

Um den chinesischen Einfluss analysieren zu können, ist es zunächst wichtig, die Verbindungen und Ähnlichkeiten zwischen den Präferenzen der Regierungen der beiden Länder zu untersuchen. Daher wird in diesem Kapitel Chinas Einfluss auf die angolanische Regierung veranschaulicht und in folgende sieben Abschnitte unterteilt: Auswirkungen Chinas auf die angolanische Regierungspartei MPLA, auf die sozio-wirtschaftliche Entwicklung Angolas, auf die angolanischen Arbeitskräfte, auf die Umwelt Angolas, auf die globale Präsenz des staatlichen angolanischen Ölkonzern Sonangols und auf traditionelle Wirtschaftspartner Angolas. In Abschnitt 4.1 werden die Auswirkungen Chinas auf die angolanische Regierungspartei MPLA untersucht. In diesem Abschnitt wird festgestellt, ob die angolanische Regierungspartei MPLA sich und ihre Entscheidungen durch die sino-angolanische wirtschaftliche Kooperation beeinflussen lässt. In Abschnitt 4.2 werden die Auswirkungen Chinas auf die sozio-wirtschaftliche Entwicklung Angolas erläutert. Trotz der Tatsache, dass China und Angola asymmetrische Mächte sind, basiert die Wechselwirkung zwischen China und Angola auf politischen und wirtschaftlichen Notwendigkeiten. Die Erhöhung der Ölexporte spielt eine große Rolle in dieser Beziehung für beide Länder. Die Erhöhung der Ölexporte und die steigenden Öleinkünfte werten die angolanische Währung, Kwanza, auf. Darüber hinaus hat Das Pro-Kopf- Einkommen sich seit dem Ende des Bürgerkrieges verzehnfacht und die Inflationsrate ist von 106 % auf 8.6 % gesunken. Diese Entwicklung macht Angola zur am schnellsten wachsenden Wirtschaft Afrikas. Im Juli 2012 wurde Angola von der Weltbank als ein Land mit mittlerem Einkommen obere Einkommenskategorie eingestuft. Angola ist damit nach Nigeria und Südafrika der drittgrößte Subsahara- Finanzmarkt geworden, und die angolanische Hauptstadt Luanda die drittgrößte portugiesisch sprachige Stadt der Welt, nach den beiden brasilianischen Städten Rio de Janeiro und Sao Paulo. Seit der chinesischen Einflussnahme hat Angola also beachtliche Fortschritte im wirtschaftlichen Bereich gezeigt. Die Rolle Chinas in der sogenannten ‚Golden Age'-Periode Angolas wird in diesem Abschnitt analysiert. In Abschnitt 4.3 werden die Auswirkungen Chinas auf die Arbeitslosigkeit in Angola untersucht. Es wird versucht herauszufinden, ob chinesische Unternehmen Arbeitsstandards in Angola verletzt haben, und ob China langfristig positive oder negative Auswirkungen auf die Arbeitslosenrate hat. Abschnitt 4.4 analysiert kurz die Beziehungen und Bedingungen zwischen Angola und dem IWF und erläutert den Prozess der Einflussnahme Chinas auf die Gespräche zwischen Angola und dem IWF, die letztlich zum Abbruch führte Weiterhin wird die Rolle Chinas auf den Wachstum im Bankensektor Angolas untergesucht. In Abschnitt 4.5 werden die Auswirkungen Chinas auf die Umwelt Angolas analysiert. Die Frage, warum China eine negative Bilanz im Umweltschutz Angolas vorzuweisen hat, wird durch verschiedene Beispiele beantwortet. Dazu gehören der legale und illegale Handel mit Schnittholz, Elfenbein, Nashörnern, außerdem die Umweltverschmutzung durch die Erdölindustrie. Schließlich erläutert der Abschnitt chinesische Maßnahmen, die der Entwicklung der Umweltauswirkungen ausländischer Investitionen der Volksrepublik Chinas dienen. Abschnitt 4.6 konzentriert sich auf die Auswirkungen Chinas, durch die Joint Venture China Sonangol International Holding (CSIH), auf die globale Präsenz des staatlichen angolanischen Ölkonzerns Sonangols. Es stellt sich nun die Frage, ob sich Sonangol durch die Joint Venture CSIH eine signifikante Möglichkeit schuf um auf Überseemärkten zu expandieren und ihren Geschäftsbetriebs in verschiedenen Ländern diversifizieren zu können. Abschnitt 4.7 stellt die Auswirkungen Chinas auf die traditionellen Wirtschaftspartner Angolas dar. Um die Ausdehnung des wirtschaftlichen Einflusses Chinas messen zu können, ist es notwendig geworden, China mit einem von Angolas traditionellen Wirtschaftspartnern zu vergleichen. Die USA, als ein wichtiger traditioneller Wirtschaftspartner Angolas, wurde als eine abhängige Variable ausgesucht. In diesem Abschnitt wird nun versucht zu analysieren, ob die Beziehungen zwischen Angola und den USA, die vor allem vom Ölhandel und Investitionen dominiert werden, durch Chinas Einfluss in Angola beeinträchtigt werden.

Kapitel 5: Fazit

Das fünfte und letzte Kapitel bietet eine Reflexion über die ganze Forschungsarbeit. Die zentrale Frage und die drei Hypothesen der Arbeit werden erneut hergeleitet und in Bezug zu Andrew Moravciks kommerziellem Liberalismus gesetzt, um die Forschungsfrage zu beantworten. Wie oben erwähnt, beschäftigt sich die Dissertation mit der Frage, wie und inwiefern die Volksrepublik China wirtschaftlichen Einfluss auf Angola genommen hat. Im Rahmen diese Frage, werden drei hypothetische Prognosen der Dissertation überprüft, von denen Hinweise auf die gegenseitigen politischen und wirtschaftlichen Abhängigkeiten, die bilaterale Beziehung, die Rolle Chinas auf Präferenzen der angolanischen Regierung, und schließlich auf einen eventuellen Wettbewerbsvorteil, den sich China gegenüber Angolas traditionellem Partner, den USA, erkämpft hat, erwartet werden.

Chapter 1: Introduction

This chapter seeks to summarize the focal points of the research, beginning with background information regarding China-Africa relations. The essence of this dissertation is formulated by clarifying the main purpose of the study, research question, hypotheses and methodology. First, the purpose of the study and research questions will be noted. The explanation of the methodology's framework will follow. Lastly, in order to provide a brief and informative basis for the chapters, the content of the thesis will be specified.

1.1 The Background of the Relations Between China and Africa

The common belief among Chinese scholars is that the connections between China and Africa may be traced back to the Tang Dynasty (608–907 AD). Chinese scholars draw attention to the discoveries of ancient Chinese porcelain pieces, stoneware and coins from the Tang Dynasty in modern Egypt, Kenya and Zanzibar.[1] However, to this day there are no records that prove human interaction between the Chinese and African people during the Tang Dynasty. The sole Chinese traveler 'Du Huan' (杜环) during the Tang Dynasty wrote about his visit to a country named Mo-lin[2] populated with black people with rough customs in his famous memoir 'Notes on Travel' (经行记).[3]

1 Jinyuan Gao, "China and Africa: The Development of Relations over Many Centuries," *African Affairs* 83:331 (1984):243.

2 Historians have differing opinions about the location of Molin. Friedrich Hirth claims that Mo-lin was to be found along the west coast of the Red Sea or the eastern coast of Egypt (See Friedrich Hirth, China and the Roman Orient: Researches into their Ancient and Medieval Relations, 1885); H.J Fisher in the book The Cambridge History of Africa Vol. 3 claims that Mo-lin used to be located in the present day Sudan. (See H.J Fisher, The Cambridge History of Africa c.1050–c.1600, Vol. 3, 1977).

3 Jinyuan Gao, op.cit., 243.

As China's agriculture, commerce and handicraft industry advanced during the Sung Dynasty, China took advantage of higher quality ocean ships and utilized its own invention of the compass for maritime navigation. According to scholar Jinyuan Gao (高晋元集), threats from China's Northern, hostile neighbors forced the Sung emperors to encourage maritime foreign trade in the South, as a source of revenue.[4] Egypt became the epicenter of Sino-African trade, yet archeological discoveries of Chinese porcelains and coins from the Sung Dynasty on the Eastern coast of Africa and Zimbabwe prove that Chinese trade contacts with the African continent dates back to 10–13 centuries.[5] In the Yuan Dynasty (1279–1368), the great improvement of China's knowledge about Africa was visible after comparing African maps drawn by Chinese cartographer Zhu Siben (朱思本) with those drawn by Europeans and Arabs during the 14th century. It is possible to argue that China's knowledge of Africa took a further leap during the Yuan Dynasty (1270–1368).[6] While an Africa map drawn by Chinese cartographer Zhu Siben (1315) was shaped like a triangle pointed southward, African maps drawn by Europeans and Arabians were shaped with a tip pointing eastward.[7] The British scientist Joseph Needham (1900–1995) described that African map illustrated by Zhu Siben as 'marvellous.'[8] However, the most important explorations began following the Chinese Moslem admiral Zheng He's (郑和) visits to African countries during the Ming Dynasty (1368–1644), under the rule of Emperor Yongle (永楽帝) (1360–1424). The admiral Zheng He began his explorations through a huge fleet of 63 ships; 28.560 men reached the east coast of Africa and visited Mogadishu, Brava, Juba and Malindi (present-day Somalia and

---

4 Ibid., 244.

5 J. J. L. Duyvendak, China's Discovery of Africa (Arthur Probsthain: London, 1949) 3.

6 Jinyuan Gao, op.cit., 244.

7 Ibid., 244.

8 Yuan Wu, *China and Africa (1956–2006)*, (Beijing: China Intercontinental Press, 2008), 23.

Kenya) in two of seven voyages between 1416 and 1423.[9] Today, there are villages in Somalia and Kenya named after Zheng He in commemoration of his visits.[10] Zheng He played a very important role in development of trade relations between China and African countries. Zheng He's fleet carried large amounts of gold, silver, silk, porcelains, to exchange with the African products[11] and contributed toward the development of trade relations between China and Africa during the Ming Dynasty reciprocally. It is known that, the King of the East African Malin Kingdom (present-day Kenya) died on his way to the China's capital. He was buried in Fujian and he received a memorial title by the Chinese emperor.[12]

Zheng He's voyages to the African East coast were, in Gao's words, 'the climax of China's efforts to develop relations with Africa.'[13] However, from the last century of the Ming Dynasty and during the Qing Dynasty, Sino-African relations slowly came to an end. According to Gao, the reasons are twofold.[14] One reason was the power struggle between Eunuch and official people, as well as Japanese pirates' attacks on China's coastal areas in the Ming Dynasty. The second reason was the invasion of European colonialists in both Asia and Africa. Qing Dynasty's (1644–1911) closed-door policy shut down China's contacts with the outside world. With the start of the Opium War in 1839, China went into the swamp of British imperialism and China's relations with the outside world, subsequently Africa entered into a 'recession period'.

It was only after the foundation of the People's Republic of China in 1949 that China began to redevelop its relations with African countries through an active foreign policy. In September 1950, Mao expressed his support

---

9 Chinese Moslem Admiral Zheng He led seven great western maritime expeditions from South China Sea and the Indian Ocean into the Persian Gulf and Red Sea, and reaching as far as the east coast of Africa. The evidences show that Admiral Zheng He visited over thirty Asian and African countries.

10 Li Rongxia, "Significance of Zheng He's Voyages," *Beijing Review* 28 May 2005, *Date Accessed: 11 June 2012.* <http://www.bjreview.cn/EN/En-2005/05-28-e/china-2.htm>.

11 Jinyuan Gao, op.cit., 245.

12 Ibid., 245.; See also Philip Snow, *The Star Raft: China's Encounter with Africa,* (New York: Weidenfeld&Nicolson,1988).

13 Jinyuan Gao, op.cit., 245.

14 Ibid., 246.

for the South African Indian Congress (SAIC) in their fight against racial discrimination.[15] Negligible ties became stronger after the gathering of the representatives of twenty-nine African and Asian nations at the Bandung Conference in Bandung, Indonesia in 1955. The purpose of the conference was to promote economic and cultural cooperation, and to oppose colonialism. China's anti-colonialist position encouraged many African countries to stand against colonial rule. By agreeing on supporting liberation movements a common platform was created to strengthen their solidarity against colonial oppressors and associated exploitation. The Bandung Conference could be regarded not only as the starting point of growing attraction of China among Third World countries, but also the beginning of China's appreciation of Third World countries' role in gaining leverage within the international arena. It was also at this conference that China introduced The Five Principles that still are, as seen in China's Africa Policy[16], the main principles of China's foreign policy:

The Five Core Principles of Chinese Foreign Policy:

- Mutual respect for each other's territorial integrity and sovereignty
- Mutual non-aggression
- Mutual non-interference in each other's internal affairs
- Equality and mutual benefit
- Peaceful co-existence

Throughout the 1960s and the 1970s, China consistently supported liberation movements across Africa. Through their support, China reduced the Soviet Union's sphere of influence and gained leverage against Taiwan; in order to be eligible to receive Chinese foreign aid, African countries were not allowed to recognize Taiwan as a sovereign state. In 1964, Chinese Premier Zhou Enlai (周恩来), during his visit to several African countries, announced China's Eight Principles of Economic and Technical Aid[17],

15 Ian Taylor, *China and Africa: Engagement and Compromise*, (London: Routledge, 2006) 19.

16 Forum on China and Africa Cooperation (FOCAC), *China's African Policy*, 12 January 2006, Date Accessed: 11 May 2011. <http://www.focac.org/eng/zt/zgdfzzcwj/>. See Appendix 1: China's African Policy.

17 The principles were: China always bases itself on the principle of equality and mutual benefit in providing aid to other nations, China never attaches any

alongside a major foreign aid campaign. In addition, by referring to shared historical roots, Zhou Enlai attracted the attention of African people to commonality and similarity exists between two parts. For example, Zhou Enlai, in his speech in Tanzania in 1965 said: "My colleagues and I do not find ourselves in a strange land. Intercourse between our countries dated back to nine hundred years ago. Some five hundred years ago, the Chinese navigator Zheng He reached African coasts."[18]

By the end of 1965, seventeen of the thirty-eight African states had recognised China. In October 1971, China realised Africa's significant political influence when twenty-six African countries (representing one-third of countries supporting Resolution 2758) voted in favour of recognition of the legitimate status of China within the United Nations. The June 1989 Tiananmen Square incident and the end of the Cold War was a turning point in China's relations with Africa. While Western countries condemned China on its human rights record, African support continued, even extending invitations to the Chinese Foreign Minister Qian Qichen (钱其琛) from six African countries (Angola, Zambia, Botswana, Mozambique, Lesotho, and Zimbabwe) in August 1989.[19] "It was... Our African friends who stood by us and extended a helping hand in the difficult times following political

conditions or asks for any privileges, China helps lighten the burden of recipient countries as much as possible, China aims at helping recipient countries to gradually achieve self-reliance and independent development, China strives to develop aid projects that require less investment but yield quicker results, China provides the best-quality equipment and materials of its own manufacture, In providing technical assistance, China shall see to it that the personnel of the recipient country fully master such techniques, The Chinese experts are not allowed to make any special demands or enjoy any special amenities. See "Zhou Enlai Announces Eight Principles", *China Daily* 13 August 2010, Date Accessed: 11 May 2011 <http://www.chinadaily.com.cn/china/2010-08/13/content_11149131.htm%3E>.

18 New China News Agency, (5 June 1965) quoted in Ian Taylor, *China and Africa: Engagement and Compromise*, (London: Routledge, 2006) 17.

19 One month later, in September 1989 Qian Qichen was also invited to Tunisia und Egypt. For more details see Luo Jianbo, *Why Is Sino-African Relationship Important (中非关系为什么重要)*, (The Study Times, April 1, 2013), Yun Sun, *Africa in China's Foreign Policy*, (Washington: Brookings, April 2014), 1–45.

turmoil in Beijing when Western countries imposed sanctions on China."[20] After the Cold War, China's booming economy brought the relations at a scale never seen before. Foreign aid from China to African states increased from US$ 60 million in 1988 to US$ 375 million in 1990.[21] Since then, China only continued to strengthen its relations with Africa.

In the post-Cold War decade, four main goals of Chinese African policy were identified. First, after the Tiananmen incident, China started to seek diplomatic and political support of Third World countries by insisting importance of mutual respect and standing against Western 'hegemonism.' For China, Africa's fifty-three states were important partners; each African state had one vote in the United Nations, which could be used to confront international pressure China had been facing. China gained most African elites' sympathy, through Premier Li Peng's (李鹏) worthily speech at the Asian-African Law Consultative Committee meeting in Beijing, March 1990:

> "[The] new order of international politics means that all countries are equal, and must mutually respect each other ...regardless of their differences in political systems, and ideology. No country is allowed to impose its will on other countries, seek hegemony in any regions, or pursue power politics to deal with other countries. They are not allowed to interfere in the internal affairs of the developing countries, or pursue power politics in the name of 'human rights, freedom and democracy."[22]

Second, China competed with Taiwan for international recognition. Third, China saw Africa as a continent to potentially provide large market opportunities for cheap manufactured Chinese products, and an opportunity for Chinese companies to set up plants and develop markets overseas. Lastly, establishing diplomatic and political relations with African countries served China's interests, which are related to gaining significance in the global political arena.

The achievement of these grand objectives has been intensified in China's 21st century Africa policy. Regarding its competition with Taiwan (The

---

20 Qian Qichen, *Ten Episodes in China's Diplomacy,* (New York: HarperCollins, 2005) 200.

21 Paul Opoku Mensah, "China and the International Aid System: Transformation or Cooptation," in ed. Li Xing, *The Rise of China and the Capitalist World Order,* (Burlington: Ashgate Publishing Ltd., 2010) 77.

22 Xinhua News Agency, (Marchs 12, 1990), quoted in Ian Taylor, op.cit., 63.

Republic of China) for recognition, China has been successful. Today, only three of fifty-four African countries (Burkina Faso, Sao Tome and Principe, and the Kingdom of Swaziland) still maintain official relations with Taiwan. Most recently, Gambia withdrew its diplomatic recognition of Taiwan. In November 2013, Gambia announced that their official recognition of Taiwan had been terminated. Chinese Foreign Ministry needed to make an announcement denying allegations of China's intentional influence on Gambia's move.[23] What is not in doubt, however, is that a remarkable development of the African countries engaging with China has been observed by neighbor African countries who lack diplomatic ties with China. This dynamic has resulted in the realization of further opportunities offered by China. Malawi acts as a prime example of this behavior. In 2007, China offered Malawi aid and investment opportunities worth US$ 6 billion[24] and in the following year, Malawi transferred diplomatic relations from Taiwan to China.[25]

Trade relations, South-South cooperation and the enhancement of China's international status have become a central interest to China in its relations with African countries. The Forum on China-Africa Cooperation (FOCAC), was established in 2000 as a significant vehicle for China to expand its economic, trade and political ties with African countries. Chinese President Jiang Zemin (江泽民) in his speech to the newly established FOCAC in 2000 in Beijing stated: "South-South cooperation is an important means through which developing countries may effectively respond to the changes in the international situation and meet the challenges that may be brought about by economic globalization."[26] Despite those challenges and risks, President

---

23 Peter Enav, "Gambia Breaks Relations with Surprised Taiwan," *The Associated Press* 15 November 2013, Date Accessed: 5 December 2013. <http://bigstory.ap.org/article/gambia-breaks-relations-taiwan>.

24 Thomas Lum, "China's Assistance and Government-Sponsored Investment Activities in Africa, Latin America and Southeast Asia," *FAS Congressional Research Service Reports*, 25 November 2009:8, Date Accessed: 11 May 2011 <https://www.fas.org/sgp/crs/row/R40940.pdf>.

25 However, after Malawi switched diplomatic relations from Taiwan to China, Malawi acquired only 286 million dollars from China.

26 "Full Text of President Jiang's Speech at China-Africa Forum," *People's Daily* 11 October 2000, Date Accessed: 11 May 2011. <http://english.people.com.cn/english/200010/10/eng20001010_52238.html>.

Jiang Zemin did not lessen his commitment to globalisation but chose to combat against existing challenges. Jiang's Zemin's famous quotation from Sun-Yat-Sen (孫中山) makes it clearer: "the tide of world events is mighty. Those who follow it prosper, whereas those who resist it perish".[27] According to the President, developing countries should, therefore, act together to strengthen co-operation and consultation in multilateral institutions such as the UN and the WTO, so as to safeguard common interests of developing countries. The historical mission of Zheng He has become an important symbol for China to advance its soft power strategy in Africa. Forty years following the Premier Zhou Enlai's speech, Guo Chong Li (郭崇立), Chinese ambassador to Kenya, to express friendship and warm ties between China and Africa, claimed in 2005:

> "Zheng He's fleet is large, consisting of over 200 ships with 27,000 sailors. But his voyages were not for looting resources but for friendship. In the trade with foreign countries, he gave much more than he took. His seven voyages promoted understanding, friendship and trade relation between China's Ming Dynasty and foreign counties in southeast Asia, west Asia and east Africa, including Kenya."[28]

In the same year, China cancelled the bilateral debts, totaling US$ 1.27 billion, of thirty-one African countries.[29] In 2006, the Chinese government released a white paper on China's African Policy in which China characterized itself as the world's largest developing country, and expressed China's appreciation of Africa's participation in the South-South cooperation.[30] In the White Paper, the intensification of the relations is presented as "new strategic partnership" based on political equality, mutual trust, an economic

27 Zhang Zhejiang, "China's Globalization and Its Policies: Focusing on Sino-American Relations", *Journal of Ritsumeikan Social Sciences and Humanities*, Vol. 1 (March 2009): 93, Date Accessed: 11 May 2011 <http://www.ritsumei.ac.jp/acd/re/k-rsc/hss/book/pdf/vol01_05.pdf>.

28 "Kenyan Girl Offered Chance to Go to College in China," *Xinhua News Agency* 20 March 2005, Date Accessed: 11 May 2011 <http://news.xinhuanet.com/english/2005-03/20/content_2719001.htm>.

29 "FM Spokesman: China Continue Offering Aid to Poor African Countries," *People's Daily* 7 July 2005, Date Accessed: 11 May 2011 <http://english.people.com.cn/200507/07/eng20050707_194733.html>.

30 Forum on China and Africa Cooperation (FOCAC), *China's African Policy*, 12 January 2006, Date Accessed: 11 May 2011 <http://www.focac.org/eng/zt/zgdfzzcwj/>.

win-win cooperation and cultural exchange. Furthermore, China allowed African states access to Chinese markets, and promised a remarkable increase in infrastructure investment, and an intensified cooperation in the fields of education, agriculture, science, peace and security.[31]

In November 2006, heads of state and dignitaries of forty-eight African countries came together in Beijing, to attend the largest international summit ever held in Chinese capital. Beijing streets were covered up with red banners with slogans: 'Friendship, Peace, Cooperation, and Development'.[32] On November 4, 2006, China's Prime Minister Wen Jiabao（温家宝）proposed that China and Africa should seek to bring their trade volume to US$ 100 billion by 2010.[33] On the same day, China's President Hu Jintao (胡锦涛) announced a package of aid and assistance measures to Africa including US$ 3 billion of preferential loans in the next three years and the cancellation of more debt owed by poorer countries.[34] Between 2013 and 2004, the Chinese government extended lines of credit amounting to over US$ 32 billion. After President Xi Jinping (习近平) had pledged to grant US$ 20 billion to African countries in March 2013, Premier Li Keqiang (李克强) offered extra loans totalling at least US$12 billion on his four-country (Ethiopia, Nigeria, Angola and Kenya) Africa tour in May 2014.[35]

Economic relations between Africa and China have considerably expanded since the establishment of FOCAC. China has become Africa's largest trading partner, with bilateral trade growing 28 % per year from 2001 to 2010.[36] The value of trade between China and Africa had increased by 45 % from 2007 to the end of 2010; total trade for 2010 was approximately US$ 115 billion. According to current Chinese statistical data, China-Africa trade reached a

---

31 Ibid.

32 Stephan Marks, Introduction, *African Perspectives on China in Africa*, In eds. Firoze Manji and Stephan Marks, (Nairobi and Oxford: Fahamu/Pambazuka News, 2007) 1.

33 Ibid., 2.

34 Ibid., 2.

35 Ben Blanchard, "China to extend over $12bn in Aid to Africa," *Reuters* 9 May 2014, Date Accessed: 12 May 2014 <http://www.reuters.com/article/2014/05/09/us-china-africa-idUSBREA4802320140509>.

36 Cui Peng, "China Now Africa's Largest Trading Partner", *People's Daily Online* 18 November 2011, Date Accessed: 27 November 2011. <http://english.peopledaily.com.cn/90778/7649195.html>

high of more than US$ 200 billion in 2012, up 42.5 % from 2010. Imports from Africa to China reached US$ 110 billion, while exports from China to Africa reached US$ 100 billion in 2012.[37] The largest share of Chinese imports consisted of raw materials that China requires for its vast industrial development; exports to Africa mainly involve value-added commodities, machinery, and low manufactured goods. Since it is challenging to obtain reliable figures for Chinese investment in Africa, it is difficult to conclude the total investment China has made in Africa. But it is estimated that by the end of 2012 Chinese foreign direct investment in Africa reached US$ 20 billion[38] from US$ 1.5 million in 1991.[39] Chinese investment in Africa concentrated on sectors such as the finance-mining sector, business services, transportation and telecommunication. Accordingly, the amount of investment Africa has made in China should not be underestimated. According to Prof. Calestous Juma of Harvard University's Kennedy School of Government, Africa has invested an estimated US$ 10 billion in China, especially in manufacturing, information communications technology and pharmaceuticals sectors.[40]

China's growing economy has doubled the need of energy in the country. China's trade with sub-Saharan Africa is highly concentrated in a few economies. Today, one third of China's oil imports come from Angola, Nigeria, Chad, the Democratic Republic of the Congo, Sudan and Equatorial Guinea. Furthermore, five countries (Angola, South Africa, the Democratic Republic of the Congo, the Republic of Congo, and Equatorial Guinea) account for about 75 % of Sub-Saharan Africa's exports to China.[41] Angola, who became

37 Chantelle Benjamin, "Africa is not a Big Bull in China's Shop," *Mail & Guardian* 21 June 2013, Date Accessed: 21 June 2013 <http://mg.co.za/article/2013-06-21-00-africa-isnt-a-big-bull-in-chinas-shop>.

38 Ibid.

39 "China-Africa Economic and Trade Cooperation," Chinese Government's Official Web Portal, December 2010, Date Accessed: 21 June 2013 <http://www.gov.cn/english/official/2010-12/23/content_1771603.htm>.

40 Chantelle Benjamin, "Africa is not a Big Bull in China's Shop," *Mail & Guardian* 21 June 2013, Date Accessed: 21 June 2013 <http://mg.co.za/article/2013-06-21-00-africa-isnt-a-big-bull-in-chinas-shop>.

41 Paulo Drommond and Estelle Xue Liu, "If China Sneezes, Africa Can Now Catch a Cold", *IMFdirect* 24 March 2014, Date Accessed: 25 March 2014 <http://blog-imfdirect.imf.org/2014/03/20/if-china-sneezes-africa-can-now-catch-a-cold/>.

the top oil supplier of China by replacing Saudi Arabia in 2006, left its leading place once again to Saudi Arabia in 2007 and became the second biggest supplier of oil to China. Africa, in some senses, serves China's long-term energy security policy. First, oil from the Gulf Guinea region offers a comparative advantage for China because this particular oil tends to be of a higher quality and low in sulfur (sweet crude), which is suitable for existing capacities of Chinese refineries. Second, even though fifty-three African countries possess only 9 % of the world's petroleum resources, Africa is a continent remains largely unexplored.[42] It is expected by US Department of Energy that African oil production will rise by 91 % between 2002 and 2025.[43] Third, African oil is an opportunity for China, who doesn't want to rely on the Middle East as a source of oil. Fourth, with the exception of a few countries (Nigeria, Angola, Libya and Algeria), African producers are not members of OPEC, which offers easier investment facilities than elsewhere.

In order not to lose its access to African energy resources in the future, Chinese companies have signed long-term contracts with African suppliers and are investing heavily within African energy resource extraction and infrastructure, both in cooperation with African governments and in joint ventures with non-Chinese companies.[44] The Chinese government made its position clear in its official policy statement on Africa: "The Chinese Government encourages and supports Chinese enterprises' investment and business in Africa, and will continue to provide preferential loans and buyer credits to this end."[45] As Mark Sorbara points out, "Investing in African

42 The Executive Director of South Africa Oil and Gas Alliance Warwick Blyth's explanation: "Many of the world's key producing fields are now budding or seriously depleted, and continued demand means companies and governments are looking to new, often completely unknown regions for supply, and Sub-Saharan Africa remains a largely unexplored region in which there have been only modest, mainly gas, discoveries to date."

43 Michael Klare and Daniel Volman. "The African Oil Rush And American National Security," *Third World Quarterly* 27:4 (May 2006): 611.

44 Ilona Steiler, *The European Union and China in Africa: Explaining Conflict and Cooperation with International Relations Theory*, (Hamburg: Verlag Dr. Kovač, 2009) 78.

45 Forum on China and Africa Cooperation (FOCAC), *China's African Policy*, 12 January 2006, Date Accessed: 11 May 2011 <www.focac.org/eng/zt/zgdfzzcwj>.

extractive industries is a risky business, but China is desperately in need of raw materials to feed its booming its economy, hence the government is willing to shoulder most of the risk for Chinese companies looking to invest in Africa."[46] Investing in Africa as part of China's going global strategy (走出去) has extended China's target of securing energy resources for the development of its own economy and unveiled long-standing global interests of Chinese companies in various economic sectors. Chinese government allowed around 180 companies to benefit from financial and political backing and tax concessions when they go global and engage in global marketplace.

Going global strategy of China serves not only for encouraging Chinese companies to invest overseas and play a role in international markets, it also reflects the anti-hegemonic aspect of China. Chinese Prime Minister Zhu Rongji (朱镕基), at the first FOCAC meeting in Beijing in 2000 said "Sino-African ties would help build up our capacity against possible risks, which will put us in a better position to participate in economic globalization and safeguard our economic interests and economic security."[47] He also pointed out the importance of the relations in terms of facilitating the establishment of a fair and rational new international political and economic order.[48] Chinese Minister of Foreign Trade and Economic Cooperation Shi Guangsheng (石广生) stated the fact that as long as the new international economic order is not established, countries would continue to be differed in economic development.[49] "Developed countries are benefiting most from economic globalization; but the large number of developing countries are facing more risks and challenges."[50] Shi Guangsheng certainly wanted to attract the attention of the global community by reflecting the risks and challenges of globalization for developing countries. The former Minister of Commerce, Bo Xilai (薄熙来), described their going global strategy as

46 Mark Sobara, "The Nation", 14 April 2006, quoted by Stephan Marks in Introduction, in Eds. Firoze Manji and Stephan Marks, op.cit., 9.

47 Ian Taylor, *China's New Role in Africa*, (London: Lynne Rienner Publishers, 2009) 16.

48 Ibid., 17.

49 Ibid., 17.

50 Ibid., 17.

"crossing the ocean by feeling the stones."[51] In 2001, after China's admission into WTO, China published its tenth five year plan and officially started to feel the stones and stepped in a process of escalation of China's own globalization, "with Chinese characteristics."[52]

In short, China's interests in Africa have shifted from purely political and ideological considerations during the Cold War to expanding its political spheres of influence. Furthermore, their interests have focused on ensuring access to exports markets for Chinese manufactured goods and investment opportunities for Chinese state-owned companies, as well as securing energy supplies and raw materials through its new foreign policy instruments.

1.1.1 China's Foreign Policy Instruments in Africa

There are many different ways of conducting foreign affairs. As aforementioned, China traditionally used its diplomacy based on friendship, mutual respect, equality and mutual benefit in order to achieve its national foreign policy goals. However, in the new world, as China's foreign policy goals have changed, the instruments of China's foreign policy have gone beyond the 'traditional diplomacy' of China.

In this section, the instruments of China's foreign policy in Africa will be examined through a case study of Angola. China's relations with Angola are based on an economic cooperation in which economic goals mainly drive China's foreign policy instruments. China's strength of economy, human capital, and development model has facilitated China's integration process with African countries through the foreign policy instruments China has developed. By focusing on and using the foreign policy instruments of China, such as diplomacy, exchange programs, participation in multilateral institutions, engagement in media and commercials, foreign aid of 'Chinese characteristics,' China aims to be an influential, attractive and effective economic partner to African countries.

51 Deborah Brautigam, *The Dragon's Gift: The Real Story of China in Africa*, (New York: Oxford University Press, 2009) 103.

52 Ibid., 103.

1.1.1.1 Diplomatic Engagement

China's African Policy paper, released in January 2006, is quite significant as it is one of the fundamental principles claiming that China will respect African countries' development strategies and will provide assistance with no political strings attached. That principle was significant because it has created a great deal of debate and criticism from other states. They were the critiques coming from the Western world, seeing China's growing role as a challenge that ignores human rights and environmental standards when lending to Africa. For example, the former World Bank President Paul Wolfowitz criticized large Chinese banks for ignoring the so-called Equator Principles and warned Chinese banks that are relatively new to this kind of activity, not to make the same mistakes as France and the US did with Zaire's (today the Democratic Republic of Congo).[53] President Joseph Mobutu, who became the President of Zaire by coup in 1960, bankrupted the country after borrowing heavily from Western banks and institutions, including World Bank.[54] However, for many African leaders, China has emerged as an alternative and positive stance, in contrast to the unwelcome conditions of Western donors and international financial institutions, including the IMF and World Bank. Sahr Johnny, Sierra Leones's Ambassador in Beijing explained the whole situation: "If a G8 country had wanted to rebuild the stadium [in Freetown], for example, we'd still be holding meetings! The Chinese just come and do it. They do not start to hold meetings about environmental impact assessment, human rights, bad governance and good governance. I am not saying that is right, I am just saying Chinese investment is succeeding because they do not set high benchmarks."[55]

---

53 Francoise Crouigneau and Richard Hiault, "Wolfowitz Slams China Banks on Africa Lending", *Financial Times* 23 October 2006, Date Accessed: 22 June 2011 <http://www.ft.com/intl/cms/s/0/45e594e0-62fc-11db-8faa-0000779e2340.html#axzz311VCmAUd>.

54 Ibid.

55 Lindsey Hilsum, "China and Africa and the G8-or Why Bob Geldorf Needs to Wake Up", in eds. Leni Wild and David Mepham, The *New Sinosphere: China in Africa*, (London: Institute for Public Policy Research-IPPR, 2006) 7.

Table 1.1: Bilateral Visits of State Officials between China and Angola

Official Visitors to Angola from China	Official visitors to China from Angola
Yang Wenchang (杨文昌), Vice Foreign Minister (July 2002)	Manuel Vicente, CEO, Sonangol (March 2004)
Zheng Peiyan (曾培炎), Deputy Prime Minister (March 2004 and February 2005)	Fernando da Piedade dos Santos, Prime Minister (May 2004 and November 2006)
Yang Zilin (羊子林), President, China Exim Bank (September 2004)	João Bernardo de Miranda, minister of foreign affairs (May 2004)
Lü Xinhua (吕新华), Vice Minister Foreign Affairs (July 2005)	General Agostinho Nelumba Sanjar, Commander of the Angolan Armed Forces (June 2005)
Wen Jiabao (温家宝), Prime Minister (June 2006)	Joaquim Icuma Muafuma, Minister of Commerce (September 2006)
Li Ruogu (李若谷), President, China Exim Bank (September 2007)	Irene Neto, Vice Minister of Foreign Affairs (September 2006)
Hu Jintao (胡锦涛), President of China (December 2008)	Antonio Burity da Silva, Minister of Education (October 2007)
Xi Jinping (习近平), Vice President (November, 2010)	President Eduardo dos Santos visits China twice (August & Dec 2008)
Liu Qi (刘淇), member of the Political Bureau of the CPC Central Committee, Beijing Party Secretary (March 2012)	Carlos Maria Feijo, Angolan Minister of State (October 2011)
Zhang Ming (张明), Vice Foreign Minister, (April 2014)	Georges Chikoti, Foreign Minister, (September 2013)
Li Keqiang (李克强), Prime Minister, (May 2014)	

The official political discourse of the Chinese government is that it wishes to establish a win-win cooperation with African countries. China declared in the White Paper of China's African Policy (2006) that China's diplomatic engagement with African countries is based on solidarity and cooperation. China highlighted the importance of the development of exchanges on the basis of principles of independence, equality, mutual respect and non-interference in each other's internal affairs reflects the ancient Chinese philosophy: "Overseas territories should be treated based on the friendship principle."[56]

56 Chuka Enuka, "Aid in Sino-Africa Relations: An Analysis of the Promptings, Pluses and Problems of China's Aid to Africa," *IUP* 55 (2011): 45.

The number of high-level official visits of China to Africa has been more than that of the world's significant countries. For instance, during president Obama's first term, Obama visited only one African country, Ghana, whilst China's former president, Hu Jintao, visited Africa seven times. Hu Jintao's successor Xi Jinping, as part of his first overseas tour, went on a three-nation tour of Africa (Tanzania, South Africa and the Republic of Congo).

China has strengthened its soft power by establishing multilateral institutions with African countries. Forum on China and Africa Cooperation (FOCAC), which was established in 2000, aims to promote collective dialogue and multilateral cooperation between China and Africa. Sino-African cooperative relations have experienced rapid development since the establishment of FOCAC. In 2004, China made a diplomatic success by establishing Macau Forum, the Forum for Economic and Commercial Cooperation between China and Portuguese speaking countries. It is made up of eight countries; Angola, Brazil, Cape Verde, China, Guinean Bissau, Mozambique, Portugal and Timor-Leste, with Macau as an observer member. Thus, Macau Forum turned out to be the second forum in which three African Lusophone countries (Angola, Guinean Bissau and Mozambique) participated with China. In 2011, China and Africa took another step to strengthen relations by launching the China Africa Think Tank Forum (CATTF). It was established to promote research and exchanges among think tanks from both regions, as well as join scholars from other parts of the world who have an interest in Sino-Africa relations. To boost bilateral diplomatic relations between China and Angola, since April 2015, the Angolan and Chinese holders of diplomatic and service passports have been exempted from visas.

Subsequently, the partnership between China and African countries shifted from ideological and strategic considerations in 1980s and 1990s to a higher degree of political and economic cooperation. Besides their interests in boosting economic cooperation, there also exists a mutual effort among China and African countries to support each other within the international political arena. For example, China is destined to play a major role in several cases to counterweight international pressure against some African countries. In 2004, China came forth with its financial assistance of US$ 2 billion to Angola, despite the fact that Western donors such as IMF and World Bank rejected the request due to non-transparency. By 2007,

China provided US$ 2 billion loan to Angola, allowing the country to turn down the IMF's offer. Similarly, Zimbabwe took arms and fighter planes from China following the arms embargo applied by Western countries in 2002.[57] Similarly, in 2014, China leveraged its influence at the United Nations to block the US-French proposal to impose sanctions on the former President of Central African Republic, Francois Bozize.[58] The relationship has remained to mutual advantage, as China has also required diplomatic support from African countries. African countries account for 25 % of the UN General Assembly votes, which play a vital role for China. Its application can be noted when China gained African support in accession to the UN General Assembly and the Security Council in 1972 and to the World Trade Organization in 2001. One also cannot ignore the support of African countries in a successful bid of China to host the 2008 Olympics, despite the Western critiques linked to China's role in the Darfur crisis through its military co-operation with the government in early 2007.

1.1.1.2 *Exchange and Cultural Programs*

The Beijing Declaration of 2000 is the starting point of China-Africa cooperation in economic and social development, which includes human resource development and education. During the first FOCAC meeting in Beijing in 2001, Chinese officials and delegates expressed China's will to focus on the exchange programs between Chinese and African students, as well as training programs for African teachers and projects to build schools across the continent. In the most recent meeting of the FOCAC, China declared the opening of one of the world's largest short-term training programmes, which plans to bring 30.000 African personnel in various sectors to China from 2013 to 2015.[59] China had also previously offered to increase the number

57 Robert I. Robertberg, ed. *China into Africa: Trade, Aid and Influence*, (Baltimore: Brookings Institution Press 2008) 174.

58 Louis Charbonneau and Michelle Nichols, "Exclusive: Russia, China block Central African Republic Blacklist at U.N.," *Reuters* 23 April 2014, Date Accessed: 24 April 2014. <http://www.reuters.com/article/2014/04/23/us-centralafrica-un-sanctions-idUSBREA3M1GA20140423>.

59 Kenneth King, *China's Aid and Soft Power in Africa: In Case of Education and Training* (New York: James Currey, 2013) 69.

of full scholarships for Africans to study in its universities, a total of 18,000 between 2013 and 2015.[60]

Table 1.2: Comparison of Number of African Students in Several Countries (2005–2009)

COUNTRIES	2005	2009	Evolution Rate (%)
FRANCE	107,707	105,766	–1.80
US	36,029	34,400	–4.52
GERMANY	21,909	15,698	–28.35
CHINA	2,757	11,909	**+339.9**

Sources: Chiffres Cles, Campus France, 2011 and Ministry of Education of PRC, China Daily

Table 1.3: Number of African Students in China (2005–2012)

Year	2005	2008	2009	2010	2011	2012
Number of African Students in China	2,757	8,799	11,909	16,403	20,744	27,052

Sources: Ministry of Education of the PRC, China Daily

As shown in Table 1.3, the number of African students in China has been decupled between 2005 and 2012. Accordingly, the number of African students in Western countries (France, Germany, US) has decreased year by year. (See Table 1.2). China's cultural diplomacy was extended with the establishment of several Confucius Institutes in Africa. There are already thirty-three Confucius Institutes[61] teaching Mandarin and Chinese language and culture at many of Africa's top universities, and there are five Confucius classrooms within secondary schools. Angola, which does not host any Confucius Institute, is currently working for the establishment of the Confucius Institute in

60 FOCAC, *Fifth Ministerial Conference of the Forum on China- Africa Cooperation Beijing Action Plan (2013–2015)*, Date Accessed: 23 May 2013 <www.focac.org/eng/ltda/dwjbzjjhys/>.

61 In Egypt, Kenya, Nigeria, and South Africa exists more than one Confucius Institutes. That means, it is more likely that not more than 25 countries in the entire continent have a Confucius Institute.

its capital city of Luanda through a cooperation between the Chinese CITIC Construction and Angola's Neto University.[62] In March 2014, Confucius Institute Headquarters signed the cooperation agreement with Agostinho Neto University in Luanda and CITIC Construction has become a sponsor for the Confucius Institute at Agostinho Neto University. Thus, for the first time, a Chinese funded enterprise participated in the construction of a Confucius Institute.[63]

Across China's main universities, there is a centre focused on China-Africa cooperation. The University of Beijing, one of the top universities in China, opened the first Institute of Afro-Asian Studies in 1964.

Similar to students from other African countries, every year students from Angola are invited to study in China. Ten scholarships are granted for ten Angolan students to study in China on an annual basis. Additionally, five scholarships are given by the Macau Foundation for the Angolan students to pursue studies in Macau.[64] By the end of 2007, sixty-eight Angolan students were in Mainland China pursuing a university diploma and seven more in Macau.[65] Computer Science and Civil Engineering are the top priorities for the Angolan Government, which also invests in this new generation of academic studies. With scholarships from the Chinese Government and Chinese state-owned companies, such as Sinohydro[66], Angolan students return home after four years of education as engineers. The return of twenty-nine Angolan students, who completed degrees in civil

---

62 "Feature: Angolan Student Realizing Chinese Dream," *Xinhuanet* 5 May 2014, Date Accessed: 5 May 2014. <http://news.xinhuanet.com/english/china/2014-05/05/c_133311725.htm>.

63 "Confucius Institute Headquarters Signs Agreements with Agostinho Neto University and CITIC Construction," *Hanban News* 28 March 2014, Date Accessed: 5 May 2014. <http://english.hanban.org/article/2014-03/28/content_530183.htm>.

64 Ana Cristina Alves, "The Oil Factor in Sino-Angolan Relations at the Start of the 21st Century," SAIIA Occasional Paper 55 (February 2010):7. *Voltairenet.* Date Accessed: 12 January 2012. <www.voltairenet.org/IMG/pdf/Sino-Angolan_Relations.pdf>.

65 Ibid., 7.

66 Since 2009, China's Sinohydro Company offers scholarship to 60 Angolan students to study in China. See: <http://www.sinohydro.com/736-1818-658081.aspx> Date Accessed: 12 January 2014>.

engineering in 2012, made headlines in Angolan newspapers. In June 2013, it was reported that the first Angolan students funded by Sinohydro had graduated and returned back to their homeland.[67] In May 2014 the success of a young Angolan man who studied in China's Science and Technology University and earned his Master's Degree from Qinghua University, was published by China's state news agency, Xinhua. He returned to Angola and is now working for the Chinese company CITIC Construction.[68]

The inauguration of the Angola/China Friendship School (Escola de Amizade Angola/China) was announced in early 2014, which will provide instruction for 200 students in the Angolan province of Huambo. The Angolan Foreign minister, Geoges Rebelo Pinto Chikoti, said:

> "This infrastructure represents above all, the living witness of the strong ties of friendship and solidarity and cooperation existing between the peoples and governments of Angola and China. The school shows the evidence of the fruits that the cooperation between the two countries has been producing in the various spheres, including the reconstruction of the country, construction of infrastructures, relaunch of the national economy and training of staff."[69]

Chinese training programs target both students and various professions from doctors to journalists; 45,000 professionals from Africa have been invited to attend short courses in China over the last nine years.[70] Additionally, African journalists and press officers are often invited on all-expenses-paid training sessions in Beijing.[71] Scholarships and training courses offered

---

67 Zhong Nan, "Power Giants Work on Local Touch," China *Daily* 20 December 2013, Date Accessed: 21 December 2013 <http://africa.chinadaily.com.cn/weekly/2013-12/20/content_17187099.htm>.

68 "Feature: Angolan Student Realizing Chinese Dream," *Xinhuanet (新华网)* 5 May 2014, Date Accessed: 5 May 2014. <http://news.xinhuanet.com/english/china/2014-05/05/c_133311725.htm>.

69 "Angola: Huambo-Angola/China Friendship School Shows Government Commitment," *all Africa* 24 February 2014, Date Accessed: 24 February 2014 <http://allafrica.com/stories/201402250252.html>.

70 Kenneth King, op.cit., 207.

71 Geoffrey York, "Why China is Making a Big Play to Control Africa's Media," *The Globe and Mail* 11 September 2013, Date Accessed: 13 September 2013 <http://www.theglobeandmail.com/news/world/media-agenda-china-buys-newsrooms-influence-in-africa/article14269323/>.

for African journalists play a crucial role in the development of an important foreign policy tool for China: Media and Commercials.

1.1.1.3 Engagement in Media and Commercials

From newspapers to satellite television and radio stations, China is investing heavily within African media. Africa has recently emerged as one of the significant media frontiers of China. As a result of a ten yearlong relationship of China in Africa, Chinese media has emerged as a new voice in Africa.

China's engagement in the media and commercial sector basically serves three main purposes: i) to reach overseas audiences ii) to diminish the control of non-Chinese media channels iii) to advance its image in the global arena.

The Western media's organization of the informational flow on a global scale has been seen as a threat to China's global rise. China had especially experienced it when following its support in the Darfur Crisis before the Olympic games of 2008. On 14 December 2006, it was argued by a Washington Post article that:

> "China seeks acceptance at the world's diplomatic top table – and this cause is unlikely to be advanced if China is perceived to be complicit in genocide. Imagine the newspaper ads leading up to the Beijing Games in 2008: Human rights campaigners will call on the world to boycott the Genocide Olympics."[72]

However one year after, Jean Marie Guehenno, the UN undersecretary-general for peacekeeping, said: "Beijing was playing a very important and constructive role in the Security Council to help bring consensus to end the fighting."[73] While UN officials saw China's role in Sudan more constructive than a year ago, Director Steven Spielberg had declared its resignation as the Games' artistic consultant. Director Steven Spielberg's resignation made headlines in many Western papers and steadily destroyed China's image. Ambassador Liu Guijin (刘贵今) said in an interview: "On the Darfur issue,

---

72 "China and Darfur," *The Washington Post* 14 December 2006, Date Accessed: 13 May 2013 <http://www.washingtonpost.com/wp-dyn/content/article/2006/12/13/AR2006121302008.html>.

73 "China Keen to Play Role in Ending Darfur Crisis-UN," *Sudan Tribune* 10 September 2007, Date Accessed: 13 May 2013 <http://www.sudantribune.com/spip.php?article23688>.

some Western media and particularly some non-governmental organizations have distorted China's role, which influenced some important rebel factions."[74] The Darfur issue is only one example of similar challenges China faces in terms of the circulation of information within international media. In general, China's presence in Africa has been widely criticized by Western news portals. China has mostly been reported as a neo-colonialist power that exploits resources to drive its own economic growth, while offering little in return. US assistant secretary for African Affairs, Johnnue Carson, and Former US State of Secretary, Hillary Clinton's warnings respectively against China's aggressive and pernicious competition with no morals and neo-colonialism in Africa hit the headlines in the Western press.[75] China knew that the expansion of its international influence depends on its ability to present a favorable picture of itself to the world. The necessity was the existence of a globally extended Chinese media.

A very important year for Sino-Africa media cooperation was 2006, when state-run media signed agreements regarding information exchange with some African countries, such as the Democratic Republic of Congo, Mali, Djibouti, and Equatorial Guinea. China also published official China's African Policy document on China's role in Africa, in which the nature of media cooperation was outlined:

> "China wishes to encourage multi-tired and multi-formed exchanges and cooperation between the media on both sides, so as to enhance mutual understanding and enable objective and balanced media coverage of each other. It will facilitate the communication and contacts between relevant government departments for the purpose of sharing experiences on ways to handle the relations with both domestic and foreign, and guiding and facilitating media exchanges."[76]

---

74 Anita Chang, "China: Media, Organizations Distorting Darfur," *USA Today* 26 June 2008, Date Accessed: 13 May 2013 <http://usatoday30.usatoday.com/news/world/2008-06-26-1059955913_x.htm>.

75 "US: China Lacks Morals in Africa," *Aljazeera* 9 December 2010, Date Accessed: 30 June 2013 <http://www.aljazeera.com/news/africa/2010/12/201012981346664660.html>; "Clinton Warns against New Colonialism in Africa," *Reuters* 11 June 2011, Date Accessed: 13 May 2013 <http://www.reuters.com/article/2011/06/11/us-clinton-africa-idUSTRE75A0RI20110611>.

76 Forum on China and Africa Cooperation (FOCAC), *China's African Policy*, 12 January 2006, Date Accessed: 11 May 2011 <www.focac.org/eng/zt/zgdfzzcwj>.

Kenya turned out to be the China's African media center. In 2006, China launched its first overseas FM radio, China Radio International (CRI) in Nairobi and moved Xinhua's Regional Editorial office that provides content to French-speaking Africa to Nairobi. In November 2010, CCTV opened its Africa Bureau in Nairobi, In April 2011, the Xinhua news agency partnered with a Kenyan network operator to provide news for mobile phones. That was followed nine months later by CCTV Africa in Nairobi, the first broadcast hub to be established by China Central Television (CCTV) outside Beijing. A joint venture, Xian Media Company, was set up in Hefei (in China's Anhui province) between China's Anhui Daily Group and South Africa's MIH Media Group in 2008. It was the first joint venture of a provincial-level newspaper group with a foreign company that was authorized by the central government.[77]

China has also been supporting African journalists to attend several training courses in China. In 2006, twenty radio and TV journalists from Africa were invited by the Chinese Media University.[78] Xinhua hosted African journalists by invitation in Beijing, and in 2007, thirty French speaking African journalists attended a training course at the Chinese Media University.[79]

Commercials, along with the media, play a significant role in the transformation of China's hard power into soft power. The relations driven mainly by infrastructure projects made China's use of those hard instruments of power for soft power purposes. Today in Africa, it is possible to see Chinese symbols, figures and various commercials of Chinese companies or their projects on the streets and even on the uniforms of some African national football teams.[80] Those visible constructions soften China's hard

---

77 Iginio Gagliardone, Maria Repnikova, Nicole Sremlau, "China in Africa: "A New Approach to Media Development?" *University of Oxford Programme in Comparative Media Law and Policy* (2010):9 Date Accessed 21 June 2013. <http://pcmlp.socleg.ox.ac.uk/sites/pcmlp.socleg.ox.ac.uk/files/China%20 in%20Africa_2010.pdf>.

78 Ibid., 7.

79 Ibid., 7.

80 Chinese networking and telecommunications company, Huawei, became the official sponsor of Ghana's national football team, the Black Stars, for the FIFA World Cup in Brazil in 2014, after a US$ 100.000 deal signed.

power instruments, such as the Headquarter of China International Fund (CIF) in Luanda, which lights up during the night to show Angolans various Chinese figures.[81]

Not only visible Chinese constructions, but also visible Chinese characters serve China's soft power strategy in Africa. China's president Xi Jinping's wife Peng Liyuan (彭丽媛) has emerged as a very strong soft power icon of China. Peng Liyuan, along with president Xi Jinping, received a place on TIME's list of the most influential people in the world.[82] Furthermore, for the first time in Chinese history a President's wife was referred to as the 'First Lady' by Chinese and American presses.[83]

Wall Street Journal highlighted the expectations by many political analysts and diplomats: "Ms. Peng will bolster and soften her husband's image by becoming the first wife of a Communist Chinese leader to play a role similar to that of a US First Lady."[84] Former NBA player Yao Ming (姚明) also emerged as a Chinese icon and projection of Chinese soft power on the world stage. Most recently, he has been very popular with efforts against the trade of ivory products. His visit to Kenya in 2012 and in September 2013 regarding the curb of the ivory trade and the relentless poaching of elephants attracted the attention of African people.

China's massive media investments in Africa, including journalist trainings, media aid programs and commercials with visible constructions and characters are resulting in increased Chinese influence in Africa. The headlines in the South African weekly newspaper Mail & Guardian "Chinese

81 See Appendix 2.

82 Hannah Beech, "The 2013 Time 100," *Time,* 18 April 2013, Date Accessed: 21 June 2013 <http://time100.time.com/2013/04/18/time-100/slide/peng-liyuan/>.

83 "Meet China's Folk Star First Lady in Waiting," *The Wall Street Journal* 13 February 2012, Date Accessed: 21 June 2013 <http://blogs.wsj.com/china-realtime/2012/02/13/peng-liyuan-meet-chinas-folk-song-singing-first-lady-in-waiting/>.

84 Jeremy Page, "China Swoons over New First Lady," *The Wall Street Journal* 22 March 2013, Date Accessed: 21 June 2013 <http://online.wsj.com/news/articles/SB10001424127887324103504578376201701604218>; "第一夫人着装大气受赞誉 例外就彭丽媛服饰发公告", *Guhantai (古汉台)* 30 March 2013, Date Accessed: 21 June 2013 <http://news.guhantai.com/2013/0330/222106.shtml>.

Dream is for a Better World"[85] and in the New York Times included a two page advert from China Daily entitled "Diaoyu Islands belong to China"[86] and another two pages advert entitled "Racing Abroad: While China remains a major recipient of foreign investment, its firms are making an increasing number of big acquisitions abroad"[87] are examples of China's growing global media influence.

So far, China's role in the Angolan Media, compared to these African countries, is very much limited. In Angola, Chinese TV and radio does not have any broadcasts in the Portuguese language. However, in June 2014, the Angolan Public Television (TPA) and China Central Television (CCTV) signed a cooperation protocol to share information programmes of mutual interest between Angola and China.[88] In January 2015, the online edition of the People's Daily, the central organ of the Chinese Communist Party, launched a portal in Portuguese to "promote communication and interchange" with Portuguese-language countries, especially with Angola, Brazil and Portugal.[89]

1.1.1.4 Foreign Aid in Chinese Characteristics

Foreign aid is another well-known foreign policy tool, despite attempts of Chinese foreign aid to distinguish itself from traditional foreign aid in two main principles. First, Chinese foreign aid policy is based on the principle

---

85 "Chinese Dream is for a Better World," *Mail & Guardian* 20 September 2013, Date Accessed: 20 September 2013 <http://mg.co.za/article/2013-09-20-00-chinese-dream-is-for-a-better-world>.

86 "Diaoyu Islands belong to China," *New York Times* 28 September 2012, Section A:16–17 (Advertisement)

87 "Racing Abroad: While China remains a major recipient of foreign investment, its firms are making an increasing number of big acquisitions abroad." *New York Times* 26 August 2011, Section A: 16–17. (Advertisement)

88 "Media Minister Ends Visit to China," *Agência Angola Press ANGOP* 23 June 2014, Date Accessed: 23 June 2014 <http://www.portalangop.co.ao/angola/en_us/noticias/sociedade/2014/5/26/Media-Minister-ends-visit-China,31407300-f367-47cf-b3f0-98e99020e77d.html>.

89 "China's People Daily Online Launches Portuguese-Language Portal," *The Portugal News Online* 8 January 2015, Date Accessed: 8 January 2015 <http://theportugalnews.com/news/chinas-peoples-daily-online-launches-portuguese-language-portal/33633>.

of non-interference in domestic affairs of other countries. Second, aid must be given without conditionality; aid cannot be combined with any political conditions. China, by publishing the White Paper on Africa, made it clear that foreign aid in Chinese characteristics "is based on the principles of equality, mutual benefit and mutual development and not-strings attached."[90]

In 1995, China undertook major reforms in its aid policy and launched an entirely new system of concessional loans.[91] Although, today China offers foreign aid in three forms: financial and material grants, zero interest loans, and low interest concessional loans with subsidized interest rate,[92] concessional aid loans dominate the total aid to Africa and are used mainly to finance infrastructure projects in over thirty-five African countries.[93] In the case of concessional loans, China preferred to follow a model known as the 'Angola Mode', which refers to the oil for infrastructure projects. The model mainly serves as the establishment of a reciprocal platform between China and the recipient countries by securing the natural resources of recipient countries with low-interest loans and infrastructure projects. As Brautigam noted: "The Chinese now wanted to channel their aid money more directly as support for 'mutually beneficial' business."[94] Connecting aid money to the 'mutually beneficial business' demanded bilateral negotiations, which generally created some economic conditions. Therefore, it's possible to argue that, the aid given by China, eliminated political conditions but not economic. The Concessional Loan Department of the Exim Bank of China published the basic criteria for the projects as follows:[95]

90 Forum on China and Africa Cooperation (FOCAC), *China's African Policy*, 12 January 2006, Date Accessed: 11 May 2011. <www.focac.org/eng/zt/zgdfzzcwj>.

91 Deborah Brautigam, op.cit., 80.

92 Deborah Brautigam, op.cit., 105.

93 Thomas Lum, op.cit., 10.

94 Deborah Brautigam, op.cit., 81.

95 Takaaki Kobayashi, "Evolution of China's Aid Policy," *JBIC Institute (JBICI)* 27 (2008):16.

i) The project should be approved by both the Chinese and the government of the borrowing country.
ii) The project should be technically feasible and generate favorable economic returns.
iii) The projects should have good social benefits.
iv) Chinese enterprises should be selected as contractor/exporter.
v) Equipment, materials, technology or services needed for the project should be acquired from China ahead of other countries.

In principle, no less than 50 % of the material procurement should come from China. Cleary, China has created new terms of conditions serving their own economic ends. However, those conditions are similar to what OECD economically demands from recipient countries. For example, according to figures published by the Development Assistance Committee of the OECD in 2001, Italy's official development aid was 92 % tied and Canada's 68 % tied; and in 2007, 50 % of procurement aid from Portugal and Greece was tied to their own goods and services.[96] Thus, China's competitive deals let China preserve its favorable position in Africa. Kenyan government officials put it better: "China is perhaps one of the most price-competitive sources whether its development aid is tied or not tied."[97]

1.2 China in Angola

Angola faced twenty-seven years of civil war (1975–2002) and is today among the fastest growing economies in the world. The vast expanded territory of Angola makes Angola the third largest country in the Sub-Saharan Africa in terms of its territory. It contains a huge amount of natural resources, particularly minerals and oil as well as thirty-five million hectares of arable land. Although the country is Sub-Saharan Africa's second-largest oil producer and has great agricultural potentials such as fertile agricultural lands and suitable climatic conditions, one-third of the population live below the poverty line.

96 Deborah Brautigam, op.cit., 152.
97 Joseph Onjala, "A Scoping Study on China – Africa Economic Relations: The Case of Kenya," *African Economic Research Consortium (AERC)* (2008): 41.

The conflicts in Angola date back to 1961 when a struggle for independence from Portugal commenced after the uprising of the local people against coercion in cotton cultivation. Increasing cotton production caused food shortages and left people at risk of hunger. That situation developed into a multi-faction struggle for the control of Portugal's former colony. The conflict arose among three nationalist movements; *Frente Nacional de Libertação de Angola* (FNLA), *União Nacional para a Independência Total de Angola* (UNITA), and *Movimento Popular de Libertação de Angola* (MPLA). In the 1970s and 80s the MPLA government was supported by Cuba and the Soviet Union, while the United States provided large amounts of aid first to the FNLA and then UNITA. The conflict came to an end in 1974 when a leftist military coup in Lisbon overthrew Portugal's Estado Novo regime. However, not long after the declaration of Angolan independence, Angola had to deal with another conflict which arose as a power struggle between two former liberation movements, the People's Movement for the Liberation of Angola (MPLA) and the National Union for the Total Independence of Angola (UNITA).

Since the end of the civil war in 2002, the MPLA government entered in a transition process from war to peace, from single-party to a multiparty system, from a centralized and planned socialist economy to a free market economy. Beyond a doubt, when the civil war ended in 2002, the country was completely devastated. The inflation rate was recorded in 2003 at 106 %, and GDP was recorded as only US$ 16.9 billion. Agricultural production seriously decreased, and the manufacturing sector, which accounted for 10 % of GDP at the time of independence, almost disappeared.[98] The economic transformation of Angola is still suffering from a number of problems, including corruption and constraints to private sector development. Human Rights Watch estimates that "from 1997 to 2002, an estimated US$ 4.2 billion in oil revenues disappeared from government coffers, roughly equal to all foreign and domestic social and humanitarian spending in Angola over

98 "Who is Benefiting from Trade Liberalization in Angola?: A Gender Perspective," *UNCTAD* (2013):vi, Date Accessed: 13 February 2014. <http://unctad.org/en/PublicationsLibrary/ditc2013d3_en.pdf>.

the same period."[99] Devastated land and a corrupted economy resulted in the breaking of assistance expectations of the Angolan government from Western countries. Asis Malaquias argues that "the government expected that Western countries in particular, would rush in with assistance because they were perceived as being partly responsible for the destruction inflicted upon Angola, owing to their support for UNITA rebels during much of the conflict."[100] However, Angola with its high reputation as one of the most corrupt countries in the world[101], received no positive signals from the Western states in terms of providing funds for reconstruction of the country. At that point in time, China stepped in Angola to fill the vacuum left by Western states. As Assis Malaquias argues, "China's significant oil-backed line of credit (2004) to Angola could not have come at a better time for the MPLA government."[102] Angola, with China's engagement, has given a start not only to the effective use of natural resources but also to the process of diversification of economy by investing in other sectors such as the construction and fishing industries, in order to avoid the 'paradox of plenty'.[103]

As multiple deep-water blocks opened up, the production of crude oil boomed between 2003 and 2008. Angola's total oil (petroleum and other liquids) production peaked in 2008, reaching nearly 2.0 million bbl/d, of which more than 1.9 million bbl/d was crude oil. However, since 2008, the oil production has gradually declined. In recent years, the total oil production averaged around 1.8 million bbl/d (crude oil: 1.7 million bbl/d). It is argued that, "Angola's production has been stagnant as a result of persistent

---

99 "Transparency and Accountability in Angola," *Human Rights Watch* (2010):1, Date Accessed: 13 February 2014. <http://www.hrw.org/sites/default/files/reports/angola0410webwcover_1.pdf>.

100 Assis Malaquias, "China is Angola's New Best Friend-for Now," *China and Angola: A Marriage of Convenience?*, eds. Marcus Power and Ana Cristina Alves, (Cape Town, Dakar, Nairobi and Oxford: Pambazuka Press, 2012) 35.

101 Angola ranked 157th out of the 176 countries reviewed by the Transparency International Corruption Index in 2012.

102 Asis Malaques, op.cit., 38.

103 The term refers to the paradox that countries with an abundance natural resources tend to have less economic growth than countries with fewer resources and they experience remarkably similar economic and political problems. See: Terry L. Karl, *The Paradox of Plenty: Oil Boom and Petro-States*, (Berkeley: University of California Press, 1997).

technical problems related to water injection systems, gas cooling, and floating, production, storage, and offloading (FPSO) units associated with some projects."[104] Despite the technical problems, in order to increase the production, Angola has several oil projects, which are expected to start producing oil in the next few years. (See Table 1.4).

Table 1.4: Upcoming Oil Projects in Angola

Project	Peak Production (thousand bbl/d)	Operator	Est. start	Location
CLOV (Cravo-Lirio-Orquidea-Voleta)	160	TOTAL	2014	Block 17 deepwater
West Hub Project (Sangos, N'Goma, Cinguwu	80	Eni	2014+	Block 15/06 deepwater
Mafumeira Sul	120	Chevron	2015	Block 0 offshore
Lianzi field	46	Chevron	2015	Block 14 deepwater
Kizombo Satellites Phase II	125	ExxonMobil	2016	Block 15 deepwater
Negage	75	Chevron	2016+	Block 14 deepwater
Lucapa	100	Chevron	2016+	Block 14 deepwater
East Hub Project (Cabaca Norte, Sout-East)	80+	Eni	2016+	Block 15 deepwater
B31 SE	200+	BP	2016+	Block 31 ultra deepwater
Kaombo Project	200	Total	2017	Block 32 ultra deep water

Source: U.S Energy Information Administration based on company reports and Oil & Gas Journal, retrieved from http://www.eia.gov/countries/cab.cfm?fips=AO, April 2014.

104 U.S Energy Information Administration. *A Report on Angola*. EIA, February 2014:9 Date Accessed: 20 April 2014 <http://www.eia.gov/countries/analysisbriefs/Angola/angola.pdf>.

As mentioned above, Angola today produces 1.7 million bbl/d crude oil and exports all of its productions to other countries. China receives nearly half of its production, which accounted for 47 % in 2013.

Angola's GDP increased from US$ 12.86 billion in 2003 to US$ 115.86 billion in 2013 and has become one of the fastest growing economies in the world. (See Figure 1.1).

Figure 1.1: GDP Growth in Angola (2003–2013)

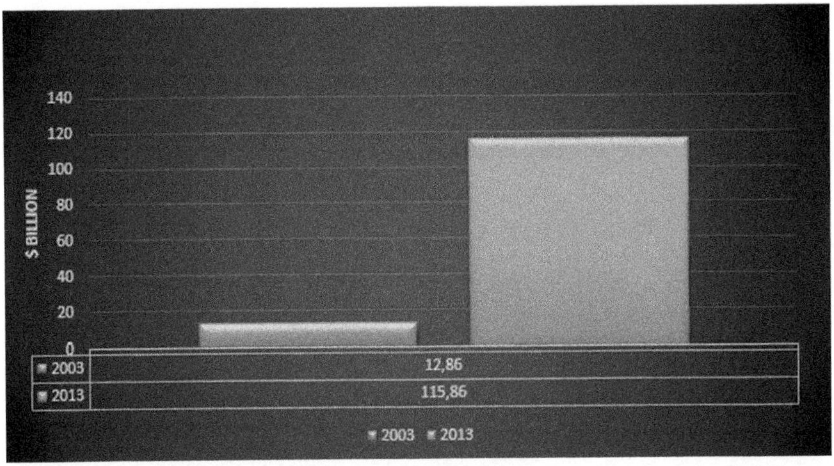

Source: AFDB

The inflation rate was over 100 % in 2003 and decreased to one-digit percentage. The inflation rate in Angola decelerated to 7.22 % in April 2014 from 7.84 % recorded in January of 2014 by the Instituto Nacional de Estatística, Angola.[105] The rapid growth rate and decrease in the inflation rate have permitted an increase in the GDP per capita. However, there is a significant difference in the evolution of the GDP per capita when comparing GDP based on purchasing power parity per capita (PPP), in other words, purchasing capacity of income per capita. While GDP per capita increased by 595 % from 2003 to 2012, GDP based on PPP has only increased by

105 Isabel Felino, "Angola Inflation Rate," *Trading Economics* 16 April 2014, Date Accessed: 08 May 2014. <http://www.tradingeconomics.com/angola/inflation-cpi>.

128 %. (See Figure 1.2). This reflects the fact that despite the huge growth in GDP per capita and quick notable decrease in inflation rate, the growth in purchasing capacity of income per capita remains far behind the growth in GDP per capita. In a survey –Cost of Living Survey- conducted by Mercer in 2013, Luanda was ranked as the most expensive city for expatriates in the world.[106] The reasons lie above all in the lack of competition in some economic sectors, poor transport conditions, large import dependency and high salaries in the oil sector.

Figure 1.2: Socio-Economic Development of Angola (2003–2012)

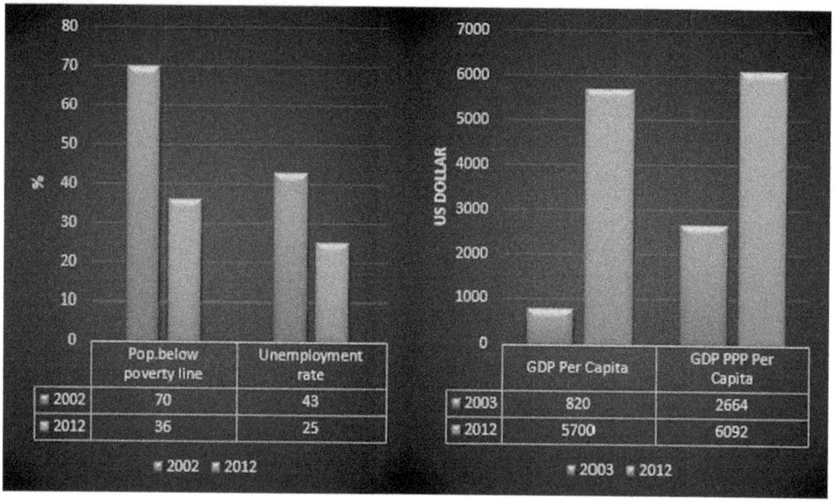

Source: IMF World Economic Outlook, Index Mundi, UNDP, AFDB

The total population of Angola was recorded at 20.6 million people in 2012 and the rate of the people who live below the poverty line decreased to 36 % in 2012, which was recorded at 70 % in 2003. Furthermore, in the same period of time (2003–2012), unemployment rate dropped from 43 %

106 "Cost of Living Survey," *Newsroom: Cost of Living Survey*, Mercer, 23 July 2013, Date Accessed: 24 July 2013 <http://www.mercer.com/newsroom/cost-of-living-survey-2013.html>.

to 25 %. According to the World Bank's report in 2012[107], Angola climbed into 'upper middle income' countries from 'the lower income' group.

1.2.1 Historical Background of the Relations between China and Angola

In order to fully understand the main characteristics of the relations between China and Angola, it is worth explaining the historical development of bilateral relations. Although the same party has ruled Angola since 1975, its relations with China did not stay same. When independence from Portugal was declared in November 1975, the MPLA controlled the capital and its leader, Agnostinho Neto, became the first president of Angola. During the struggle against Portuguese colonial rule from 1961 to 1975, China had 'hot and cold' relations with the three rival national liberation movements in Angola. First, China approached the MPLA, the largest liberation movement, however, pro-Soviet tendency of MPLA made China switch its support to the FNLA in 1963. FNLA was a movement that was based in Zaire (now Democratic Republic of Congo) and was allowed to run military camps on the DRC territory in which the entrance of Chinese delegates to the Democratic Republic of Congo was not allowed.[108] That situation had eventually broken the relations between China and FNLA. In 1964, China switched its side once again and started supporting UNITA, which was formed by a rebel group that had split from the FNLA. UNITA was led by Jonas Sawimbi. Sawimbi had trained in China in 1964–1965, and adopted Maoist approaches such as self-sufficiency and tactics such as multiple military fronts. However, in the early 1970s, anti-Soviet sentiment in China, which had started right after Kruschev's revisionist policies in the aftermath of Stalin's death, reached its peak. In order to break Soviet Union's power in Angola, China tried to improve its relations with Soviet-backed MPLA. In 1971, China invited MPLA's leader Agostinho Neto for a visit to Beijing. The negotiations resulted in disappointed Chinese authorities who believed

107 "The World Bank: Classification of Countries," *The World Bank Data* July 2012, Date Accessed: 08 May 2014 <http://data.worldbank.org/about/country-classifications/country-and-lending-groups>.

108 Ana Cristina Alves, op.cit., 5.

that the MPLA leader Agostinho Neto was too 'pro-Russian'.[109] Following that, China made another strategic return towards UNITA, which was considered more likely to come into power in the future. The improving relations with Zaire's Mobutu government resulted in China turning its attention to FNLA. After President Mobutu's visit to Beijing, FNLA managed to receive a promise of aid from China in 1973.[110]

The Carnation Revolution (*Revolução dos Cravos)* in Portugal, the 1974 military coup, caused Chinese concerns regarding the Soviet's growing influence in Angola. China, at that time, followed a strategy based on unification of three organizations. In that context, China had organized meetings in Beijing for representatives of all three organizations, commenting that, "overcoming difficulties and getting united would bring the liberation movements success."[111] The military-coup in Portugal and other issues accelerated the declaration of independence of Angola from Portugal. On November 11, 1975, Soviet-military backed MPLA declared its independence. The country was immediately recognized by the USSR. However, China refused to build any formal diplomatic relations with Angola until 1983. The improving relations between China and the USSR played a major role in the establishment of diplomatic ties between China and Angola. On the political level, the first meeting between the leaders of Angola (President José Eduardo dos Santos) and China (President Deng Xiaoping 邓小平) was held in October 1988 in Beijing. During the meeting, Angola's President José Eduardo dos Santos expressed his party MPLA's main goal, based on repairing the broken Angolan economy to "improve our economic leadership, readjust our policies for construction and straighten out our financial affairs."[112] Deng Xiaoping stressed the importance of the peaceful end of the civil war for the promotion of economic construction and development in the country, "dialogue is better than confrontation, and relaxation is

---

109 W Schneidman, "Confronto em África- Washington e a Quedo do Império Colonial Português," (Lisboa: *Edições* Tribuna, 2007) cited in Sofia Fernandes, "China and Angola: a strategic partnership?," *China and Angola: A Marriage of Convenience?*, Marcus Power and Ana Cristina Alves eds., (Cape Town, Dakar, Nairobi and Oxford: Pambazuka Press, 2012) 69.

110 Ian Taylor (2006), op.cit., 77.

111 People's Daily, (January 22, 1975) quoted in Ian Taylor, 2006, op.cit., 79.

112 Renmin Ribao, (October 22, 1988) quoted in Ian Taylor, 2006, op.cit., 88.

better than tension."[113] Following that visit, trade flows between two countries increased and the second meeting between two countries was held in 1999 at the Economic and Trade Joint Commission meeting. That meeting gave signals of the growing weight of economic cooperation and trade in the bilateral relations of China and Angola. The end of the twenty-seven yearlong civil war in 2002 and the launch of China's going-out strategy occurred at the same time.[114] During that time, Angola was busy with the IMF negotiations; US$ 11 billion of debt could be relieved through Paris Club if Angola would comply with IMF's requirements. Angola negotiated at least four IMF programs between 1995 and 2004, but could not manage to come up with a sufficient conclusion.[115] The bilateral relations between IMF and Angola turned into a vicious cycle. Angola promised the IMF to create greater transparency in oil revenues, reduce fuel subsidies, raise water rates, rein in borrowing and privatize several money-losing enterprises. However, despite the promises of Angola, IMF declared Angola's failure in meeting its demands.

According to an estimate from the international watchdog group Global Witness, between September 2000 and October 2001 alone, international banks provided Angola up to 3.55 billion in high cost, oil-backed loans.[116] As a high-risk country, Angola had borrowed at LIBOR (the London Inter-Bank Offered Rate) plus 2.5 % from the international banks.[117] Therefore, China's entrance to Angola with cost-less oil-backed loans attracted attention of the Angolan government. China offered Angola oil-backed loans at LIBOR plus 1.5 %.[118] Furthermore, China offered an exceptional loan model, called 'Angola Mode'-oil for infrastructure. The devastated economy and infrastructure in the country, alongside rising oil prices, paved Angola's way to turn its face

113 Xinhua News, (October 22, 1988) quoted in Ian Taylor, 2006, op.cit., 88.

114 According to a UN report in 2004, Chinese direct foreign investments rose from US$ 3 billion in 1991 to US$ 35 billion in 2003, see "UN Report: China becoming major investor abroad" *People's Daily* 07 January 2004, Date Accessed: 12 April2014 <http://english.peopledaily.com.cn/200401/07/eng20040107_132003.shtml>.

115 Deborah Brauutigam, op.cit., 274.

116 Ibid., 275.

117 Ibid., 275.

118 Ibid., 275.

towards China and ultimately turning its back on IMF. As the Angolan Ambassador to Portugal, José Marcos Barrica, stated in his speech at a meeting with Portuguese business people in April 2014: "China promptly stood by Angola at the time the country was going through a crucial and distressing moment and hardly needed external aid to rise from the ruins of a fierce war."[119] All these developments present that, the vacuum left by international financial institutions and Western countries had been filled by an auspicious Chinese strategy, which would later bring profitable deals for both nations.

1.2.2 Angola's Importance for China

Angola, as Africa's second largest oil producer with an average 1.75 million barrels per day, attracted the attention of energy-hungry China. However, economic interdependence between China and Angola initially arose when China's increasing energy demand merged with a challenge the Angolan government confronted in reconstruction of the country since the end of the civil war in 2002. In other words, Angola has emerged as more than an energy hub for China. Decades of civil war had destroyed infrastructure, halted economic expansion and prevented any progress on social development indicators. Angola's needy situation in terms of rebuilding its country and economy made China diversify its interests in the country.

Angola is endowed not only with oil resources but also other resources such as diamond and natural gas. This allowed China to develop its business activities with the country. Apart from the existence of underground treasures, such as diamond, oil and gas reserves, Angola is located over fertile soils and arable lands offering great potential for commercial agricultural development. Before the start of the twenty-seven yearlong civil war, Angola was the world's fourth largest coffee producer, a top exporter in sisal, sugarcane, banana and cotton and self-sufficient in all food crops except wheat.[120]

119 "Ambassador Praises Cooperation with China," *Agência Angola Press ANGOP* 11 April 2014, Date Accessed: 12 April 2014 <http://www.portalangop.co.ao/angola/en_us/noticias/politica/2014/3/15/Ambassador-praises-cooperation-with-China,83e5422e-3811-4ac6-aad3-b73c4e700681.html>.

120 "Country Profile: Angola," *Country Profile,* New Agriculturist, July 2009, 21 April 2013 <http://www.newag.info/en/country/profile.php?a=781>.

Angola's strategic location and abundant dynamic young population are also providing opportunities for China. Angola has a potentially huge labor force capable of generating a strong domestic market. According to the African Development Bank 2011 Report, 45 % of its 18 million population is under 15 years old.[121] However, its heavily oil-dependent economy, 97 % of its oil exports, provides job opportunities for only about 20,000 people.[122]

Figure 1.3: Export Goods of Angola, 2013

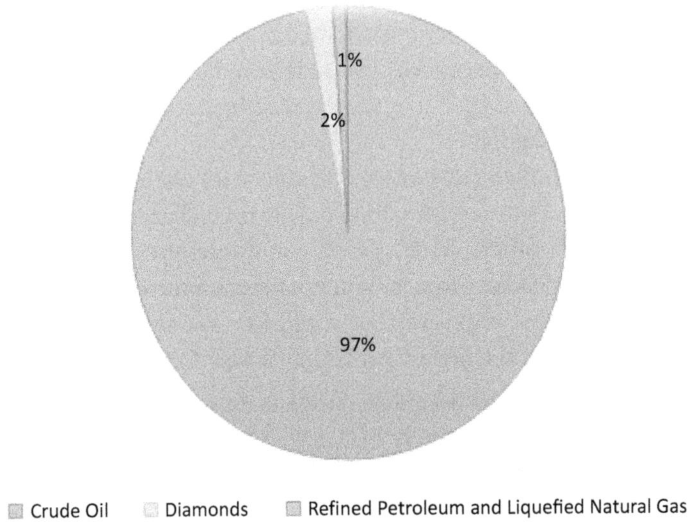

Source: Banco Nacional de Angola and www.diamonds.net

Angola's tremendous potential in almost every sector of the economy has resulted in its rising importance for China, a country needing resources for its own growing economy. On the other hand, Angola has emerged as an ideal market for Chinese products and the place for China to strengthen the

121 "2011 Annual Report," AFDB, 1 June 2012, Date Accessed: 31 March 2013. <www.afdb.org>.

122 Ricardo Soares de Oliveira, "Business Success, Angola-Style: Postcolonial Politics and the Rise of Sonangol," *F. of Modern African Studies* 45:4 (2007): 616.

global presence of its state-owned companies and to locate its own citizens to solve the problems associated with China's overpopulation.

1.2.3 China's Importance for Angola

China's burgeoning global influence and emergence as the world's second largest economy has resulted in capturing the attention of several developing countries. As American political scientist Horace Campbell argued: "The rapid rise of China is a testament that poor societies can rise beyond colonial exploitation."[123] On the one hand, China emerged as an encouraging factor for many developing countries. On the other hand, China's increasing demand for energy with its large population and high economic growth rates, positioned itself as a crucial trading partner for many oil rich countries, such as Angola.

In contrast to similar relations of Angola with each of its traditional donors, Angola's relations with China has its own characteristics that distinguish itself from others. First, China's non-interference principle, and granting of financial aid to Angola with no-strings attached, has challenged the traditional donors' imposition of conditions on aid provision. As the Beijing Declaration of the Forum on China-Africa Cooperation stated:

> "[C]ountries that vary from one another in the social system, stages of development, historical and cultural background, and values, have the right to choose their own approaches and models in promoting and protecting human rights in their own countries."[124]

Second, China's way of doing business differs from that of Angola's former trade partners. It is based on a deal structure known as Angola Mode or Resource for Infrastructure, referring to the repayment of loans for Angola's infrastructure development. It consists of natural resources, similar to the oil-for-infrastructure model Japan used in China three decades prior. The interdependent structure of the Angola Mode has been challenging the attraction of the Western type of 'top-down aid.' China's former Ambassador Ji Peiding (吉佩定), who served in various African countries such as Nigeria, Zimbabwe, Namibia and South Africa, offered advice to US President

123 Firoze Manji and Stephan Marks eds., op.cit., 132.
124 Ian Taylor (2009), op.cit., 17.

Barack Obama: "You must take Africa as an equal. This is the basic condition of success."[125] Thus, the mutual benefits gained through the engagement increased China's popularity in the eyes of Angolan government, which requires an equal relationship, opposed to the West's top-down attitudes. As Ethiopian Minister of State underlines the difference between China and the West:

> "They have one major advantage *vis–à–vis* the West (US) –they are always prepared to engage with African countries theoretically and in principle on the basis of respect and equality. This, for a continent and for a people colonized, and used to the double standards of the West, has a lot of impacts."[126]

Third, by providing export sellers and buyers credits, the Chinese government is building a healthier balance of trade than most Western countries. Chinese financial institutes, such as China Exim Bank, support Chinese companies, this creates a competitive advantage for Chinese companies against Western companies. Furthermore, the presence of Chinese companies as contractors or exporters, has allowed local people to reach many products for lower prices.

1.3 Literature Review

China's engagement with African countries has been attracting the attention of many scholars. There is a wide-range of literature analyzing China's growing involvement in Africa from various perspectives. In the Literature Review, it is aimed to summarize the different perspectives of scholars on the Chinese role in Africa and to display their gaps and flaws.

Studies are mainly concentrated on two focal points: The first interpretation of China's role in Africa reflects a negative perspective that sees China as a resource grabber who places its interests on gaining access to natural resources and breaking the influence of the traditional Western states in the continent, while putting aside Africa's initial needs which are accompanied with human-rights, democracy and good-governance. The second

---

125 Nicholas Kotch, "China 'like a brother' to Africa, says former envoy as US summit approaches," *Business Day Live* 30 April 2014, Date Accessed 30 April 2014 <http://www.bdlive.co.za/africa/africanbusiness/2014/04/30/china-like-a-brother-to-africa-says-former-envoy-as-us-summit-approaches>.

126 Kenneth King, op.cit., 40.

point scholars concentrate on is the Chinese way of aid and their effects on development and economic growth in Africa.

1.3.1 Negative Perspective: China as a Resource Grabber and a Neo-Colonialist Power

China's interest in securing energy resources in oil-rich countries has become the main asset of the negative arguments. Some significant scholars in the China-Africa field, Chris Alden, Dan Large and Soares de Oliveira claim that the relations between China and African countries are primarily driven by China's interests to secure a long-term import of oil.[127] Similarly, Kopinski, Polus and Taylor argue that: "Resource security is undoubtedly the biggest driving force behind China's increased involvement in Africa."[128] Furthermore, they explain their concerns from a view of a dependency theorists: "By focusing on primarily on exporting natural resources, in particular oil, African states may find themselves open to market shocks which may devastate fragile developing economies."[129]

In addition to that, some scholars put emphasis on the similarities between China and Western predecessors of Africa who exploited the natural resources and left nothing for the local people.[130] The resemblance lies in the exchange of unequal values: African raw materials in exchange for processed, cheap Chinese products. While some scholars see the low-cost Chinese goods as an opportunity, as they enable local people to reach some luxury goods which were not affordable for many African people; some other scholars, such as Manji and Marks and Rutendo Dhliwayo

---

127 Chris Alden, Dan Large and Ricardo Soares de Oliveira, "China Returns to Africa: Anatomy of an Expansive Engagement." *Real Instituto Elcano* (2008):8.

128 Dominik Kopinski, Andrzej Polus and Ian Taylor, *China's Rise in Africa: Perspectives on a Developing Connection*, (Routledge: New York, 2013) 4.

129 Ibid., 4.

130 Ian Taylor, *China and Africa: Engagement and Compromise.* (London: Routledge, 2006); Michelle Chan- Fishel, "Environment Impact: More of the Same," in Firoze Manji and Stephen Marks eds., *African Perspectives on China in Africa,*139–152; Raphael Kaplinsky, Dorothy McCormick and Mike Morris, *China and Sub Saharan Africa: Impacts and Challenges of a Growing Relationship,* SAIS Working Papers in African Studies, 2008.

and Kaplinsky, McCormick and Morris stress on the challenges African industry faces. "The overwhelming domination of China in Africa and the global textile and clothing industry has frustrated local manufacturers who find it exceedingly difficult to compete."[131] Kaplinsky, McCormick and Morris, similarly draw our attention on the sectors such as clothing and furniture in which China's growing competitiveness is having a very harmful impact on many SSA exporting economies.[132]

Likewise, Alden, who uses the concept of hegemony when analyzing China's presence in Africa, pointed out the closure of South African and Nigerian textile mills, resulting in job losses for thousands of Africans due to cheap Chinese imports.[133] Furthermore, Jenkins and Edwards in their article "Chinese Competition and the Restructuring of South African Manufacturing" claim that the Chinese competition would harm the South African economy in a serious way and that Chinese engagement would lead to the destruction of the whole industry sector.[134]

According to some other scholars, such as Alden, Alves as well as Jansson, China has been paying very little attention to the development necessities of Africa such as improvement in human rights, governance transparency and democratic values.[135] David Zweig and Bi Jianhai also

---

131 Rutendo Dhliwayo,"A Continent vs. A Country: China putting strain on Africa's Clothing and Textile Industries, Consultancy African Intelligence, 2012 <http://www.consultancyafrica.com/index.php?option=com_content&view=article&id=1111:a-continent-vs-a-country-china-putting-strain-on-africas-clothing-and-textile-industries-&catid=82:african-industry-a-business&Itemid=266>.

132 Kaplinsky, R., McCormick, D. and Morris, M. (2008) 'China and Sub-Saharan Africa: Impacts and Challenges of a Growing Relationship', SAIS Working Paper in African Studies 05–08, Johns Hopkins University, 6.

133 Chris Alden, *China in Africa*, (Zed Books: London, 2007):80.

134 Lawrence Edwards and Rhys Jenkins, "Chinese Competition and the Restructuring of South African Manufacturing," Dev Research Briefing, 4 August 2012, Date Accessed: 1 July 2014 <http://www.uea.ac.uk/polopoly_fs/1.220503.1346400476!DEV%20research%20briefing%2008-2012-RJ-final.pdf>.

135 Johanna Jansson, 'Chinese investment in Gabon's extractive industries' *Pambazuka News*, 2010, Date Accessed: 1 July 2014 <http://www.pambazuka.org/en/category/africa_china/65779>.

note that what China doing in Africa has left little room for morality.[136] China's non-interference policy pushes more the dictators in Africa to resist against Western governments and institutions that are using economic pressure to provide improvement to human rights and governance transparency.[137] Similarly, Penhelt explains his concerns about China's involvement in Africa without taking into account the quality of governance by arguing that China's aid serves only in unstable, problematic and rogue countries.[138] Bhola also points to that China has no experience in good governance, fails to understand the value of human rights and associated principles, it lacks respect for the rule of law and property rights. Thus, China cannot be a responsible actor in Africa.[139]

Another negative argument is related with China's so-called efforts to play a neo-colonialist role in the continent and simultaneously in the world. Under the motto of South-South cooperation, China is seeking to gain political control over the African states and create a new set of alliances in order to form a multi-polar world. Based on this logic, Robert Kagan expresses his fears that China is trying hard to develop like-minded dictators. He supports his view by purporting that "China aims in the near term to replace the United States as the dominant power in East Asia and plans to challenge America's position as the dominant power in the world in the long-term."[140]

Most of the negative approaches on China's engagement in Africa originate from Western-based scholars to whom China is primarily conducting a zero-sum game in which it is the one leading a strategy that serves only its

---

136 David Zweig and Bi Jianhai, "China's Global Hunt for Energy," *Foreign Affairs*, 2005.

137 Kenneth Roth, "China's Silence Boost Tyrants," *International Herald Tribune*, 19 April 2006, Date Accessed: 1 July 2014 <http://www.iht.com/articles/2006/04/19/opinion/edroth.php>.

138 Gernot Penhelt, "The Political Economy of China's Aid Policy in Africa", *Jena Economic Research Paper n°2007-051*, 2007, 16.

139 Gaurav Bhola, "China and India Battle for Influence in Africa: Part 4," 15 October 2007, Date Accessed: 1 July 2014 <http://www.gimmiethescoop.com/china-and-india-battle-for-influence-in-africa-part-4>.

140 Robert Kagan, "What China Knows and We Don't: The Case for a New Strategy of Containment," *The Weekly Standard,* 20 January 1997:24.

interests. These scholars are supporting the argument that China is taking advantage of Africans through uneven partnership agreements. They argue that China is plundering the African resources. However, there are other scholars who share the view that it would be unfair to accuse China of practicing a new form of exploitation as Chinese aid may carry more potential for bringing development and economic growth in Africa.

1.3.2 Chinese Way of Aid and its Effects on Development, Economic Growth in Africa

The Chinese way of aid differs sharply from Western aid. Thus, scholars began to focus on China's lending and their results on the development of African states. Scholars in this field see energy resources as main drivers for China's way of aid. "Since China's large overseas investments are executed by state-owned enterprises, and backed by state-controlled banks, many observers posit that Beijing uses aid and soft loans to secure access to natural resources."[141] The majority of China-Africa scholars share the common perspective which regards to China's need of oil and other natural resources as the starting point of China's financial assistance to African countries and to Angola in particular. Despite these viewpoints, there are two conflicting perspectives among scholars. The first group of scholars, such as Lyman, Dreher, Fuchs, Power and Mohan, see Chinese way of aid as rogue aid, driven by Chinese interests and not by the recipients' needs.[142] Onjala expresses his concerns about the type of Chinese aid, which is closely bundled with infrastructural projects and often connected to the extraction and export of minerals and oil to China. He believes this kind of aid will

141 Michelle Chan-Fishel & Roxanne Lawson, "Quid Pro Quo? China's Investment-for-Resource Swaps in Africa," *Development* 50 (2007):64.

142 Princeton Lyman, "China's Rising Role in Africa", *Council on Foreign Relations*, 21 June 2005, Date Accessed: 4 July 2014 <http://www.cfr.org/china/chinas-rising-role-africa/p8436>.; Alex Dreher & Andreas Fuchs, "Rogue Aid? The Determinants of China's Aid Allocation," *Working Papers CEB 11-035*, ULB – Universite Libre de Bruxelle, 2011; Marcus Power & Giles Mohan, "Towards a Critical Geopolitics of China's Engagement with African Development," *Geopolitics* 15.3 (2010): 462–495.

hurt African countries in the long-run.[143] As an example, the concerns on China's involvement in Angola increased among some scholars especially after the emergence of cracks outside of the Luanda General Hospital. Some scholars, among them an Angolan scholar Rafel Marques de Morais, refer to the poor quality of Chinese constructions and expressed his concerns over China's growing presence in Angola in the following words: "Beyond the low engineering and construction standards, the Chinese intervention in Angola is widely seen as fostering social stultification and regression."[144]

The second group of scholars sees the Chinese way of aid from a win-win perspective. Through the FOCAC process, China has cancelled African debt, facilitated expanded market access and provided a wide range of new opportunities for positive engagement.[145] In short, while some scholars argue that the aid given in absence of any political conditions makes China a rogue donor state, some other scholars note that it is not fair to call China a rogue donor due to differences between Chinese and Western aid. According to Brautigam, "many of the fears about Chinese aid and engagement are misinformed."[146] For example, in contrast to the critiques claim that China is interested in giving aid only to resource-rich countries, Brautigam in her book 'The Dragon's Gift: The Real Story of China in Africa, put emphasis on small countries like Sierra Leone which receives the same amount of financial support and investment from China as larger

---

143 Joseph Onjala, "A Scoping Study of on China-Africa Economic Relations: The Case of Kenya," *African Economic Research Consortium (AERC)*, 5 March 2008:42.

144 Rafael Marques de Morais, The New Imperialism: China in Angola, *World Affairs*, 2011, Date Accessed: 4 July 2014 <http://www.worldaffairsjournal.org/article/new-imperialism-china-angola>.

145 Hon et. al., Evaluating China's FOCAC commitments to Africa and Mapping the Way Ahead, *Report by the Centre for Chinese studies at Stellenbosch University*, (2010):4–5.

146 Deborah Brautigam, "China in Africa: Seven Myths," *ARI*, 2011, Date Accessed: 4 July 2014 <http://www.realinstitutoelcano.org/wps/wcm/connect/07b4c88045b474b89aa7df5e7489e10f/ARI23-2011_Brautigam_ChinaAfrica_Seven_Myths.pdf?MOD=AJPERES&CACHEID=07b4c88045b474b89aa7df5e7489e10f>.

countries like Angola and DRC.[147] The Chinese way of aid is based on China's experiences from Japan, using large credits given at competitive market rates, tied to the Chinese equipment and construction services with repayment in oil or other resources promotes more of a win-win situation than a zero-sum game.[148] Furthermore, Sautman and Hairong assert that the distinguishing characteristics of Chinese links with African countries make China's perspective better than the Western in terms of support for Africa's development and the respect for African nations.[149] Brautigam, Sautman and Hairong could be referred as the leading scholars of the second group of scholars in analyzing Chinese way of aid in Africa. Another well-known scholar in that field, Lucy Corkin confirms Brautigam, Sautman and Hairong's win-win aspect but places an exemption on the direction of the win-win route. According to Corkin, Chinese credit lines are win-win for Angola's elite but not its people.[150] Two scholars, Raine and Åberg underline the contentment of African governments by demonstrating South African, Angolan governments' praises over China's involvement in Africa and how they see China as the best alternative to the Western donors.[151] Cheru and Obi also see Sino-African relationship, focusing mainly on reconstruction finance and rehabilitation of infrastructure in exchange for oil as a great opportunity for African development.[152] "China presents an enormous economic opportunity for Africa, given its potential large purchasing power, its links to export markets, and its commitment to increase investment and

147 Deborah Brautigam, *The Dragon's Gift: The Real Story of China in Africa*, (New York: Oxford University Press, 2009).

148 Deborah Brautigam, op.cit., 86.

149 Barry Sautman & Yan Hairong, "Friends and Interests: China's Distinctive Links with Africa," *African Studies Review* 50.3 (December 2007): 75–114.

150 Lucy Corkin, *Uncovering African Agency: Angola's Management of Credit Lines* (London: Ashgate Pub.Co., 2013): 121.

151 Sarah Raine, *China's African Challenges*, (New York: Routledge, 2009); John Åberg, "Chinese Financial Assistance in Angola: Promise, Curse or an Uncertain Venture," A Minor Field Study: Master Thesis in Global Studies at Lund University, 2010.

152 Fantu Cheru & Cyril Obi, eds., *The Rise of China and India in Africa* (London: Zedbooks, 2010); Fantu Cheru & Cyril Obi, "De-Coding China-Africa Relations: Partnership for Development or Neo-Colonialism by Invitation," *World Financial Review*, September-October 2011.

trade."[153] Unlike Corkin, Chen et al. points to several examples of Chinese state-owned companies invested in the African construction sector and their impacts on local Africans' access to cheap Chinese goods and building materials.[154] However, Onjala analyzes the impact of Chinese trade and aid with its gains and losses and argues that while local producers are being challenged due to competitive pressure from cheaper Chinese goods, local people enjoy the affordable prices of various products extended throughout the continent.[155]

So far, bilateral trade has become the center focus of the most scholars in the Sino-Africa field. Zafar, Alden and Berthelemy discuss the impacts of bilateral trade on African economy. In a recent study, Alden focuses on the mutual benefits of Sino-Africa relations and notes that while Chinese manufacturing firms are finding new outlets for their products, African consumers are capturing an opportunity to reach low cost goods such as bicycles, radios and watches that were once out of reach of the majority of the population.[156] Zafar considers China both an opportunity and a challenge for Africa as China assists African countries in increasing revenue from natural resources, but at the same time prevents their poverty-reducing economic development at home by filling the continent with Chinese goods.[157] However, Berthelemy sees that the usual 'Dutch disease' argument is debatable. In his study, Berthelemy shows that the growing importation of Chinese products in Africa can be interpreted as a trade creation rather

153 Fantu Cheru & Cyril Obi, "De-Coding China-Africa Relations:Partnership for Development or Neo-Colonialism by Invitation," *World Financial Review*, September-October 2011, 75.

154 Chuan Chen, Pi-Chu Chiu, Ryan J. Orr and Andrea Goldstein, "An Empirical Analysis of Chinese Construction Firm's Entry into Africa," *CRIOCM 2007 International Symposium*, 2007.

155 Joseph Onjala, op.cit., 43.

156 Chris Alden, "China and Africa: A Distant Mirror of Latin America," Colombia Internacional 75 (June 2012): 31.

157 Ali Zafar, "The Growing Relationship between China and SSA: Macroeconomic, Trade, Investment and Aid Links," *World Bank Research Observer* 22.1 (2007): 103.

than a trade diversion, and trade creation will bring positive outcomes for African countries.[158]

One important shortcoming in literature on Chinese aid in Africa is that there are only two major scholars who have contributed to the subject by publishing two significant books: The Dragon's Gift by Deborah Brautigam and Uncovering African Agency: Angola's Management of Chinese Credits by Lucy Corkin. Since it is very difficult to reach major data on aid and agreements between both countries, these two books have become crucial to knowing more about the Chinese way of aid in Africa. As Brautigam warns "sensationalism and rumors cloud our ability to understand China's growing engagement in Africa."[159] Although the two books are deeply analyzing Chinese aid, they pay limited attention to examining the expansion of Chinese wide-range influence on infrastructure, various business sectors and on the determination of political preferences of African governments. In other words, there still has yet to be an empirical analysis and explanation on whether or not there is an interdependent relationship enabling both sides in gaining.

Angola became the first recipient of China's oil-backed loans, has often been perceived as a significant country for scholars that have analyzed China's aid policy in Africa. One important study by Markus Weimar and Alex Vines examines China's success in accessing Angolan oil and securing resources through infrastructure deals. The study underlines the relationship between Angola and China as pragmatic and strategic for both states.[160] Asis Malaquias sees Chinese engagement in Angola through the oil-backed credit lines as opportunistic, especially considering the fact that Angola was not receiving responses from Western countries to "its pleas for

---

158 Jean Claude Berthelemy, "China's Engagement and Aid Effectiveness in Africa," African Development Bank Working Paper Series 129 (2011):31.

159 Deborah Brautigam, "China in Africa: Seven Myths," *ARI*, 2011, Date Accessed: 4 July 2014 <http://www.realinstitutoelcano.org/wps/wcm/connect/07b4c88045b474b89aa7df5e7489e10f/ARI23-2011_Brautigam_ChinaAfrica_Seven_Myths.pdf?MOD=AJPERES&CACHEID=07b4c88045b474b89aa7df5e7489e10f>.

160 Markus Weimer and Alex Vines, "China's Angolan Oil Deals," *China and Angola: A Marriage of Convenience,* Marcus Power and Ana Cristina Alves eds., (Cape Town, Dakar, Nairobi and Oxford: Pambazuka Press, 2012)

financial assistance."[161] He also notes that in relations between China and Angola, both sides come out as winners only if the analysis is confined to government-to-government relations.[162] "China benefits because Angola is a willing supplier of oil to help fuel China's impressive economic growth. Angola wins because China provides critical assistance in Angola's post-war reconstruction process."[163] Åberg's case study argues that the main driving factors behind the Chinese way of aid to Angola are China's quest for natural resources, as well as diversifying the sources of its energy resources.[164] Chinese aid to Angola arose through China's interests alongside Angola's need for alternative financial resources; a crucial necessity in order for Angola to rebuild its devastated economy.[165] As Brautigam notes: "The Chinese now wanted to channel their aid money more directly as support for 'mutually beneficial' business."[166] Furthermore, Brautigam claims that the Chinese deal is not without risks, but it is revolutionary for the country: "For the first time, there was hope that some of Angola's riches might actually be translated directly into development."[167] Brautigam, is a scholar that defends the China's policy based on the mutual benefit concept. She explained her perspective in an article for *Foreign Policy*, "This is an opportunity for African states to ride into the global economy on China's shirttails rather than remain natural-resource suppliers to the world."[168] Similarly Lucy Corkin sees Chinese engagement with the Angolan government as a

161 Assis Malaquias, "China is Angola's New Best Friend-for Now," *China and Angola: A Marriage of Convenience?*, eds. Marcus Power and Ana Cristina Alves, (Cape Town, Dakar, Nairobi and Oxford: Pambazuka Press, 2012) 42.

162 Ibid., 26.

163 Ibid., 26.

164 John Åberg, "Chinese Financial Assistance in Angola: Promise, Curse or an Uncertain Venture," A Minor Field Study: Master Thesis in Global Studies at Lund University, 28.

165 Ibid., 2.

166 Deborah Brautigam, The Dragon's Gift: The Real Story of China in Africa, 81.

167 Ibid., 276.

168 Deborah Brautigam, "Africa's Eastern Promise," *Foreign Affairs,* 5 January 2010 <http://www.foreignaffairs.com/articles/65916/deborah-brautigam/africa%E2%80%99s-eastern-promise>.

platform in which the Angolan government enjoys "a new-found sense of political and economic leverage."[169]

To date, the main dependency drivers between China and Angola relations are claimed to be bilateral trade, but the role of the Chinese aid and investment is partly seen as an additional matter. As is seen within most studies on China-Angola relations, there is not much of a focus on business fields other than the oil sector. Concentration on China's efforts on the diversification of Angola's economy is not found in the literature. Therefore, one major flaw in the studies to date is that Chinese influence in Angola has been concentrated on the oil sector rather than all the other sectors in which China has invested. Another flaw identified in the available research is the Angolan government's effort to maximize benefits from their engagement with China has often failed to be addressed. China has usually been seen as the only reason for development/underdevelopment of African states. In addition, the studies to date are lacking well-researched empirical evidences, as well as comparative data needed for the comprehension of China's influence in Angola. In this context, new research questions arise: How much influence has China gained in Angola? How does the Angolan government make the best use of the Chinese way of aid? In the scope of these two questions, it is aimed in this study to reach a widespread analysis of economic engagement with China and analyze its impact on the preferences of the Angolan government.

1.4 Theoretical Framework and Methodological Approach

This portion of the dissertation provides an in-depth analysis and discussion of the theoretical concepts and methodological approach used in this study, and elaborates on the adaptations made to them. In terms of the international system, Andrew Moravcsik's preference-oriented liberalism will be used to theorize China's involvement in Angola.

Andrew Moravcsik, a leading exponent of the liberal international relations theory, assumes that social preferences determine the configuration of

169 Lucy Corkin, "All's Fair in Loans and War: The Development of China-Angola Relations," in eds. Kweku Ampiah and Sanusha Naidu, *In Crouching Tiger, Hidden Dragon? Africa and China,* (Scottsville: University of KwaZulu-Natal Press, 2008) 108.

state preferences, and thus take a significant influence on the foreign policy of the respective state:

> "The state is not an actor but a representative institution constantly subject to capture and recapture, construction and reconstruction by coalitions of social actors. Representative institutions and practices constitute the critical transmission belt by which the preferences and social power of individuals and groups are translated into state policy."[170]

In contrast to realism's 'top-down' approach which argues that state behavior is determined by the structure of the international system, Moravcsik develops an approach which emphasizes a 'bottom-up' relationship: "A bottom-up view of politics in which the demands of individuals and societal groups are treated as the analytically prior to politics."[171] There are three key assumptions that explain his bottom up approach.

The first of these assumptions is a liberal view of the nature of politics as a competition between individuals and social groups in pursuit of their interests:

> "The fundamental actors in international politics are individuals and private groups, who are on the average risk-averse and who organize exchange and collective action to promote differentiated interests under constraints imposed by material scarcity, conflicting values, and variations in societal influence"[172]

Given that, as Xuewu Gu argues, this first assumption underlies the ontological logic of Moravcsik which explains the nature of the international system.[173] In the contrary of realists and institutionalists according to which states are the principal actors in the international system, Moravcsik sees individuals and social groups as the most important actors of the international system. The state's role is limited to the representative of these individuals and societal groups. Xuewu Gu puts it better: "People are not for the state, but state is for the people."[174] In addition, Moravcsik emphasizes the interests of individuals and societal groups. According to him, the interests are

170 Andrew Moravcsik, "Taking Preferences Seriously: A Liberal Theory of International Politics," *International Organization*, 51:4 (1997): 518.

171 Ibid., 517.

172 Ibid., 516.

173 Xuewu Gu, *Theorien der internationalen Beziehungen: Einführung*, (München: Oldenbourg, 2010) 125.

174 Ibid., 125.

differentiated and not all interests can be satisfied at the same time, therefore there will arise an inevitable competition for influence. Therefore, the state's role is limited as a representative of the dominant social group.

Liberals reject the idea that there is a harmony of interests between individuals and groups of a society. Generally, they believe that the individuals who are rational, gain-oriented and risk averse tend to "remain more cautious about assuming cost and risk in pursuit of new gains."[175] Thus, the society is characterized by a competition between individual and group interests. There are three factors which drive the behaviors of individuals and societal groups: i) Divergent/Complementary fundamental beliefs of individuals and societal groups over social co-existence. ii) Existence of scarce/abundant resources. iii) Inequalities/Equalities in political influences.

Moravcsik notes that the likelihood of intra-social groups and individuals conflicts is high when divergent beliefs over social-co-existence, conflicts over scarce resources, and unequal access to political opportunities exist within the state; the likelihood of harmony and cooperation among social groups and individuals is high when complementary beliefs over social co-existence, abundance in resources and equitably distributed political influence exist within the state.[176]

Second assumption reflects the fact that states interests emerged as a reflection of the social interests.

> *"States (or other political institutions) represent some subset of domestic society, on the basis of whose interests state officials define state preferences and act purposively in world politics."*[177]

The state is no longer seen as a unitary actor, but as "a representative institution constantly subject to capture and recapture, construction and reconstruction by coalitions of social actors."[178] It is a process where individuals and social groups in domestic and transnational society decide on foreign behavior of the states. Andrew Moravcsik noted: "Individuals turn to the state to achieve goals that private behavior is unable to achieve effectively."[179]

---

175 Andrew Moravcsik, op.cit., 517.
176 Ibid., 517.
177 Andrew Moravcsik, op.cit., 518.
178 Ibid., 518.
179 Ibid., 518.

The third assumption explains the interdependency in the international system.

"The configuration of interdependent state preferences determines state behavior."[180]

According to Moravcsik, the state requires a purpose in order to start a conflict, propose a cooperation, or take any other foreign policy action.[181] However, the foreign policy goals of a state are not simply composed of its own ideal policy, instead, "each state seeks to realize its distinctive preferences under varying constraints imposed by the preferences of other states."[182]

Therefore, for Moravcsik, preferences are not fixed as realists and institutionalists argue. They are neither naturally conflictual nor partially convergent. Rather liberals seek to explain variation in preferences and their significance for world politics. States are not alone; therefore, they must take other states' preferences into account prior to deciding on a course of action. Moravcsik noted that: "Policy interdependence is defined as the set of costs and benefits created for foreign societies when dominant social groups in a society seek to realize their preferences."[183] The connection between state preferences and states' behavior is provided through the concept of policy of interdependence. "Liberal theory assumes that the pattern of interdependent state preferences imposes a binding constraint on state behavior."[184] According to Moravcsik, there are three configurations of state preferences.

1. Compatible Preferences: This configuration arises when the external eff fect of unilateral policies are optimal or insignificant for other states. This creates strong incentives for coexistence with low conflict.
2. Conflicting (zero-sum/deadlocked) Preferences: This configuration arises when a dominant social group in one country attempts to realize its preferences through state action and that situation imposes costs on dominant social groups in other countries. This causes high potential for interstate tension and conflict.

180 Ibid., 520.
181 Ibid., 520.
182 Ibid., 520.
183 Ibid., 520.
184 Ibid., 520.

3. Mixed Preferences: This configuration arises when the preference of a country is so mixed that an exchange of policy concessions through coordination can improve the welfare of both parties. This constitutes strong incentives for coordination and cooperative activities.

These three configurations of state preferences illustrate Moravcsik's focus on the connection between state preferences and the international system. Moravcsik believes that the formulation of state preferences relies not only on interests of domestic dominant social groups but also on transnational civil society. As Moravcsik states: "National preferences emerge not solely from a domestic context but from a transnational civil society."[185] Since states must consider their interdependence when determining their preferences upon which they take actions, it is possible to identify liberal theory as a systemic theory.[186]

According to Moravcsik, the roles of those core assumptions are limited to reach a sharp definition of a paradigm. Therefore, it is needed to develop a set of theories or hypotheses. Moravcsik has developed three variants of liberalism. Each variant of liberal theory (ideational, commercial and republican liberalism) share the assumptions noted above, explaining interstate politics through an examining the influence of variation in pressure from domestic and transnational societal actors on constituting state preferences.[187]

Ideational Liberalism, as a bottom-up understanding of policies, social identities and values (identities and borders, commitment to political institutions, socio-economic regulation) determine state preferences. For Moravcsik, governments are nothing more than substitutes for the representative sections of society. "Government policy is [...] constrained by the underlying identities, interests, and power of individuals and groups

---

185 Andrew Moravcsik, "The New Liberalism," in Christian Reus-Smit and Duncan Snidal eds., The Oxford Handbook of International Relations (Oxford: Oxford University Press, 2010). 234–254.

186 Andrew Moravcsik, "Liberal International Relations Theory: A Scientific Assessment," in Colin Elman and Miriam Fendius Elman eds., *Progress in International Relations Theory: Appraising the Field* (Cambridge: MIT Press, 2003) 165.

187 Ibid., 160.

(inside and outside the state apparatus) who constantly pressure the central decision makers to pursue policies consistent with their preferences."[188] This means social identity is playing an essential role in the determination of the state preferences. "One source of state preferences is its set of core domestic social identities."[189]

According to Moravcsik, there are three essential sources of ideational preferences. The three domestic arrangements of identities (national identity, political ideology and the socio-economic regulation) are fundamental factors in determining state preferences.

The first type of social identity, nation, specifically refers to the legitimate location of national borders and the allocation of citizenship rights. "Where borders coincide with underlying patterns of identity, coexistence and even mutual recognition are more likely, but where there are inconsistencies between borders and underlying patterns of identity, greater potential for interstate conflict exists."[190]

The second type of social identity, political, specifically refers to individual and group commitments to particular political institutions. "Where the realization of legitimate domestic political order in one jurisdiction threatens its realization in others (a situation of negative externalities) conflict is more likely."[191]

The third type of social identity, socio-economic, specifically refers to the nature of legitimate socio-economic regulation and redistribution. The activities of the countries depends on the level of conflict or convergence perceptions about immigration, social welfare, taxation, religious freedom, families, health and safety, environmental and consumer protection, cultural promotion and many other domestic public goods.[192]

The consequences of these three domestic arrangements of identities for the international system arose when affecting the preferences of other states. In that context, Moravcsik come up with a solution: "Where national conceptions of legitimate borders, political institutions, and socio-economic equality

188 Andrew Moravcsik (1997), op.cit., 518.
189 Andrew Moravcsik (2010), op.cit., 240.
190 Ibid., 169.
191 Ibid., 170.
192 Ibid., 171.

are compatible, thus generating positive or negligible externalities, harmony is likely; where social identities are incompatible and create significant negative externalities, tension and zero-sum conflict is more likely."[193] Moravcsik's rule of thumb is explained by Xuewu Gu: "The greater the difference in the conceptual ideas of the various states, the more likely it is to draw the states into conflict and less likely there will be a harmonious end; and vice versa."[194]

Commercial Liberalism seeks to explain the international behavior of states based on economic actors and the structure of domestic and global economies. Commercial liberal theory assumes that changes in the structure of the domestic and global economy alter the costs and benefits of transnational economic exchange. Through foreign economic and security policies, it will force governments to facilitate or block such exchanges in accordance with their interests. Moravcsik believes that the expansion of the international economy and free trade capitalism would create interdependencies, and growing interdependence among state preferences influences state behaviors.[195] The basic assumption of Moravcsik's commercial liberalism is: "The greater the economic benefits for powerful private actors, the greater their incentive, all other things equal, to press governments to facilitate such transactions; the more costly the adjustment imposed by the proposed economic exchanges, the more opposition is likely to arise."[196]

In order to create a more sophisticated cost-benefit calculation, one has to take into account the potential economic costs and potential benefits of war. Moravcsik assumes:

> "Where monopolies, sanctions, slavery, plunder of natural resources, and other forms of coercive extraction backed by state power are cost-effective means of elite wealth accumulation, we should expect to see a positive relationship, between transnational economic activity and war. Where, conversely, private trade and investment within complex and well-established transnational markets provide a less costly means of accumulating wealth and one that cannot be cost-effectively appropriated-as is most strikingly the case within modern multinational investment

193 Andrew Moravcsik (1997), op.cit., 525.
194 Xuewu Gu, op.cit., 134.
195 Andrew Moravcsik (1997), op.cit., 528.
196 Ibid., 528.

and production networks-the expansion of economic opportunities will have a pacific effect."[197]

Therefore, domestic dominant private actors' interests play a crucial role in determining states' preferences and behaviors. Since political leaders seek power and want to remain in power, and dominant private actors pursue economic interests, it is more likely that governments will follow a foreign policy in accordance with the economic interests of dominant domestic private actors.

Republican Liberalism stresses how state preferences and foreign policy are determined through a governing coalition and powerful domestic groups. According to Moravcsik, Republican Liberal Theory emphasizes on the institutions transforming domestic interest groups priorities into state policy.[198] To put it another way, institutions foster either cooperative behavior or conflictual behavior. Similar to democratic peace theorists' argument, Moravcsik also supports the idea that domestic representative institutions in democratic countries tend to be more cooperative/peaceful than non-democratic countries in international behavior.

1.4.1 Explanation of the Theory in the Scope of Economic Relations between China and Angola

Commercial Liberal Theory has been chosen as the most applicable theory for the explanation of current economic relations between China and Angola, specifically due to the dissertation's concentration on economic engagement between China and Angola.

As aforementioned, the first prediction put forward by Moravcsik's commercial liberalism is that the government is under pressure from both domestic and transnational economic actors to force either a free or a protectionist economic policy and to make its foreign and security policy accordingly. In general, the greater the economic benefits for dominant private actors, the greater their incentive to press governments to facilitate such transactions; the more costly the adjustment imposed by economic

197 Ibid., 530.
198 Ibid., 530.

interchange, the more opposition is likely to arise.[199] The second prediction stressed by the Commercial Liberal Theory is that importance of economic interdependence in shaping states behavior. Moravcsik believes that the expansion of the international economy and free trade capitalism would create interdependencies, and growing interdependence among of state preferences influences state behaviors. It is possible to assume that, as a result of its growing trade relations with China, the Angolan government is under pressure from both domestic and transnational economic actors in terms of its relations with Chinese government.

Consequently, in the scope of Commercial Liberal Theory and in light of empirical evidences, economic transactions between China and Angola, as well as the role of dominant domestic and transnational economic actors in Angola in influencing the Angolan government's economic preferences would be analyzed.

1.4.2 Methodological Approach

This dissertation was conducted in order to assess and explore the economic influence China has gained in Africa, specifically in Angola. The study is based on the case-study methodology that examines the economic relations between China and Angola. The focus of the assessment has been on various economic facilities of China in Angola from trade, investment to business transactions. Using both quantitative and qualitative data, it is aimed to gather the necessary empirical information. In this dissertation, mainly secondary data is used, and it is collected from various relevant books, articles retrieved from online databases, African institutions, Chinese and Angolan state-owned newspapers, speeches and statistics from the governmental bodies and international organizations, such as the IMF and World Bank.

1.4.3 Purpose of the Study and Research Hypothesis

In the context of Commercial Liberal Theory, the main purpose of the dissertation is to determine China's economic influence in Angola. Under the guidance of the main research question, the primary argument of the thesis is that cooperation in the core economic areas between China and Angola

199 Ibid., 528.

would bring mutual benefits for both sides. Establishment of Chinese partnerships with the Angolan government, as well as the existence of Chinese footprints in Angola's economy from industry to agriculture, would lead to the emergence of a more influential Chinese presence in Angola. Mutual gains would lead to compatible policies and foster the convergence of interests. Consequently, the US' economic role in Angola would be diminished as a result of growing of China-dominated economical actors in Angola. In light of this argument and Moravcsik's Commercial Liberalism Theory, the research is based on three hypotheses:

Hypothesis 1: Cooperation of China and Angola in the core economic areas would lead to a relationship based on interdependency in which both sides stand on mutual economic and political necessities.

Hypothesis 2: China's business cooperation with Angola's domestic companies would increase their incentive to press the Angolan government to facilitate economic transactions.

Hypothesis 3: Through concepts such as Angola Mode and the principle of non-interference in the internal affairs of other sovereign countries, China has gained competitive advantage against the US and US companies.

Angola is a compelling case study for a couple of reasons. First, the Chinese way of investment in Africa, which is called Angola Mode (resources for infrastructure), is named due to its initial emergence in Angola. An investigation of the Angola Mode would help us comprehend its main characteristics, which point to an interdependent relationship between China and Angola. Second, Angola is chosen because it has been one of the most important African countries in terms of its business interactions with numerous Chinese state-owned companies in various sectors. This challenges the common belief that considers China's role in Angola solely for the purpose of natural resource extraction. China's more extensive engagement within the Angolan economy makes the case study more interesting. For this reason, Angola serves as a good example to analyze the process of China's business cooperation with domestic companies in different sectors. And third, Angola is chosen due to its strong economic relations with the U.S, mainly in the oil sector. Therefore, it is compatible to the research question in which it is targeted to measure Chinese influence in Angola. By making a comparison with another 'big power', it hopes to comprehend the extension of China's economic influence in Angola.

The following chapter of this dissertation introduces the interdependent structure of the aid given by China to Angola under the concept of Angola Mode, which refers to the idea of securing natural resources of recipient countries with low-interest loans and the projects linked to the construction of public facilities. Within the frame of Angola Mode, this part of the dissertation also demonstrates how Chinese credits serve as facilitating factors for the trade, oil and infrastructure contracts.

The third chapter sheds light on the growing business ties between China and Angola as a war-torn country being repaired through various infrastructure projects. This section evaluates the extent of China's attempt to diversify the Angolan economy and the process of establishing several joint ventures between Chinese and Angolan state-owned companies in various sectors from oil, to diamond, automotive and agricultural.

The fourth chapter assesses the influence of China on the Angolan economy by providing an in-depth analysis on the impacts of the bilateral relationships on Angola's economic preferences. This chapter explains China's impacts on the preferences of Angolan governing party MPLA, Angola's socio-economic development, the labor market, Angolan financial institutions, the environment, the Angolan state owned oil company Sonangol Ltd.'s global presence, and traditional economic partners of Angola.

The concluding chapter returns to the dissertation's central question and three hypotheses, drawing together the main findings and analyses through empirical evidence.

Chapter 2: Angola Mode as an Indicator of Economic Interdependence and a Facilitating Factor for Trade, Oil and Infrastructure Contracts

While China respects the national sovereignty of African countries by following the principle of non-interference in domestic affairs, it is also willing to find alternative payment arrangements in order to place Angola as a more attractive partner of financially poor but resource-rich African governments. Angola Mode, which could be defined as bartering natural resources for large-scale infrastructure projects, reflects the idea of cooperation and a win-win relationship. It is seen as a foreign policy instrument for both parties since the idea fulfills the interests of the Angolan and the Chinese parties.

2.1 Development of Angola Mode as an Indicator of Economic Interdependence

Historically, Japan has had an enormous role in the development of the concept 'Angola Mode' in China's economic relations with African countries. In the 1970s, when Japan began engaging in China, it was found extremely convenient to import technology and expertise from Japan while its 'vast natural resources' made China an ideal trading partner for Japan.[200] Nearing the end of 1978, Chinese officials had signed seventy-four contracts with Japan to finance significant projects that would build today's modern China.[201] Those contracts were all paid in oil and coal. In the late 1970s, China needed to modernize its own resource base and infrastructure, and Japan created a platform for these opportunities. China took advantage of Japan's interest in the Daqing oil rich region to build infrastructure for

200 Deborah Brautigam, op.cit., 47.
201 Ibid., 47.

oil transport. Japan's first package of foreign aid loans was mainly used to build railroads and ports to facilitate the export of China's oil and coal to Japan.[202] The subsidized yen loans funded hydroelectric and thermal power plants, urban water supply, telecommunications and highways and fertilizer plants in China.[203]

Beyond doubt, Japan became a role model when China began engaging African countries. However, China is not the first country to provide oil-backed loans to African countries. By the end of the war, Angola has taken out an estimated forty-eight oil-backed loans, nearly all arranged, and very profitably, by respectable Western banks: BNP Paribas of France, Standard Chartered of the UK, Commerzbank of Germany, and so on.[204] Yet, still, 'Angola Mode' (安哥拉模式), a term first coined by China Exim Bank upon entering Angola, had unique aspects which distinguished themselves from Western loans. The main distinction can be seen in the features of the contracts. First, unlike traditional oil guaranteed loans, the projects and construction teams in Angola Mode were secured by agreement. This ensured that the loans would be effectively utilized, and reduced the possibility of delays in construction. Second, the credits were paid directly to Chinese construction companies by the Chinese Exim Bank to convert oil revenues into construction contracts. In doing so, the Chinese government sought to avoid the possible risk of the loan money blindly entering the Angolan financial system, perhaps mitigating the risks of corruption. As Brautigam points out "Loans from China don't get deposited into a dictator's bank account and promptly sent to Swiss bank accounts."[205] Third, in contrast to Angola's previous deals with Western countries, oil shipments to China

202 Ibid., 48.
203 Ibid., 48.
204 Ibid., 274.
205 Deborah Brautigam and Adama Gaye, "Is Chinese Investment Good for Africa," Council on Foreign Relations, 20 February 2007, Date Accessed: 13 April 2013. <http://www.cfr.org/china/chinese-investment-good-africa/p12622>.

are priced according to the international market price of the day.[206] According to Corkin, in deals with Western countries, the price of the barrel of oil was fixed, usually at a reasonable price for the buyer, but in some cases as low as US$ 25 per barrel.[207] China's acquisition of oil according to the international market price gave Angola an advantageous status against China who would seek a lower, fixed price in such a long-term supply contract. Table 2.1 illustrates Chinese expenditure on oil, between 2007 and 2009. The table shows that China paid more for the average per barrel of oil than other two important trading partners of Angola, US and Portugal.

Table 2.1: Angola's Average Value per Barrel of Oil Exports to China, US and Portugal 2007–2009 (US Dollar)

	2007	2008	2009
CHINA	71.27	95.31	62.90
US	67.39	92.91	57.83
PORTUGAL	66.2	73.93	59.4

Source: Angolan Ministry of Petroleum (2010, p. 30–31)

In principle, the China Exim Bank and the Angolan Ministry of Finance sign a loan agreement in which both sides agree on the barter of natural resource exports for investment in infrastructure. The Angolan state oil company Sonangol sells oil to China at the international spot price on shipment day. Oil revenues are deposited in an escrow bank account in the name of the Angolan government with China Exim Bank. Thereby, the China Exim Bank directly pays the costs of Chinese companies by using the money deposited in the escrow bank account. Prior to this process, the Technical Assistance Office (*Gabinet de Apoio Técnico*-GAT), and the China Exim Bank formed a joint commission to identify priority construction projects. (See Figure 2.1).

206 Lucy Corkin, *Uncovering African Agency: Angola's Management of Credit Lines* (London: Ashgate Pub.Co., 2013) 83.
207 Ibid., 83.

Figure 2.1: Fundamental Structure of Angola Mode

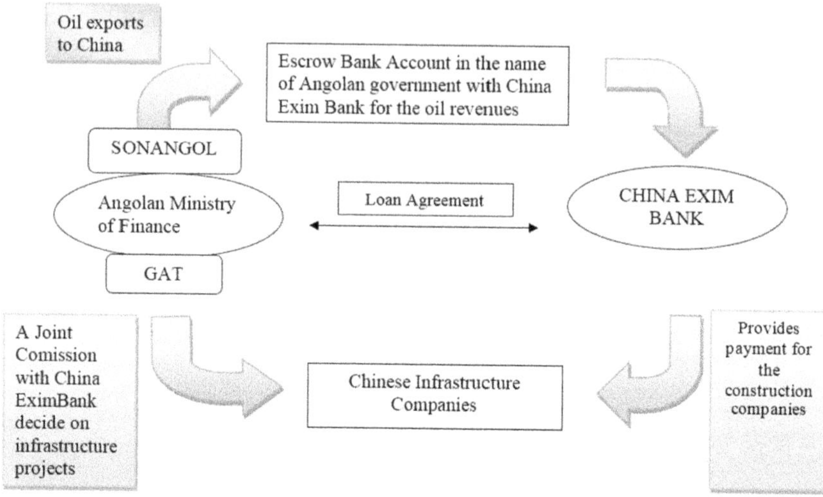

In short, under this arrangement, Angola can seize the chance to rebuild its war-torn land through infrastructure projects, and, simultaneously, China utilizes Angola to feed its energy hungry, growing economy. Another important aspect of this arrangement is that there is no cash money transfer directly to the government. In that aspect, the fundamental structure of Angola Mode reflects the idea of Moravcsik's Commercial Liberalism Theory, which stresses economic interdependence results from economic necessities. China's most competitive construction companies and limited natural resources are then proportionate to Angola's infrastructure deficit and wealth of resources. As Charles Montesquieu in his book *The Spirit of Law* argued, "two nations who traffic with each other become reciprocally dependent; for if one has an interest in buying, the other has an interest of selling; and thus their union is founded on mutual necessities"[208]

208 Charles de Secondat baron de Montesquieu, *Montesquieu: The Spirit of the Laws* (Cambridge: Cambridge University Press, 1989) 316.

Figure 2.2: Explanation of Interdependent Structure of Angola Mode with a Future Risk of Unilateral Dependence

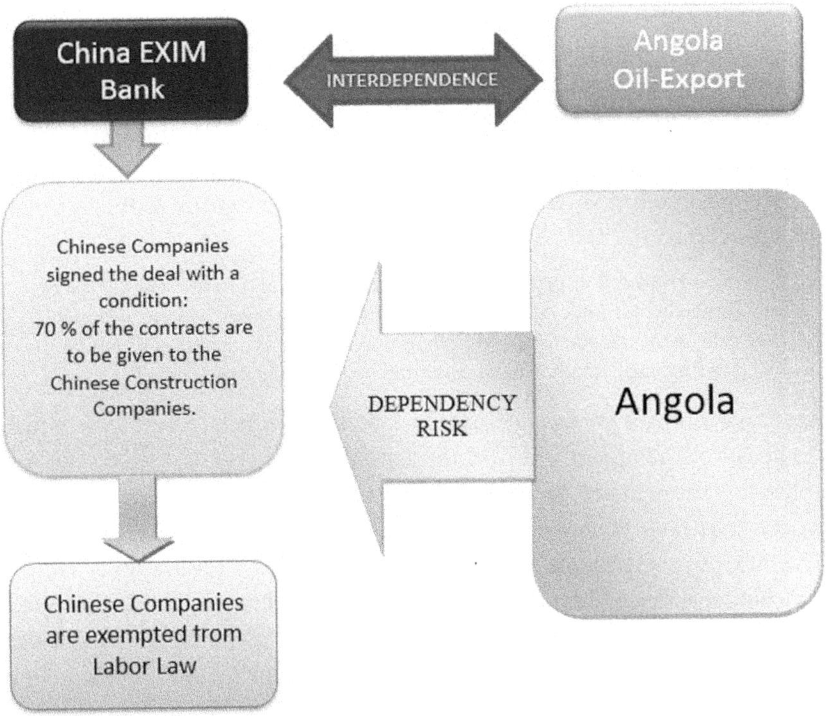

As it is seen in Figure 2.1 and Figure 2.2, there are three dimensions of Angola Mode: i) The completion of the infrastructure projects ii) Local employment iii) Oil contracts. The majority of Chinese credits are invested in infrastructure projects and the projects are contracted to some of China's biggest enterprises, such as China Road Bridge Cooperation, China Railway, Huawei or China International Trust and Investment Corporation (CITIC). The agreement between China and Angola has enabled Chinese Enterprises to have access to 70 % of contracts in Angola and to bring 50 % of the whole equipment, materials, technology needed for the projects. Therefore, the stipulated criteria is that Chinese enterprises should be selected as contractors/exporters and at least 50 % of the equipment, materials and technology needed for the project should be procured from

China.[209] Furthermore, Chinese enterprises are exempted from Labor Law which allows Chinese enterprises not to be required to maintain a low quota of foreign workers. That means Chinese enterprises are not obliged to adapt the law based on low quota of expatriate workers.[210] However, Chinese companies when they enter the Angolan economy on their own (not through Exim Bank or the CIF credit lines), they must register at the National Agency for Private Investment, which requires that 70 % of the labor force has to be Angolan.[211] The only exception is made under the consideration that:

> "National construction projects such as water supply and road construction are urgently needed for Angolan's daily life and should be finished as soon as possible; while other projects, such as power plants and telecom, require a large number of skilled technicians, which Angola cannot provide for the time being."[212]

Therefore, only the companies that work under the official credit lines (which are given for the urgently needed infrastructure projects decided by the Angolan government itself) are exempted from that law and they hire few local labors only if they don't engage into any private projects in Angola. The lack of professionals and time and language barriers are other factors that hinder China's intent to hire more Angolan labors. Third dimension of the Angola Mode is related to the acquisition of oil assets by Chinese National Oil Companies. China's oil contracts with Angola are characterized by loans and credit lines in connection with infrastructure projects. Important to note that, the oil-trade intensity in the relationships between China and Angola plus the deals with conditions more favorable to China could lead to a dependency risk of Angola to China. A work of an IMF blog,

---

209 Dr. Martyn Davies, et al., *How China Delivers Development Assistance to Africa* (Stellenbosch: Centre for Chinese Studies, 2008) 57.

210 "Evaluating China's FOCAC Commitments to Africa and Mapping the Way Ahead," *Centre for Chinese Studies*, 2010: 28, Report prepared for the Rockefeller Foundation, Date accessed: 14 April 2013 <http://www.ccs.org.za/wp-content/uploads/2010/03/ENGLISH-Evaluating-Chinas-FOCAC-commitments-to-Africa-2010.pdf>.

211 Dr. Martyn Davies et al., op.cit., 59.

212 Xiaoyang Tang, "Bulldozer or Locomotive? The Impact of Chinese Enterprises on the Local Employment in Angola and the DRC," *Journal of Asian and African Studies* 45:3 (2010): 353.

which analyzes the way of China's domestic investment and its impacts on Sub-Saharan African countries' export growth in between 1995 and 2011, notes: "For the top five resource-rich sub-Saharan African countries ranked by exports to China as a share of GDP—Angola, South Africa, the Republic of Congo, Equatorial Guinea, the Democratic Republic of the Congo—a 1 percentage point change in China's domestic investment growth would be accompanied by a 0.8 percentage point change in their export growth rate."[213] That means, as a significant resource-rich country in Sub-Saharan Africa, Angola's growing presence in global trade would let it avoid neither its interdependent relationship with China nor the possible risks arise from a possible economic downturn in China. Those possible risks involve a decrease in Chinese investments into Angola as well as a decline in oil prices. The slowdown in the Chinese economy, undoubtedly, lead to a drop in global oil prices and push down Angolan oil revenues. However, as it is seen in the Table 2.2 the oil-backed China Exim Bank loans are no longer the only Chinese official financing in Angola. That could be the sign of that, as Angolan economy improves, Angola doesn't need to have an oil guarantee to secure credits from China. For example, in February 2009, when Angolan Finance Minister, Severim de Morais, visited China to conclude the negotiations about the new loans from China. A condition of the Angolan Finance Minister is worth noting: "the loans will not be oil-backed, but linked to sovereign guarantees."[214] This implies that both Chinese and Angolan needs play equally crucial roles in determining the direction of the relationship.

---

213 Paulo Drommond and Estelle Xue Liu, "If China Sneezes, Africa Can Now Catch a Cold", *IMFdirect* 24 March 2014, Date Accessed: 25 March 2014. <http://blog-imfdirect.imf.org/2014/03/20/if-china-sneezes-africa-can-now-catch-a-cold/>.

214 "China in Africa: A Strategic Overview," October 2009, Executive Research Associates (ERA), Date Accesses: 1 May 2013 <http://www.ide.go.jp/English/Data/Africa_file/Manualreport/pdf/china_all.pdf>.

Table 2.2: Chinese Official Financing to Angola[215]

YEAR	Amount of the Credits	Name of the Financial Institute	Angola Mode? Yes/No	Purpose
2002	$ 145 million	China Exim Bank, China Construction Bank	NO	Infrastructure
2004	$ 2 billion	China Exim Bank	YES	Infrastructure
2005	$ 2 billion	China Exim Bank	YES	Infrastructure
2006	$ 1 billion	China Exim Bank	YES	Infrastructure
2007	$ 2 billion	China Exim Bank	YES	Infrastructure
2007	$ 500 million	China Exim Bank	YES	Infrastructure
2009	$ 1.5 billion	China Development Bank	NO	Agriculture
2010	$ 6 billion	China Exim Bank	Not Known	Infrastructure
2010	$ 2.5 billion	China Industrial and Commercial Bank	NO	Support Development
2011	$ 3 billion	China Exim Bank	YES	Support Development
2012	$ 500 million	China Exim Bank	YES	Infrastructure
2013	$ 1.32 billion	China Development Bank	NO	Support Development
2014	$ 170 million	China Exim Bank	YES	Infrastructure, Agriculture
2014	$ 30 million	Chinese Government	NO	Support Development
2014	$ 120 million	China Industrial and Commercial Bank	NO	Infrastructure, Urban Development
2014	$ 2 billion	China Development Bank	NO	Support Development in the Oil and Gas Industry

215 2002 figure is from Indira Campos & Alex Vines, "Angola and China: A Pragmatic Partnership", *Center for Strategic and International Studies* (March 2008):6; 2004 and 2005 and 2007 numbers from Lucy Corkin 2013, op.cit., 81–82; 2006 numbers from Lucy Corkin, "China's Contribution to the Development of African Infrastructure through Investment in the Extractive

2.2 Chinese Credits as a Key to Success in Obtaining Contracts in Three Sectors: Trade, Oil and Infrastructure

In December 2011, the Busan Partnership for Effective Development Cooperation was adopted at the end of the 4th High-Level Forum on Aid Effectiveness, in Busan, South Korea, to establish a worldwide partnership on aid effectiveness. However, China preferred to stay outside of OECD by expressing its desire to keep its distinct policy and pursue its aid regime independent of OECD's framework.[216] China's attitude has created an alternative aid model, which challenges the long-standing traditional understanding of aid.

The credits primarily granted by the China Exim Bank consist of concessional oil-backed loans, as well as government-backed investments in

---

Industries," *AFRODAD Occasional Papers*, 8 (December 2007): 2, *Centre for China Studies*, Date Accessed: 20 April 2013, <http://www.ccs.org.za/downloads/China%20Occasional%20Paper.pdf>; 2009 and 2010 figures are from Angolan weekly newspaper *Expansão*; 2012 figure is from "Angola takes out US$ 500 million in loans from China Exim Bank," *Macauhub* 9 July 2012, Date Accessed: 20 April 2013 <http://www.macauhub.com.mo/en/2012/07/09/angola-takes-out-us500-million-in-loans-from-china-exim-bank/>; 2013 figure is from "Loan from China Development Bank to Sonangol is a sign of the close relationship between Angola and China," *Macauhub* 11 March 2013, Date Accessed: 20 April 2013 <http://www.macauhub.com.mo/en/2013/03/11/loan-from-china-development-bank-to-sonangol-is-a-sign-of-the-%E2%80%9Cclose-relationship%E2%80%9D-between-angola-and-china/>; 2014 figures are from "Eximbank Releases USD170 million for Projects in Angola," *Agência Angola Press ANGOP* 10 May 2014, Date Accessed: 10 May 2014 <http://www.portalangop.co.ao/angola/en_us/noticias/economia/2014/4/19/Eximbank-relases-Usd170-million-for-projects-Angola,42355548-b41a-4ab5-976f-7caf43bd251b.html>, "Angola Takes on Loan from Chinese Bank for Real Estate Project," *Macauhub* 25 November 2014, Date Accessed: 25 November 2014 <http://www.macauhub.com.mo/en/2014/11/25/angola-takes-on-loan-from-chinese-bank-for-real-estate-project/>, "Angola Gets USD 2 Billion Credit From China," *ANGOP* 12 December 2014, Date Accessed: 12 December 2014 <http://www.portalangop.co.ao/angola/en_us/noticias/economia/2014/11/50/Angola-gets-Usd-billion-credit-from-China,db7b0e75-e943-4e16-a131-72dbc5b8f26d.html>.

216 Mark Tran, "China pulls out of aid partnership," *The Guardian* 29 November 2011, Date Accessed 1 June 2013 <http://www.theguardian.com/world/2011/nov/29/china-pulls-out-aid-partnership-bUSn?intcmp=239>.

the infrastructure and energy sectors. These features of Chinese aid are enough to distinguish itself from the OECD-defined 'Official Development Assistance (ODA).' (See Table 2.3).

Table 2.3: Similarities and Differences between OECD-Defined "Official Development Assistance" (ODA) and "Chinese Aid"[217]

	Government to Government	Financing through Development Agency	Strong Links to Donor Country Economy	Concessional or Favorable Lending Terms	Receives Payment of Debt in Kind	Private or Corporate Financing
OECD Aid Donor	yes (a)	yes	no	yes	no	no
CHINA	yes	no (b)	yes (c)	yes	yes (d)	no

a. Grants may be awarded to NGOs based in either the donor country or recipient country.
b. Chinese aid is largely provided in the form of concessional loans administered by the China Exim Bank
c. Aid projects facilitate the export of natural resources and commodities to China, as well as utilize Chinese companies, materials and labor
d. In some cases, aid recipients make payments on loans from China with oil or minerals.

As Table 2.3 demonstrates, China Exim Bank's credits do not really fit into OECD's definition of aid. Chinese credits distinguish themselves from development assistance, by creating a strong link between given aid and commercial activities. As Berthelemy points out: "Development assistance is usually granted in kind, while financial assistance is given to finance contracts that are implemented by Chinese companies."[218] Given this point, Chinese credits could be defined as trade, oil and infrastructure contracts facilitators of China. In other words, trade, oil and infrastructure contracts could be taken as three components of oil-backed Chinese credits (Angola Mode).

2.2.1 Chinese Credits as Trade Facilitating Factors

There has been a high correlation between Chinese credit lines and increasing trade figures between China and Angola. Davies noted: "China's foreign

217 Table is retrieved from Thomas Lum, op.cit., 2.
218 Jean Claude Berthelemy, "China's Engagement and Aid Effectiveness in Africa," *African Development Bank Working Paper Series* 129 (2011): 16.

policy and aid commitments are becoming an increasingly sophisticated instrument that helps to entrench China's commercial engagement."[219] Chinese credits are closely tied to the bilateral trade in oil as credits were given only when guaranteed by a specific long-term trade agreement on oil. Corkin stated: "Chinese credits are a means with which to secure an oil supply and open up markets for Chinese companies' (predominantly state-owned) good and services."[220] Aid-based relations between China and Angola are driven by China's economic interests, but due to the attractiveness and competitiveness of the Chinese way of aid it did not lose its effectiveness in the country, instead it promoted the growth and strength of bilateral trade relations.

Relations between Angola and China gradually improved in the 1990s. Primarily due to China's hunger for oil, Angola became China's major trading partner in Africa, displacing South Africa by 2006. According to the figures from Angola's National Statistics Institute (INE), by the end of 2012, China became the destination of 49 % of Angola's exports, an increase from 35 % in 2011.[221] Despite the increase in Chinese imports from Angola, Chinese exports to Angola remained at a low level, which caused a significant trade deficit.

In order to reduce the trade deficit with Angola, the China Exim Bank introduced credits for export buyers, which were issued at commercial rates to foreign buyers of Chinese products. Corkin noted: "The Chinese government has developed this financing mechanism to encourage their risk-averse companies to enter the Angolan market and stimulate Chinese exports Angola through procurement of goods and services"[222] In other words, export credits from the China Exim Bank offered to sellers and buyers to support the purchase of Chinese goods. In an agreement with Angola, at least 50 % of equipment, materials, service and technology needed in completion of the project should be provided by China.[223] In 2012, China

219 Dr. Martyn Davies, et al., op.cit., 52.
220 Lucy Corkin (2013), op.cit., 97.
221 "Half of Angola's Exports are Sent to China," *Macauhub* 12 November 2012, Date Accessed: 1 June 2013 <http://www.macauhub.com.mo/en/2012/11/12/half-of-angola%E2%80%99s-exports-are-sent-to-china/>.
222 Lucy Corkin (2013), op.cit., 96.
223 In Angola, the figure is even higher at 70 %. See "China in Africa: A Strategic Overview," October 2009, Executive Research Associates (ERA), Date Accessed:

surpassed Portugal as the leading supplier of products imported by Angola, accounting for 21 percent of total Angolan imports.[224] In short, the Chinese credits came as export credits, tied to Chinese goods and services. Different from Western credits, Chinese credits do not arrive as cash and are given with a much lower interest rate than previous Western financiers extended to the Angolan government. China Exim Bank's US$ 2billion oil-backed credit offered to Angola in 2004 was unlike most oil-backed loans.[225] It differed itself from traditional oil-backed credits with its low interest rates. The Chinese loan is given at LIBOR (London Inter-Bank Offered Rate) plus 1.5 %, compared to the Western banks, including the World Bank, which were charging an interest rate of LIBOR plus 2.5–3 %.[226] For example, in 2004, the UK's Standard Chartered Bank acted as the lead arranger of a consortium of European Banks (Calyon, Commerzbank, Deutsche Bank, KBC, Natexis, the Royal Bank of Scotland, and Portuguese bank Banco Espirito Santo) in US$ 2.35 billion oil-backed credits with an interest rate of LIBOR plus 2.5 %.[227] Therefore, the Chinese credits at far below market rates became an effective way for the Angolan government to avoid spending huge amounts on interest and sever the strength of Western institutions in Angola. For example, as noted in previous chapter, in 2004, prior to China offering its first US$ 2 billion oil-backed loan to Angola, Angola was close to agreeing to IMF's conditions related to the improvement of oil revenue transparency, thus opening itself to tangled accounts of inspection. However, after China's no strings-attached offer, including favorable repayment terms, Angola turned its back on the IMF and welcomed China.[228]

---

1 May 2013 <http://www.ide.go.jp/English/Data/Africa_file/Manualreport/pdf/china_all.pdf>.

224 "Learn More about Trade in Angola" The Observatory of Economic Complexity (Harvard HKS/CDI – MIT Media Lab), Date Accessed: 1 June 2014. <http://atlas.media.mit.edu/profile/country/ago/>.

225 Deborah Brautigam, op.cit., 275.

226 Ibid., 275.

227 Ibid., 276.

228 Angola negotiated at least four IMF programs between 1995 and 2004, but failed to stick with any of them.

Figure 2.3: Angola-China Trade (2005–2013) US$ millions

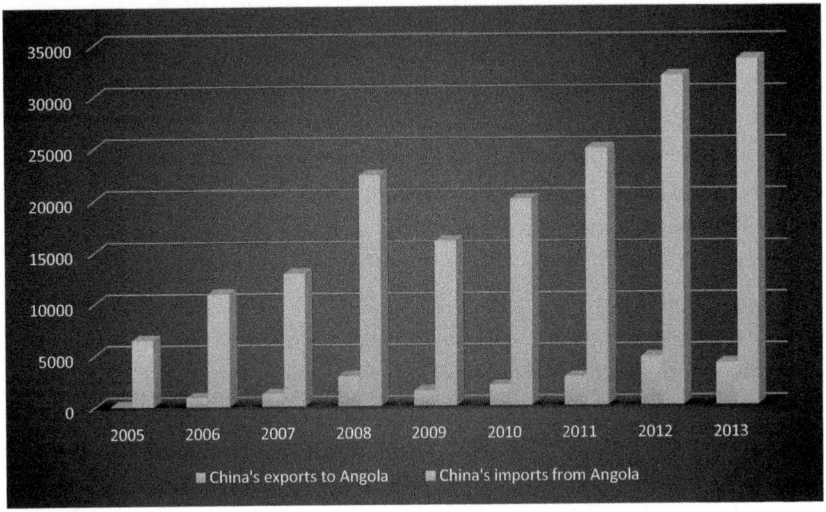

Source: World Trade Atlas and China's Customs Service

Figure 2.4: Comparison of China's and the US's Bilateral Trade with Angola (2005–2013)

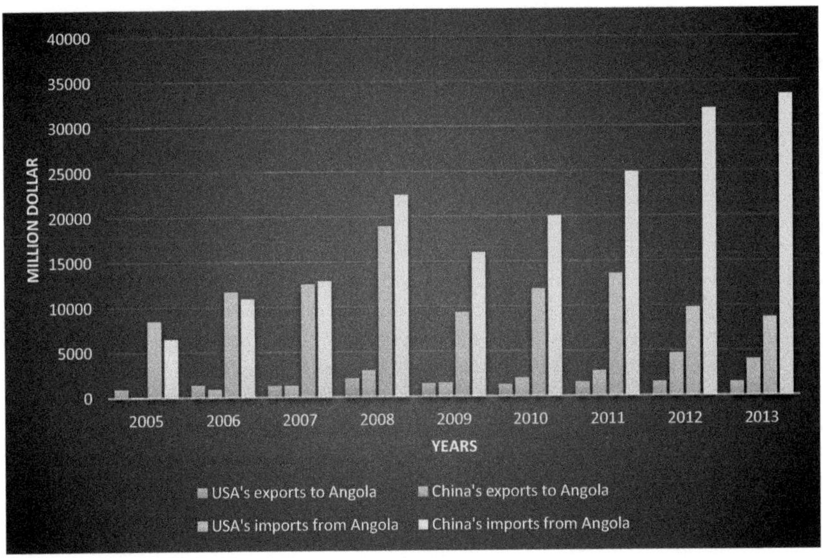

Source: United States' Census Bureau, US Department of Commerce World Trade Atlas and Office of the US Trade Representative.

In 2003, China announced that it would be given duty-free status for some goods imported from least developed countries. That means, almost all Chinese imports from Angola enter China without tariffs. By eliminating customs tariffs on Angolan exports, China attempted to encourage Angolan businessmen to export various products to China. By 2007, 98 % of the total value of Chinese imports from least developed countries, which include Angola, entered China tariff-free.[229]

In 2004, Angola was entitled to benefit from the African Growth and Opportunity Act (AGOA), the US trade-preference program which paved the way for tariff-free trade in 52 % of all US imports from Angola.[230] However, the US' tariff-free trade policies were not enough to break China's growing influence in Angola. Not only China's imports, but also its exports to Angola exceeded US' activity. (See Figure 2.4). Chinese loans tied to trade in oil promoted a substantial increase in the quantum of annual bilateral trade as Angolan exports-imports to the US declined. As Petroleum Minister of Angola, José Botelho de Vasconcelos pointed out, there was a reduction in oil exports to the United States.[231] According to data from the U.S Energy Information Administration, Angola's crude oil exports to the US fell by 57 % in the first two months of the year 2014 (January and February) compared to the year-ago period.[232] In 2013, India overtook the USA as Angola's second biggest export market. (See Figure 2.5).

---

229 "US GAO - Sub-Saharan Africa: Case Studies of U.S and Chinese Economic Engagement in Angola, Ghana, and Kenya; a Supplement to GAO-13-199," *United States Government Accountability Office* (February 2013):5, Date Accessed: 14 May 2014. <http://www.gao.gov/assets/660/652043.pdf>.

230 Ibid., 4.

231 Neanda Salvaterra, "Angola Looks to China as Oil Sales to US Decline," *The Wall Street Journal* 13 May 2013, Date Accessed: 13 August 2013 <http://online.wsj.com/news/articles/SB100014241278873237163045784814025 47990718>.

232 US Energy Information Administration, *U.S Imports of Angola of Crude Oil,* EIA, 29 April 2014, Date Accessed: 30 April 2014 <http://www.eia.gov/dnav/pet/hist/LeafHandler.ashx?n=PET&s=MCRIMUSO1&f=M>.

Figure 2.5: Major Export Destinations of Angola, 2013

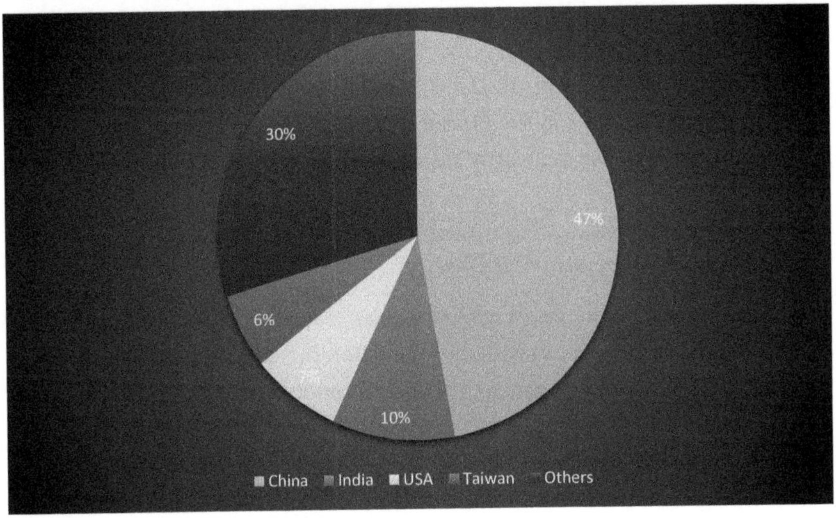

Source: Instituto Nacional de Estatistico Angola

In 2007, by importing US$ 12.8 billion worth of products, Chinese imports from Angola exceeded US imports for the first time. It was a slight exceed which was recorded for China as US$ 12.8 billion, whereas US$ 12.5 billion for the US. However, China imported US$ 33.4 billion worth of production in 2013, a 27 % annually average increase in between 2007 and 2013, whereas the US imported only US$ 8.7 billion worth of production, a 5 % annually average decline in the same period. Moreover, in 2008, the US was overtaken by China in terms of exports to Angola. Between 2008 and 2013, China increased its exports from US$ 2.9 billion to US$ 4 billion, while U.S exports decreased from US$ 2 billion to US$ 1.5 billion. In 2011, top Chinese exports included manufactured goods (e.g., cement, iron and steel rails), machinery and transport equipment (e.g., electric generators, motorcycles). Top US exports to Angola were mostly machinery and transport equipment such as civil engineering equipment.[233] In terms of imports,

233 "US GAO - Sub-Saharan Africa: Case Studies of U.S and Chinese Economic Engagement in Angola, Ghana, and Kenya; a Supplement to GAO-13-199," *United States Government Accountability Office* (February 2013): 5, 14 May 2014. <http://www.gao.gov/assets/660/652043.pdf>.

crude oil makes up 96 % of the US imports and 99 % of China's imports from Angola.[234] In addition to importing crude oil, both countries have imported diamonds since 2003. In 2009, China became the top importer of the Angolan diamond production, overtaking the United States.[235] These patterns reflect the shift in the bilateral trade from the US to China despite the longer distance between Angola and China.

2.2.2 Chinese credits as Facilitating Factors for China's Access to Angolan Oil Blocks

In 2013, Angola's daily oil production was recorded at 1.7 million barrels and according to Petroleum Minister, José Botelho de Vasconcelos, Angola's government forecasted an increase to 2 million bbl/d due to upcoming fields in just the next year. Oil accounts for approximately 95 % of Angolan export earnings, 43 % of GDP[236] and 80 % of government revenue.[237] This means that the Angolan economy is driven by oil production, concentrated in Angola's Cabinda Province.

Angola's Cabinda Province, a politically disputed area, is the main location for oil exploration. Cabinda, alone, produces approximately 70 % of Angola's oil output. The US has played an important role in Cabinda's oil exploration and production. For example, in 1968, for first time in Angolan history, oil production began in the Cabinda province and the US firm Gulf Oil (later Chevron) owned 49 % of the shares in offshore Cabinda

234 In 2011 the US imported US$ 510 million in non-crude oil, whereas China imported none.

235 "Chinese Demand Helping Angolan Industry," *Macauhub* 24 May 2010, Date Accessed: 11 August 2013 <http://www.macauhub.com.mo/en/2010/05/24/9127/>.

236 Angola's GDP dependency on petroleum has dropped from around 65 % in 2009 to 43 % in 2014. See: "Oil Accounts for Smaller Portion of Angola's GDP as Production in Other Sectors Increases," *Macauhub* 7 November 2014, Date Accessed: 7 November 2014 <http://www.macauhub.com.mo/en/2014/11/07/oil-accounts-for-smaller-portion-of-angolas-gdp-as-production-in-other-sectors-increases/>.

237 Joel Muzima & Domingos Mazivila, "Angola 2014," *African Economic Outlook*, (2014):2.

blocks.[238] Today, the US firms act as operators for eleven of the forty-nine oil blocks, maintaining primary responsibility for operations such as drilling, maintenance and complying with required rules and regulations.[239] Despite the strong role of the US in Angola's oil industry, the Angolan government has followed a strategy based on distributing ownership stakes of its blocks among multiple companies.

In 1976, Angola's government created a national oil company, the Sociedade Nacional de Combustiveis de Angola (Sonangol). In 1978, Sonangol became the sole concessionaire and majority shareholder in all oil and gas exploration in Angola. Eventually foreign companies involved in Angola purchased stakes in Angolan oil blocks. Apart from US' Chevron, ExxonMobil, UK's British Petroleum (BP), Norwegian Statoil, Italian ENI and French TOTAL, Chinese oil companies, such as China Petroleum and Chemical Corporation (Sinopec) and China National Offshore Oil Corporation (CNOOC) entered in the Angolan oil block market.

Chinese oil companies gained access to Angolan oil blocks following the announcement of Chinese Exim Bank's first US$ 2 billion oil-backed loan agreement with the Angolan government in March 2004. Chinese oil companies currently act as non-operators for thirteen oil blocks. Having non-operator roles in Angolan oil assets can be comprehensible when we take it into account that Chinese firms, compared to US firms, lack the technology and capacity to manage offshore oil operations.[240] Angola, which still needs operators, prefers a strategy that does not depend solely on one part.

Chinese oil company, Sinopec, sought to acquire a controversial 50 % stake in Block 18, previously owned by Royal Dutch Shell. Block 18 was controversial because in October 2013, Royal Dutch Shell Company agreed to sell its 50 % share to the Indian state owned oil company ONGC-Videsh, the international branch of India's state-owned Oil and Natural Gas

---

238 "Chronology for Cabinda in Angola," 16 July 2010, University of Maryland Centre for International Development and Conflict Management, 11 August 2013 <http://www.cidcm.umd.edu/mar/chronology.asp?groupId=54003>.

239 "US GAO - Sub-Saharan Africa: Case Studies of U.S and Chinese Economic Engagement in Angola, Ghana, and Kenya; a Supplement to GAO-13-199," *United States Government Accountability Office*, (February 2013): 17 Date Accessed: 14 August 2013 <http://www.gao.gov/assets/660/652043.pdf>.

240 Ibid., 18.

Corporation (ONGC). Lasting meetings between executives from Sinopec and Sonangol in Angola and China during the next months made the Angolan government shift its objective toward a point that made the exploration of Block 18 in partnership with Sinopec possible. It is interesting to note that, during the same period, President José Eduardo dos Santos not only refused India's invitation to visit New Delhi, but also rejected to receive Indian Oil Minister Mani Shankar Aiyar in Angola's capital, Luanda.[241]

In August 2004, Sinopec announced that it signed an agreement with Sonangol to establish a joint venture; Sonangol Sinopec International Ltd. (SSI). Right after the establishment of the joint venture, Sonangol Sinopec International formally exercised its own rights to buy the 50 % stake in oil Block 18 in which British Petroleum (BP) owns the remaining 50 %. It was the oil block that Sinopec would gain rights to own a 27.5 % stake under the joint venture Sonangol Sinopec International (SSI) in February 2005. Block 18, with its highest reserves, huge exploration potential and production volumes is one of the most significant oil blocks in Angola. Therefore, SSI's procurement of 50 % interest in Block 18 could be considered an outstanding achievement. According to a press release of Sinopec Corp., in March 2010, with the completion of this transaction, Sinopec Corp.'s proven reserves were expected to increase by 102 million barrels, up 3.6 %; its daily crude oil production was expected to increase by 72,520 barrels, up 8.8 %.[242]

In March 2005, Chinese Vice Premier Zheng Peiyan's visit to Angola resulted in signing nine cooperation agreements and a memorandum of understanding to work together for the exploration of the shallow offshore blocks 3/05 and 3/05A (previously owned by TOTAL and known as block 3/80). In the same year, the China Exim Bank extended US$ 2 billion oil-backed loans, immediately following the visit of Manuel Vicente to Beijing in July 2005. In the following days, a 25 % stake in block 3/05 and a 25 %

241 Lee Levkovitz, Marta McLellan, J.R. Warner, "The 88 Queensway Group: A Case Study in Chinese Investors' Operations in Angola and Beyond," *US-China Economic and Security Review Commission*, 10 July 2009:19.

242 "Sinopec's First Acquisition of Overseas Upstream Assets," *News*, SINOPEC, 28 March 2010, Date Accessed: 13 August 2013 <http://english.sinopec.com/media_center/news/20100329/download/en-news100329d.pdf>.

stake in block 3/05A were conceded to China Sonangol (CSIH). However, in 2007, these shareholdings were, briefly handed over to SSI.[243]

In 2006, China increased its previous oil-backed loan by US$ 1 billion and in the same year, Sonangol announced the winners of exploration licenses for seven offshore and deep-water concessions.[244] SSI was awarded to three new Angolan offshore oil blocks. SSI gained access to 20 % of ENI-operated block 15/06 by offering US$ 750 million and to 27 % of block 17/06 and 40 % of block 18/06, offering a record price of $1.1 billion for each (totaling $2.2 billion).[245] SSI made headlines with its record price and its success to win two relinquished offshore blocks by outbidding ExxonMobil and BP. It is believed that blocks 15/06, 17/06 and 18/06 have proven reserves of 3.2 billion barrels of oil; 1.5 billion, 1 billion and 700 million barrels of oil respectively.[246] Following the acquisitions of oil blocks, both companies also agreed to work on a new project of a new US$ 3 billion oil refinery in Lobito (Sonaref) with a capacity of 240.000 barrels per day.[247] However, in early March 2007, the deal was cancelled due to disagreements between Sinopec and Sonangol over which markets would be designated to receive Sonaref's refined petroleum products. It is claimed that China's demand of 80 % of Sonaref's production to be exported to foreign markets was strictly rejected by Angola, which imports over 70 % of its refined oil.[248] Manuel

243 Ana Cristina Alves, "China's Oil Diplomacy: Comparing Chinese Economic Statecraft in Angola and Brazil," A PhD Thesis for International Relations Department of London School of Economics, June 2011, date Accessed: 13 August 2013 <http://etheses.lse.ac.uk/206/1/Alves_China%E2%80%99s_Oil_Diplomacy.pdf>.

244 Markus Weimer and Alex Vines, "China's Angolan Oil Deals," *China and Angola: A Marriage of Convenience,* Marcus Power and Ana Cristina Alves eds., (Cape Town, Dakar, Nairobi and Oxford: Pambazuka Press, 2012) 89.

245 Ibid., 89.

246 Ibid., 89.

247 "Sonangol Rubrica Acordo para Desenvolvimento de Refinaria do Lobito," *Agência Angola Press ANGOP* 16 March 2006, Date Accessed: 30 August 2013 <http://www.portalangop.co.ao/angola/pt_pt/noticias/economia/2006/2/11/Sonangol-rubrica-acordo-para-desenvolvimento-refinaria-Lobito,4fd78bb4-05cd-47c7-a212-b184d8efb6b2.html>.

248 Lee Levkovitz, Marta McLellan, J.R. Warner, op.cit., 22; "Sonangol 35 Year Milestone of Success Beckons," *Sonangol Universo*, December 2010: 39, Date

Vicente, chairman of Sonangol, criticized the Chinese company in the Angolan media, claiming, "We cannot construct a refinery just to make products for China."[249] At the end of 2008, the technical implementation of the project was awarded to an American company, Kellogg Brown & Root (KBR). This situation exemplifies situations in which China and Angola's relationship is adjusted to Angolan interests.

According to a report in the Angolan weekly newspaper Expansão, between 2009 and 2010, China provided Angola with funding totaling US$ 10 billion; US$ 1.5 billion was paid out by the China Development Bank, US$ 2.5 billion by the Commercial and Industrial Bank of China and US$ 6 billion by the China Exim Bank.[250] In March 2010, the Chinese company Sinopec signed a US$ 2.46 billion deal to acquire a 55 % stake of Sonangol Sinopec International Ltd. (SSI) from Sinopec Overseas Oil & Gas Ltd. (SOOG), a subsidiary of Sinopec registered in the Cayman Islands.[251] It was expected that Sinopec's oil reserves would have grown by 102 million barrels.[252] In February 2010, Sonangol bought Marathon's 20 % stake (valued at US$ 1.3bn) in ultra-deep water oil Block 32, but later the stake was placed under China Sonangol (CSIH).[253] In December 2010, Sinopec, via China Sonangol (CSIH), purchased TOTAL's 5 % stake for US$ 983 million in ultra-deep water Block 31.

Accessed: 13 August 2013 <http://www.sonangol.co.uk/wps/wcm/connect/c4b95a00475d1922ac54fd7c37a37d2d/SU28-web.pdf?MOD=AJPERES>.

249 Alex Vines, "China in Africa: A Mixed Blessing," *Current History*, May 2007:218.

250 "China Provides Angola with US$ 10 billion between 2009 and 2010, Expansão Reports," *Macauhub* 8 February 2011, Date Accessed: 13 August 2013 <http://www.macauhub.com.mo/en/2011/02/08/china-provides-angola-with-us10-billion-between-2009-and-2010-expansao-reports/>.

251 Yvonne Lee, "Sinopec to Acquire Angolan Oil Assets," *The Wall Street Journal* 29 March 2013, Date Accessed: 13 August 2013 <http://online.wsj.com/news/articles/SB10001424052702303429804575149714050757630>.

252 "Sinopec's First Acquisition of Overseas Upstream Assets." *News*. SINOPEC, 28 March 2010. 13 August 2013. <http://english.sinopec.com/media_center/news/20100329/download/en-news100329d.pdf>.

253 Ana Cristina Alves, "Taming the Dragon: China's Oil Interests in Angola," in Marcus Power and Ana Cristina Alves eds., op.cit., 116.

Table 2.4: Correlation between Chinese Credit Lines and China's Access to Angolan oil blocks

March 2004: China offered US$ 2 billion oil-backed loan to fund reconstruction projects	**March 2004-February 2005:** – A joint venture between Sinopec and Sonangol (SSI) established. – SSI bought Royal Dutch Shell's 50 % stake in oil Block 18, despite a purchase agreement between Shell and Indian oil company ODGC Videsh. – A joint venture between Sonangol E.P. and Hong Kong-based company, New Bright International Development established: China Sonangol International Holding (CSIH).
2005: US$ 2 billion oil-backed loan	**In 2005***, China Sonangol purchased TOTAL's 25 % of oil assets in Block 3/05 and 25 % of oil assets in Block 3/05A (previously known as Block 3/80).
2006: US$ 1 billion	**In 2006,** SSI purchased 20 % of oil assets in oil block 15/06 and 27.5 % of oil assets in oil block 17/06, 40 % of oil assets in Block 18/06.
Between 2009–2010: US$ 10 billion[252]	**In 2010,** China Sonangol acquired Marathon Oil's 20 % assets in oil block 32. SSI, China Sonangol purchased TOTAL's 5 % assets in oil block 31. **In 2011** China Sonangol acquired: 10 % assets in Block 19/11 20 % assets in Block 36/11 15 % stake in Block 38/11
March 2013: US$ 1.32 billion	**In June 2013,** SSI acquired Marathon Oil's 10 % assets in oil block 31.

Note* the stakes purchased by China Sonangol in 2005, handed over to SSI in 2007.

In January 2011, China Sonangol was listed as the winner of stakes in four oil blocks, namely 10 % stakes in oil block 19/11, 20 % stakes in oil block 36/11

254 See Table 2.2.

and 15 % stakes in oil block 38/1. (See Table 2.4). In June 2013, approximately three months after the China Development Bank granted a US$ 1.32 billion to Angolan oil company *Sociedade Nacional de Combustíveis de Angola* (Sonangol), their joint venture, Sonangol Sinopec International (SSI), acquired a 10 % stake of Marathon Oil on the Angolan Block 31.[255]

As shown in Table 2.4, there is a high correlation between Chinese credit lines and Chinese companies' access to Angolan oil blocks. Almost every time China extended credit lines to the Angolan government, the doors of Angolan oil blocks were simultaneously opened for China.

2.2.3 Chinese credits as Facilitating Factors for Infrastructure Contracts

As explained in the previous chapter, the focus of the Angolan-Mode is to solve Angola's infrastructure problems through the loans provided by Chinese government. These loans were given under the terms that Chinese companies have to be awarded to 70 % of the infrastructure contracts. Chinese companies are paid directly by China Exim Bank following the negotiations with Angolan GAT, in which final decisions are made regarding the amount and classification of infrastructure contracts against oil sales made to the Chinese government.

In 2002, the first infrastructure loan was provided by the China Construction Bank (CCB) and the China Exim Bank; the financial support was worth US$ 145 million and was not an oil-backed loan. The loan was reserved for key public investment projects to assist Angola's post-war reconstruction. The projects are recorded as:[256]

- The rehabilitation of the 444 km Luanda Railway, worth US$ 90 million
- The rehabilitation of and expansion of the electrical network of Luanda, worth at US$ 15 million

255 "China's Sinopec Buys Marathon's Angola Oil Fields for $ 1.52 billion," *Reuters* 23 June 2013, Date Accessed: 14 August 2013 <http://uk.reuters.com/article/2013/06/23/uk-china-cnpc-idUKBRE95M07B20130623>.

256 Vete Willy Emmanuel, "Chinese Investments in Angola," in eds. Anthony Yaw Baah and Herbert Jauch, *Chinese Investments in Africa: A Labour Perspective*, (African Labour Research Network, 2009) 369.

- The rehabilitation of electricity networks of Lubango, worth at US$ 15 million
- The rehabilitation of electricity networks of Namibe and Tombwa, worth at US$ 25 million.

Chinese construction companies entered into the Angolan market in 2004 right after China's Exim Bank offered a US$ 2 billion oil-backed loan to Angola on favorable terms. By entering the Angolan market in 2004, China Road and Bridge Corporation (CRBC) became the first Chinese Corporation in the infrastructure rebuilding area following the end of Angola's civil war.

Since 2004, Chinese companies participated in various projects in four significant Angolan economic fields: 1. Construction of Roads, Bridges and Railways, 2. Construction of Telecommunication Facilities, 3. Urban Construction, 4. Construction of Power Plants.

2.2.3.1 Construction of Roads, Bridges and Railways

By entering the Angolan market in 2004, China Road and Bridge Corporation (CRBC) became the first Chinese corporation in the infrastructure rebuilding area. Connecting the country through roads, bridges and railways were the priority of the Angolan government to repair the devastation of the 1975–2002 civil war.

The most important project awarded to the Chinese construction company, CRBC, with the injection of the first phase of credit lines from China Exim Bank (US$ 1.1 billion), is the rehabilitation of the 371-kilometer road from the capital Luanda to the northern agricultural and mining province of Uíge. The project includes the repair of twelve bridges on the road and represents an investment of US$ 211 million. In 2006, CRBC also started to build a 172-kilometer road (Highway 211) between towns of Ondjiva and Huambo; the project was completed in June 2009. The construction of the road between Ondjiva and Huambo is significant as it connects Luanda to its neighboring country of Namibia.

808-metre long bridge over the Cunene River in South Angola links two main cities of Lubango and Ondjiva in South-Western Angola has also been completed by CRBC. The Cunene River Bridge, which cost US$ 29 million, is currently the longest bridge in Angola and makes it possible to travel by road to the provinces of Huila, Huambo, Benguela, Bengo and Luanda, as well as to neighboring South Africa and Namibia since the construction was completed in June 2009. In 2012, the Cunene River Bridge Project left fifty-eight projects behind and won the 2012 China Communication Construction Company (CCCC) high-quality project awards.[257]

In September 2007, Angola and China signed another oil-backed agreement for another US$ 2 billion. The deal under the Angola Mode stipulates that Chinese companies were awarded to complete 70 % of the projects with input from the Angolan Ministry of Finance and Technical Assistance Office (GAT). In 2008, CRBC was awarded another project for the construction of a 20-kilometer long bridge over the Congo River, linking the province of Cabinda to the rest of Angola by crossing the territory of the Democratic Republic of Congo. In May 2011, CRBC completed the construction of a 44-meter long bridge over the Mponzo River on the road (Highway 210) between M'banza Congo (the capital of Angola's northwestern Zaire Province) and Luanda.

Another important project concluded by CRBC is the rehabilitation of 371-kilometer long Kifangondo-Negage road. The project aimed to link three provinces and included the repair of twelve bridges on the road. As it was pointed out in Angola daily paper, ANGOP, one of the goals of the project was to build a road considered as basis for launching of farming in the region in order to better meet the local populations' needs.[258] In 2012, the road rehabilitation project won the silver award of National High-Quality Project of China Association of Construction Enterprise Management (CACEM).[259] By 2013, with the help of Chinese companies, Angola

---

257 "Two Projects of CRBC in Cambodia and Angola win 2012 CCCC High Quality Project Awards," *China Road and Bridge Corporation (中国路桥工程有限责任公司)*, 9 January 2013, Date Accessed: 15 August 2013 <http://www.crbc.com/site/crbcEN/achievenments/info/2013/1571.html>

258 "Angola: Rehabilitation of Kifangondo/Caxito/Uije Road Complete by 2008," *Agência Angola Press ANGOP* 26 June 2006, Date Accessed: 15 August 2013 <http://www.portalangop.co.ao/angola/en_us/noticias/economia/2006/5/26/Rehabilitation-Kifangondo-Caxito-Uije-Road-Complete-2008,2fed05ff-5309-4eef-aab3-2194c897e018.html>.

259 "A Project of CRBC in Angola wins the Silver Award of 2012 CACEM National High-Quality Project," *China Road and Bridge Corporation*, 4 January 2013, Date Accessed: 15 August 2013 <http://www.crbc.com/site/crbcEN/achievenments/info/2013/1579.html>.

completed the reconstruction of 13,000 kilometers of highways throughout the country.[260]

The China Railway Construction Corporation (CRCC) is the second most important company, which played a significant role in China's engagement within overseas construction projects. The reconstruction of Benguela, Luanda and Moçâmedes Railway (Namibe Railway), which connect the interior eastern parts of Angola to port cities, has been funded by the China International Fund. (See Map 2.1). In 2005, a US$ 350 million rehabilitation project was launched with China International Fund's assistance for the construction of 424-kilometer long Luanda Railway (Angola railway). The Luanda Railway, just like other transportation routes, plays an essential role for the development and diversification of the Angolan economy since it provides an inland route toward Eastern Angola, but ends halfway in Malanje. In July 2010, after a decade break, the Luanda Railway was reopened for the first time; another important railway rehabilitation project awarded to the Chinese Railway Construction Corporation is the Benguela Railway (*Caminho de Ferro de Benguela (*CFB*)*) project. According to Liu Feng, head of China Railway Construction's Angola railway project, China won over the US, Portugal, Russia, and Brazil by attracting the interests of Angolan officials, especially the chief of Angola Railway Bureau who was invited to travel on China's high-speed railways (Qinghai-Tibet Railway, Beijing-Shanghai Express) when he came to China for observation and analysis.[261] The Benguela Railway begins at the port of Lobito and heads 1,344 kilometers to the East, crossing the provinces of Huambo and Bié to the Eastern border, Luau in Moxico province, which lies 15 kilometers from the Democratic Republic of Congo (DRC) border. After twenty-nine years of interruption due to the armed conflict in Angola, the railway reopened for the first time in February 2012 and enabled passengers to travel from Lobito to Huambo. (See Map 2.1). In August 2014, the Chinese Company, China Railway Construction, succeeded in completing Angola's fastest railway, making it possible to travel

260 "Angola-China: Mutual Benefits," *Sonangol Universo* September 2013:8.

261 "China Outperforms Europe, Completes Fastest Angolan Railway," *People's Daily Online* 15 August 2014, 16 August 2014 <http://english.peopledaily.com.cn/n/2014/0815/c98649-8770415.html>.

at a speed of 90 km per hour.[262] Benguela Railway, with sixty-seven stations is reopened with a capacity to carry over four million passengers and twenty million tons of cargo per year, becoming the second-longest railroad built by a Chinese company overseas.[263] In addition, Benguela Railway was reopened with a pledge of 3,000 new job opportunities.[264] Benguela Railway, together with the Angolan port of Lobito, makes the main components of Lobito Corridor, designated by the Southern African Development Community (SADC) as the most strategic of the fifteen corridors.[265] (See Map 2.3).

---

262 "China Outperforms Europe, Completes Fastest Angolan Railway," *People's Daily Online* 15 August 2014, 16 August 2014 <http://english.peopledaily.com.cn/n/2014/0815/c98649-8770415.html>.

263 1,344 km Benguela Railway is shorter only than the 1,860 km Tanzania-Zambia Railway built by Chinese in the 1970s. See: "Chinese Company Completes Massive Angolan Railway," *Shanghai Daily* 13 August 2014, Date Accessed: 14 August 2014 <http://www.shanghaidaily.com/article/article_xinhua.aspx?id=235113>.

264 "Benguela Railway to Offer 3,000 New Jobs," *Agência Angola Press ANGOP* 22 August 2012, Date Accessed: 15 August 2013 <http://www.portalangop.co.ao/angola/en_us/noticias/transporte/2012/7/34/Benguela-Railway-offer-000-new-jobs,00b35b49-d4c9-418c-b259-7044f047fddb.html>.

265 "Route to Riches: The Lobito Corridor," *Sonangol Universo* September 2013: 26.

Map 2.1: Railways in Angola: Luanda Railway, Lobito Railway and Moçâmedes Railway

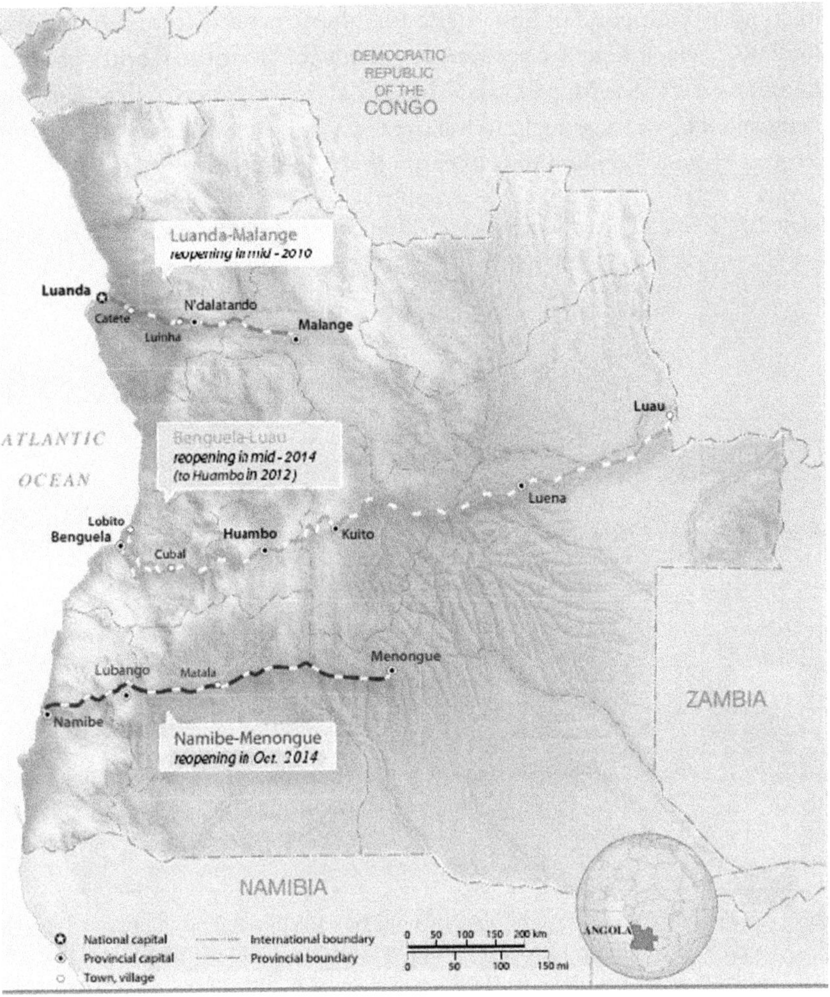

Source: Sonangol Universo, 2010- a Revised Edition by the Author

The reconstruction of the Benguela Railway plays a crucial role not only for leading to an increase in commercial exchanges between provinces of Angola, but also in commercial exchange with the bordering countries such as the DRC and Zambia. When the Zambian project (together with a South African company Grindrod) to build a new 590 km railway[266] connecting Zambia's copper belt region with the Angolan border is completed, Lobito will be able to compete with ports in East Africa for copper exports from Zambia and the DRC, which together account for about 9.6 % of the world's production of metal.[267] (See Map 2.2 and Map 2.3). It is also expected that, once the Benguela Railway is brought to full capacity, the port of Lobito's capacity is to grow from 3.7 million tons of cargo to 4.1 million tons.[268]

Map 2.2: China's Contribution to the Transcontinental Railway Lines in Africa

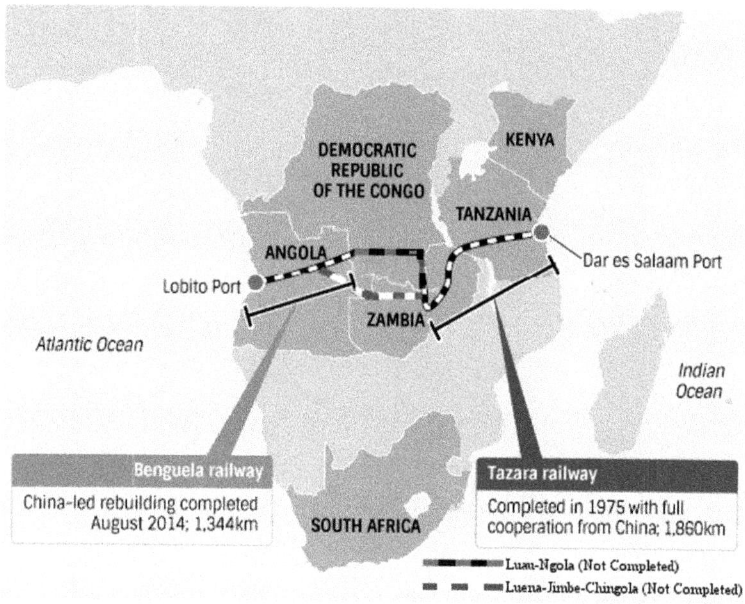

266 In February 2014, South African Logistics Company and Zambian Northwest Rail Company agreed on building, operating and maintaining a 590 km railway from Chingola to the Benguela railway line on the Zambia-Angola border near Jimbe (See Map 2.2).

267 U.S Geological Survey (USGS), *Copper Data 2013*, USGS Mineral Commodity Summaries, February 2014: 48–49. <http://minerals.usgs.gov/minerals/pubs/commodity/copper/mcs-2014-coppe.pdf>.

268 Mugdha S. Kelkar, "Reopening of Benguela Railway Brings Economic Hope to Angola," *The National Law Review* 29 January 2015, Date Accessed: 30 January 2015 <http://www.natlareview.com/article/reopening-benguela-railway-brings-economic-hope-to-angola>.

Angola can enjoy the opportunity to export its oil directly to its 'landlocked' neighbor Zambia, and after a successful upgrade of the two railway lines in Congo and Zambia is achieved, the Benguela Railway would be linked to the Tazara Railway and create a transcontinental railway connection between the Atlantic (East coast of Africa) and Indian Oceans (West coast of Africa). (See Map 2.2). That railway connection will subsequently facilitate the transport of raw materials, not only to the neighboring countries, but also to the other parts of the world, particularly to China.

Map 2.3: The Lobito Corridor

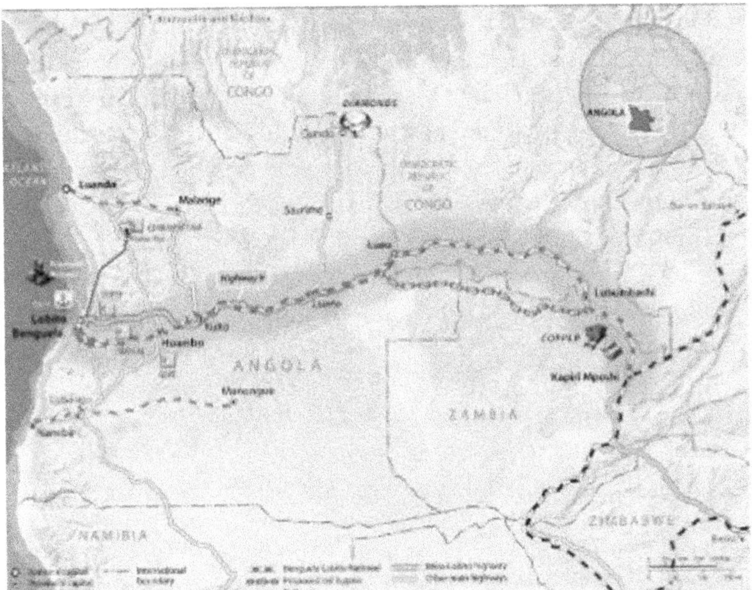

Source: Sonangol Universo, 2013

In late 2005, it was announced that the Chinese Hywai Group was in charge of the construction of fifty-six new stations and total rehabilitation of the 1003.1-kilometer Moçâmedes Railway.[269] The railway begins with

269 "Moçâmedes Railway Project," *Subordinate Corporate*, China Hyway Group (中国浩远), n.d., Date Accessed: 15 August 2013 <http://www.hyway-china.com/En_aboutHY.asp?lm=45&newsid=37>.

coast city Namibe from the West, via Lubango and Matala, and reaching Menongue to the East. The project, just like other construction projects, is part of oil for infrastructure loans. According to an agreement between the Chinese CNR Dalian Locomotive and Rolling Stock Company and the Angolan government, Angola, which formerly used to import locomotives from the United States, would buy fifteen diesel locomotives from CNR Dalian in total. Shortly after the delivery of fifteen diesel Chinese locomotives[270] to Angola, in August 2012, it is reported that Moçâmedes Railway's last station Menongue was reopened in a ceremony with the participation of Angolan President José Eduardo dos Santos.[271] The final delivery of the reconstruction and modernization of fifty-six stations, the telecommunications systems of railway line project of the Moçâmedes Railroad (CFM), which began in 2006, is scheduled for October 2014.[272]

Railways and highways are now bringing the network back to life with thousands of kilometers of new service for both passengers and cargo. The accurate number of Chinese and Angolan workers that participated during the rehabilitation of three railways is unknown, but according to Angolan Minister of Transport Augusto da Silva Tomás, the revival of the country's three rail systems would provide more than 4,000 jobs for Angolan people.[273] Besides creating more local jobs, every single project in construction

---

270 Rated at 1715 kW, the 1067 mm gauge CKD8F locomotives have a top speed of 160 km/h and compartments are air conditioned and equipped with dust filters which make them suitable for the desert environment. Angola has become the first African country imported Chinese locomotives.

271 "Head of State inaugurates Moçâmedes Railway Station in Menongue," *Agência Angola Press ANGOP* 26 August 2012, Date Accessed: 15 August 2013 <http://www.portalangop.co.ao/angola/en_us/noticias/politica/2012/7/34/Head-State-inaugurates-Mocamedes-Railway-station-Menongue,f2621ea8-d13d-42d4-ad85-f97f8cc732ac.html>.

272 "China Hyway due to Deliver Angola's Moçâmedes Railroad in October," *Macauhub* 5 September 2014, Date Accessed: 5 September 2014 <http://www.macauhub.com.mo/en/2014/09/05/china-hyway-due-to-deliver-angolas-mocamedes-railroad-in-october/>.

273 "4,000 Related Jobs in Angola," *Railways Africa*, 14 August 2012, Date Accessed: 15 August 2013 <http://www.railwaysafrica.com/blog/2012/08/14/4000-rail-related-jobs-in-angola/>.

of various transportation routes is one of the fundamental ways that would enable Angola to create more developed and diversified economy.

2.2.3.2 *Construction of Telecommunication Facilities*

Construction of telecommunication facilities has also taken place among the priorities of the Angolan government, which was very much interested in rebuilding the country's infrastructure. In 2001, Angola Telecom (Multitel), which until then had a monopoly in the telecommunication sector, had been liberalized following the Angolan government's new regulations within the sector. The end of the civil war in 2002 facilitated those liberalization attempts of Angolan government. Following the liberalization of the telecommunication sector, other state-owned as well as private companies emerged, such as Mundo Startel Telecom (a subsidiary of the state-owned petroleum company Sonangol) and two mobile service providers, Movicel (partly privatized) and Unitel[274] (the first private mobile telephone operator, previously owned by Sonangol).

In contrast to other construction companies of China, Alcatel Shanghai Bell and ZTE had already signed its first deals with the Angolan government in order to begin laying down fiber-optic cables in 2002 and 2003, even before China's first oil-backed US$ 2 billion loan. However, Huawei, which is today the largest telecommunication equipment maker in the world[275], has been involved in Angola only after the installation of large-scale Chinese loans in 2004.

In 2002, Alcatel Shanghai Bell (ASB) and Angolan Telecom signed a US$ 60 million contract for the Angola Telecom Network Expansion Project

---

274 Unitel counts among the shareholders of the President dos Santos' daughter, Isabel dos Santos. The company is owned by Sonangol, Isabel dos Santos and Portugal Telecom. See Kerry Dolan, "Daddy's Girl: How an African 'Princess' Banked $3 billion in a Country Living on $2 a Day," *Forbes* 2 September 2013, Date Accessed: 13 October 2013 <http://www.forbes.com/sites/kerryadolan/2013/08/14/how-isabel-dos-santos-took-the-short-route-to-become-africas-richest-woman/2/>.

275 Huawei Technologies Ltd. overtook Ericsson as the largest telecommunication equipment maker in the world in 2012, See: "Who's afraid of Huawei?", *The Economist* 3 August 2012, Date Accessed: 15 August 2013 <http://www.economist.com/node/21559922>.

in the provinces of Namibe, Huila, Cunene and Lunda Norte; the project was funded by China Exim Bank.

China's deals with the Angolan government under the arrangement of Angola Mode, exchanging infrastructure for resources, has led to a growth in the telecommunication sector. In March 2005, the Chinese company ZTE Corporation International signed an agreement with Mundo Startel Telecom for the sale of telecommunications equipment. As a consequence of that agreement, ZTE invested US$ 400 million to build Angola's telecom network, upgrade the military telecommunications system, and construct a mobile phone factory.[276] Furthermore, ZTE, which already owns a growing patent portfolio in the WiMAX field, pledged to provide the Angolan company Mundo Startel Telecom with the equipment to build a nationwide WiMAX network by January 2006. The network covers three cities (Luanda, Benguela and Lobito) and provides broadband and VoIP services for more than six million people.[277] In addition, the network provides Next Generation Network (NGN) technology, which allows one network to transport all information and services such as voice, data and all sorts of media. It would be among the first of its kind in Africa.[278]

In 2005, the China International Telecommunication Construction Corporation (CITCC) completed four phase projects for the improvement of Angola Telecom's telephone network in Luanda. CITCC also built 42 kilometers of

---

276 US$ 300 million of the amount will be used to modernize and expand Angola Telecom's fixed-line network, and the remaining US$100 million will be invested in military communications, the construction of a mobile devices factory, the creation of a telecommunications training institute for Angolan employees, and a laboratory for research activities in telecommunications field. See "China vai investir USD 400 milhões em telecomunicaçoes," *Angonoticias* 24 February 2005, Date Accessed: 15 August 2013 <http://www.angonoticias.com/Artigos/item/3944/china-vai-investir-usd-400-milhoes-em-telecomunicacoes>.

277 "ZTE to Deploy its First Commercial African WiMAX Network," *Total Telecom* 14 October 2005, Date Accessed: 15 August 2013 <http://www.totaltele.com/view.aspx?ID=441981>.

278 "ZTE Lands Angola network Deal," *Shenzhen Daily* 28 July 2005 retrieved from *china.org.cn* (中国网), 15 August 2013 <http://www.china.org.cn/english/BAT/136508.htm>.

new telecom ducts, as well as laid 366 kilometers of telephone cables and supplied telephone lines for approximately 200,000 people.[279]

China's other telecommunication company, Huawei, took a start in Angola shortly after the first extension of a billion dollar oil-backed loan by China Exim Bank. In 2006, during the Beijing Summit of Sino-Africa Cooperation Forum, leaders of many African countries visited Huawei's Shenzhen headquarters and Beijing Institute. The leaders had high praise for Huawei's contribution to their telecom industry. Angola Prime Minister Fernando dos Santos noted: "Huawei has entered the Angola market, and I believe that they will play an important role in the development of Angola's telecom industry. I am certain that we will have a win-win future."[280] Huawei entered into the Angolan market by selling technology to operators Angola Telecom and MSTelcom. Huawei also has executed the project of e-Government and the Private Network of State which has been seen as an important tool to combat poverty and achieve Millennium Development Goals by the Vice Minister of Information Technologies, Pedro Sebastião Teta.[281] In 2008, Huawei announced an investment of US$ 7 million to build a technical telecommunications training centre to transform the Angola Telecommunications Institute into a Telecommunications University.[282] Before that investment announcement, it was reported that Huawei had been training about 400 local technicians in the company's headquarters in

---

279 "China in Africa: A Strategic Overview," October 2009, Executive Research Associates (ERA), Date Accesses: 1 May 2013 <http://www.ide.go.jp/English/Data/Africa_file/Manualreport/pdf/china_all.pdf>.

280 "Realize Your Potential: Annual Report 2006," *Huawei Technologies Co., Ltd.* (2006):35, Date accessed: 15 August 2013 <http://www.huawei.com/ucmf/groups/public/documents/annual_report/092583.pdf>.

281 "New Technologies to Boost Country's Development-Vice Minister," *Agência Angola Press ANGOP* 25 April 2011, Date Accessed: 15 August 2013 <http://www.portalangop.co.ao/angola/en_us/noticias/ciencia-e-tecnologia/2011/3/17/New-technologies-boost-country-development-vice-minister,1b9714be-215d-470d-8673-bc33711b4e26.html>.

282 "Angola: China's Huawei Opens Training Centre in Angola," *Macauhub* 29 October 2008, Date Accessed: 15 August 2013 <http://www.macauhub.com.mo/en/2008/10/29/5983/>.

Shenzhen.[283] As of 2015, Huawei has provided training in telecommunications to over 800 Angolan technicians.[284]

In 2011, the National Institute of Telecommunications (ITEL) and Huawei signed a cooperation agreement for the training of Angolans in the field of telecommunications. Therefore, Angola would reduce the shortage in well-trained technicians in the telecommunications sector and information technology. In February 2012, Huawei and Movicel announced their partnership to launch Africa's first 4G services in Angola.[285] Under this contract, with support from ZTE and Huawei in terms of transferring knowledge and experience, Movicel has deployed a 4G LTE FDD 1.8 GHz network in the oil-rich province of Cabinda, and has become the first African country where the LTE service has been launched.

Moreira da Silva Junior, CEO of Movicel, expressed the central role telecoms and technology plays: "Movicel is doing its share to pave the future of Angola and Africa with this state-of-the-art communication infrastructure. It will remove the gap between Northern and Southern hemispheres' networks."[286] Similarly, Chief Operations Officer, Antonio Francisco, remarked on the importance of telecoms sector: "The telecoms sector is a strategic sector, we can't think about the growth of the economy unless we have telecoms infrastructure well done."[287]

---

283 "Angola: China's Huawei Opens Training Centre in Angola," *Macauhub* 29 October 2008, Date Accessed: 15 August 2013 <http://www.macauhub.com.mo/en/2008/10/29/5983/>.

284 "China's Huawei Group Trains 800 Technicians in Angola," *Macauhub* 21 January 2015, Date Accessed: 21 January 2015 <http://www.macauhub.com.mo/en/2015/01/21/chinas-huawei-group-trains-800-technicians-in-angola/>.

285 "Huawei Partners with Angola's Movicel to Deploy Africa's First 4G Network," *Tech Mtaa* 27 February 2012, Date Accessed: 15 August 2013 <http://www.techmtaa.com/2012/02/27/huawei-partners-with-angolas-movicel-to-deploy-africas-first-4g-network/>.

286 "MWC: Huawei Wins Movicel LTE Contract," *CommsMEA* 27 February 2012, Date Accessed: 15 August 2013 <http://www.commsmea.com/11957-mwc-huawei-wins-movicel-lte contract/?utm_source=twitterfeed&utm_medium=twitter#.UpUlm8Q2bRs>.

287 Egon Cossou, "Angola's Businesses Beat Most of Europe to 4G Mobile Services," *BBC News* 30 April 2012, Date Accessed 15 August 2013 <http://www.bbc.com/news/business-17898861>.

Map 2.4: The Countries with 4G Technology, As of December 2012

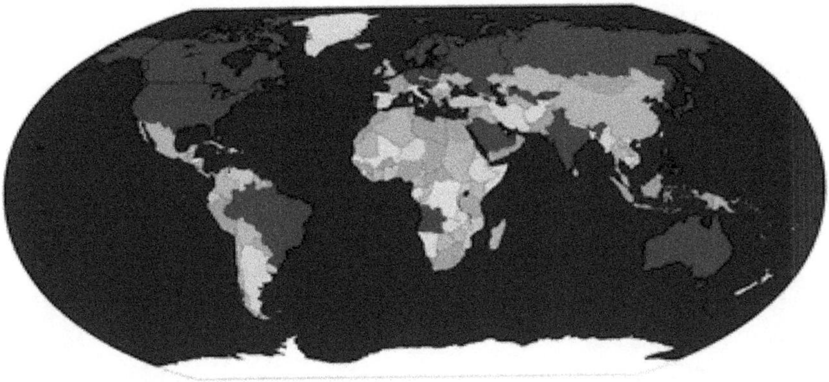

■ Countries with Commercial LTE (4G) Service

Source: Global Mobile Suppliers Association (GSA)

As shown in Map 2.4, 4G technology arrived in Angola before coming to many European countries. Chief Executive Officer of Movicel, Yon Júnior stated that, "The fact that 4G has arrived here in advance of arriving in Europe shows not only the power of a rapidly expanding market, but the power of an overloaded economy."[288] He also pointed out the positive effects of launching of LTE (4G) services on the labor market by noticing the fact that "more than 95 % of his technical team comes from Angola."[289]

In June 2012, the Angolan Ministry of Education, Angola's leading mobile telecommunications company Unitel and Huawei signed a project contract to launch free internet access (E-net) for secondary schools in eighteen provinces. It is estimated by the Angolan company Unitel that "such a project would fit into its action of social responsibility, will benefit more than 18,000 adolescents and young adults by promoting habits in academic research among the students."[290] After the completion of the first phase of

288 Ibid.

289 Ibid.

290 "Angola: Education Ministry, Unitel, Huawei Create Joint Internet Project," *allAfrica* 5 June 2012, Date Accessed: 15 August 2013 <http://allafrica.com/stories/201206060708.html?utm_source=twitterfeed&utm_medium=twitter>.

the project[291], Huawei and Unitel came together to start the second phase of the project in October 2013.

Figure 2.6: Number of Internet Users in Angola (2002–2013)

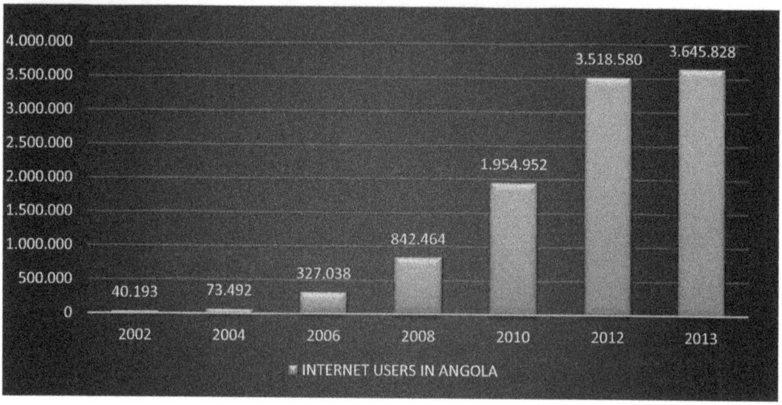

Source: World Bank & Internet World Stats

As shown in Figure 2.6, initiatives such as E-net project played a significant role in increasing the country's Internet usage. According to data from the World Bank, from 2008 to 2013, the number of Internet users in Angola increased approximately 332 %. In addition to that, mobile phone users in Angola increased 50 % from 2010 to 2013. (See Figure 2.7).

According to the Minister of Telecommunication and Information Technology, the country is expected to grow to fourteen million mobile users and twelve million Internet users by 2017.[292] As smartphones represent very small percentage of total phones in Angola, Huawei and Microsoft together introduced their new smartphone model, Huawei4Africa, which

291 The first phase of the project has already connected 9 provinces, namely Luanda, Uige, Cabinda, Bié, Benguela, Kuanda-Kubango, Huambo, Malanje and Kuanzo Norte and the second phase is expected to connect the provinces of Zaire, Moxico, Kubango, Kwanza Sul, Bengo, Lunda Norte, Lunda Sul, Namibe and Cunene.

292 "Mobile Phone Users Reach 14 Million in 2017," *Agência Angola Press ANGOP* 31 October 2013, Date Accessed: 15 August 2013 <http://www.portalangop.co.ao/angola/en_us/noticias/ciencia-e-tecnologia/2013/9/44/Mobile-phone-users-reach-million-2017,585c0a1c-fb27-4fe7-addb-43b37718f5aa.html>.

is produced only for Africa. Huawei4Africa, with its affordable price, is expected to give the opportunity for more Africans to connect markets and opportunities online.

Figure 2.7: Number of Mobile Phone Users in Angola (2010–2013)

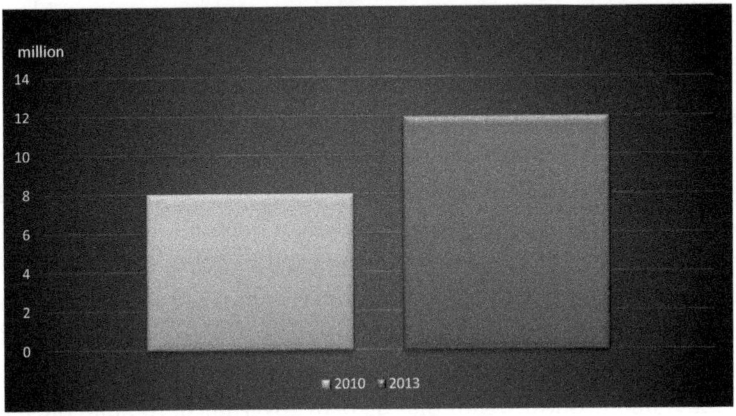

Source: Agência Angola Press ANGOP

In December 2014, it is declared by the director of Huawei Angola, James Yang, that Huawei has a share of 42 percent of the mobile phone market in Angola[293] and since 2006, the company has created more than 500 jobs in the country.[294]

The consequences of Chinese investments in Angola's telecommunication sector can be seen in Angola's recent endeavor. Today, Angola is making an effort to be the technology and Internet hub of Africa by developing two significant projects to serve as a connection to Africa and South America through fiber-optic cable.[295] These two projects play a significant role in decreasing Africa's dependence on Europe for telecommunications and Internet.

293 "Chinese Group Huawei has 42 pct of Angola's Mobile Phone Market," *Macauhub* 17 December 2014, Date Accessed: 17 December 2014 <http://www.macauhub.com.mo/en/2014/12/17/chinese-group-huawei-has-42-pct-of-angolas-mobile-phone-market/>.

294 "China's Huawei Group Trains 800 Technicians in Angola," *Macauhub* 21 January 2015, Date Accessed: 21 January 2015 <http://www.macauhub.com.mo/en/2015/01/21/chinas-huawei-group-trains-800-technicians-in-angola/>.

295 "Hub Role for Angola," *Sonangol Universo* September 2013: 4.

2.2.3.3 *Urban Construction*

Under the terms of oil-backed loans, China has also contributed toward the urbanization of the country, which includes various housing, stadium, convention center projects. As Mario Osava from Inter Press Service described, it is shocking for the visitors to see such a war-torn county with those "shiny new cars on brand-new roads and highways lined by thousands of still-empty or half-built office buildings, apartment blocks and residential towers stand in sharp contrast to the sprawling slums around the city."[296]

In December 2007, the Chinese company Sinohydro Corporation signed two separate US$ 69 million and US$ 116.8 million stadium projects in Huila Province and Benguela Provinces.[297] Lubango Stadium, in Huila Province, with a 20,000 seating capacity was completed in 2010. Ombaka Stadium, in Benguela Province, with 35,000 seats, was completed in 2010 and hosted some events for the African Cup of Nations (CAN2010). In March 2008, the Chinese company Shanghai Urban Construction Group (SCG) signed a US$ 226 million contract with the Angolan government to build the biggest stadium in Angola within the capital city of Luanda.[298] The stadium has a seating capacity for 50,000 people, was handed over to the Angolan government in December 2009 and hosted Group A matches in the Africa Cup of Nations 2010. Chiazi Stadium (with a 20,000 people capacity) in Cabinda Province, which was built by China Jiangsu International, was also inaugurated in December 2009 to be ready for the Africa Cup of Nations Soccer Championship. According to Lucy Corkin, this is not the first prestigious event China has been a part of in Angola.[299] In 2007, Angola hosted the African basketball championships, Afro-Basket, and the Chinese company

---

296 Mario Osava, "Building the New Angola: How Chinese and Brazilian Firms Rise Up to the Challenge," *Newstime Africa* 30 November 2012, Date Accessed: 15 August 2013 <http://www.newstimeafrica.com/archives/29924>.

297 Business Portfolio, Sinohydro: http://eng.sinohydro.com/index.php?m=content&c=index&a=show&catid=50&id=168.

298 "Hub Role for Angola," *Sonangol Universo* September 2013: 9.

299 Lucy Corkin, "China and the Macau Forum," *Pambazuka News* 7 May 2009, Date Accessed: 15 August 2013 <http://www.pambazuka.org/en/category/africa_china/56116/print>.

China National Electronics Import and Export Corporation (CEIEC) was contracted to build four basketball stadiums in Cabinda, Benguela, Huila and Huambo provinces, financed by the Chinese credit line.[300]

In November 2009, China Communication Construction Company (CCCC) is awarded to the construction of Angolan Port, Lobito, and rehabilitation project. In 2013, the same company started to implement the second stage of the project, which includes the rehabilitation of water supply system, sewerage, fire hydrants, construction of Namibe's dry port and logistical activity zones, as well as the construction of the coastal navigation terminal.[301] Another important project is the construction of new major Luanda International Airport. The airport, which will have an annual passenger capacity of fifteen million, is being built by China International Fund Construction Ltd.; the opening of the airport is scheduled for 2015.[302]

The Kilamba Kiaxi[303] Housing Project (Nova Cidade de Kilamba)[304] is another important construction project launched by a Chinese company, CITIC Construction in Angola. It is known as part of China's programme to build approximately 100,000 new houses in Angola's ten provinces. Kilamba Kiaxi contains 710 blocks, 20,000 residential homes, and houses 485,000 people.[305] In September 2008, the construction of the first phase of the project is announced. The Kilamba Kiaxi housing project is the largest social housing program in Angola and in the whole world; the total investment amount is set to be US$ 10 billion to build houses on a land of 56 square kilometers in

300 Lucy Corkin, "China and the Macau Forum," *Pambazuka News* 7 May 2009, Date Accessed: 15 August 2013 <http://www.pambazuka.org/en/category/africa_china/56116/print>.

301 "Contractor to Start Lobito Port Reconstruction," *Dredging Today* 26 November 2012, Date Accessed: 15 August 2013 <http://www.dredgingtoday.com/2012/11/26/contractor-to-start-lobito-port-reconstruction-angola/>.

302 Manuel de SoUS, "Novo Aeroporto orgulha África," *Jornal de Angola* 17 May 2012, Date accessed: 15 August 2013 <http://jornaldeangola.sapo.ao/politica/novo_aeroporto_orgulha_africa>.

303 Kilamba Kiaxi is one of nine municipalities which make up the metropolitan region of Angola's capital Luanda.

304 New City of Kilamba.

305 "Angola-China: Mutual Benefits," *Sonangol Universo* September 2013:9.

Southern Luanda.[306] Liu Guigen (刘桂根), General Manager of the Angola Project of the CITIC Construction Company, said: "Some 10,000 Chinese workers and 5,000 Angolan workers are building up the project and the investment for the first-phase of the project was valued at some 35 billion dollars."[307] The hand-over ceremony of the first phase of the social housing project was presided by President José Eduardo dos Santos on July 11, 2011. Hence, CITIC Construction succeeded to hand over 115 high-rise buildings, containing 3,118 apartments, a dozen schools and more than 100 retail units on July 2011.[308] The construction of the second phase of the project began in the beginning of 2012 and in October 2012, the US$10 billion project was completed with a total of 20,000 residential homes, 200 retail stores, 24 kindergartens, 9 primary schools and 8 middle schools.[309] Since then, Kilamba Kiaxi Social Housing Project has become the main target of Western medias' critiques, insisting that the town is haunted. It turned out to be very usual to see the term 'Ghost City' in the news related to China's huge investment on the housing project. From BBC[310] to CNN[311], in many Western media networks, Kilamba Kiaxi Housing Project is portrayed as a 'Chinese built ghost-town.' The main argument of those critiques are that the prices of the apartments in those buildings are too high (US$ 120,000–200,000), in comparison to an average Angolan who lives on less than US$ 2 a day.[312]

---

306 Wang Bingfei, "Interview: China plays active, responsible role in Angola's post-war reconstruction," *Xinhuanet (新华网)* 19 August 2012, Date Accessed: 15 August 2013 <http://news.xinhuanet.com/english2010/world/2011-08/19/c_131062120.htm>.

307 Ibid.

308 Ibid.

309 Li Jing, "Changing the Face of Real Estate in Angola," *China Daily* 17 November 2014, Date Accessed: 17 November 2014. <http://usa.chinadaily.com.cn/business/2014-11/17/content_18926287.htm>.

310 Louise Redvers, "Angola's Chinese-Built Ghost Town," *BBC News* 2 July 2012, Date Accessed: 15 August 2013. <http://www.bbc.co.uk/news/world-africa-18646243>.

311 "Angola's Ghost Town: A New Town, with Few Residents," *CNN* 5 December 2012, Date Accessed: 16 August 2013 <http://edition.cnn.com/video/data/2.0/video/international/2012/12/05/angola-ghost-town.cnn.html>.

312 Louise Redvers, "Angola's Chinese-Built Ghost Town," *BBC News* 2 July 2012, Date Accessed: 15 August 2013 <http://www.bbc.co.uk/news/world-africa-18646243>.

Therefore, it is not likely to see any person from that actual area. Another common critique is related to the fact that the project acts as nothing more than a fancy instrument for the government campaigns of the last elections in 2008 and 2012.[313] A spokesperson for Angola's main opposition party UNITA, Alcidas Sakala claimed: "The project had been poorly planned because it had been aimed at middle-class people who already had homes rather than those on low-incomes who were most in need."[314] The response to the critiques came from Angola's only daily paper Jornal de Angola, in which such reporters are accused of being blind to "all the people who were happily living there".[315] From the Chinese side, the Economic and Commercial Counselor's Office of the Chinese Embassy in Angola clarified that the whole project was not yet completed, and the first sales went very well.[316] In addition, the Director of African Studies at the Chinese Academy of Social Sciences argued, "China has constructed many economic housings and infrastructure projects for African countries, including roads and bridges, which are beneficial to all African people, and serve as a base for African economic growth."[317] According to the official Angolan news agency ANGOP, as of September 2013, around 40,000 people moved into Kilamba after the families took advantage of long-term and low-cost mortgages to buy flats with prices ranging from US$ 70,000 to US$ 140,000.[318]

"At the beginning of 2013 the Angolan government substantially reduced the selling price of apartments in several of its large scale housing projects in Luanda

---

313 Ibid.

314 Louise Redvers, "Angola's Trophy City a 'Ghost Town,'" *Mail & Guardian* 23 November 2012, Date Accessed. 16 August 2013 <http://mg.co.za/print/2012-11-23-00-angolan-trophy-city-a-ghost town%E2%80%8E>.

315 Jose Ribeiro, "Casas do Kilamba: A Bolha e as Cataratas," *Jornal de Angola* 10 November 2012, Date Accesed: 16 August 2013 <http://jornaldeangola.sapo.ao/-127638>.

316 Ibid.

317 Guo Jiali, "China Refutes Ghost City Allegation," *China.org.cn (中国网)* 4 July 2012, Date Accessed: 16 August 2013 <http://www.china.org.cn/business/2012-07/04/content_25808562.htm>.

318 "Kilamba City Flats Sold Out," *Agência Angola Press ANGOP* 4 September 2013, Date Accessed: 5 September 2013 <http://www.portalangop.co.ao/angola/en_us/noticias/sociedade/2013/8/36/Kilamba-City-flats-sold-out,9a874ce7-f6fa-4f25-b35a-9d888d4c07d4.html>.

(notably Kilamba Kiaxi, Zango and Cacuaco) and set up a real estate company, SONIP, under the auspices of the state petroleum company Sonangol. Substantial subsidies were introduced and the price of a three-room apartment was brought down from US$ 120.000 to US$ 84.200, which could be purchased on a 3 % mortgage over 15 years with a US$ 14.000 down-payment and US$ 390 monthly payments. This brought apartment ownership within the reach of middle-level civil servants earning over US$ 1.500 per month."[319]

According to the announcement from CITIC in November 2014, 90 percent of the homes are already occupied.[320] It seems more likely that the rapid rise of housing-construction in Angola through the Chinese companies has slowed and decreased the rise of house prices and awakened the so-called 'ghost town'.

Another controversial construction built by the Chinese company China Overseas Engineering Group (COVEC) with funding (US$ 8 million, non-oil-backed[321]) from the Chinese Government, is the Luanda General Hospital. The Hospital, with a capacity to hospitalize 100 patients, opened in February 2006. According to a report by the Angolan government, the construction had been completed with 90 % of local labor force.[322] In 2010, Luanda General Hospital reappeared in the news, due to the cracks seen on the outside of the building. The hospital closed down and patients had to spend nights in tents on the hospital grounds.[323] China was the target of

319 Alan Kane, "Angola," *Centre for Affordable Housing Finance in Africa*, 2014, Date Accessed: 21 August 2014 <http://www.housingfinanceafrica.org/country/angola/>.

320 Li Jing, "Changing the Face of Real Estate in Angola," *China Daily* 17 November 2014, Date Accessed: 17 November 2014. <http://usa.chinadaily.com.cn/business/2014-11/17/content_18926287.htm>.

321 The decision to build the US$ 8 million Luanda General Hospital was made in 2002- It was two years before that Chinese government started to extend oil-backed credit lines to Angola.

322 "President Opens USD 8 million Luanda General Hospital," *Agência Angola Press ANGOP* 3 February 2006, Date Accessed 5 September 2013 <http://www.portalangop.co.ao/angola/en_us/noticias/sociedade/President-Opens-USD-Million-Luanda-General-Hospital,42eba8a0-3295-4017-8785-c03e78d049b3.html>.

323 Deborah Brautigam, "Chinese Aid and Luanda General Hospital in Angola: Still Falling Down?" *China in Africa Real Story*, 11 April 2011, Date Accessed: 16 August 2013 <http://www.chinaafricarealstory.com/2011/04/chinese-aid-and-luanda-general-hospital.html>.

critiques. Made in China quality, once again, caused global concern and anxiety. According to a Chinese official, however, the Chinese were not solely to blame, but rather shared responsibility with the Angolans. The Angolan government, which was responsible for geotechnical investigation and providing data for the location, did not submit accurate data.[324] In 2012, the Angolan government signed a memorandum of understanding in Beijing, formalizing the intention of cooperation for the rehabilitation, construction and expansion of the General Hospital of Luanda. The construction of the new hospital, which has the capacity of more than 250 beds, was expected to be ready in July 2014.[325] In December 2013, an economic and technical cooperation agreement was signed between China and Angola. The agreement resulted from a non-refundable aid from the Chinese Government estimated at US$ 32 million given for the rehabilitation of and equipping of the Luanda General Hospital.[326]

In March 2014, in addition to both controversial construction projects, CITIC announced its new project of building 6,000 apartments on the outskirts of the city of Malanje, located 380 km East of Luanda.[327] The project includes the construction of roads with domestic sewage and drainage systems, water and telecommunications networks, as well as electricity and a petrol station, police station, health centre and a public lighting system.

In 2013, a memorandum for the bilateral cooperation for the construction of the Zoo/Botanic Project was signed in Luanda by the Angolan Ministry of Environment and the China Far East Investment Group. The project is to be built over an area of 55 hectares of reserved land in the Kilamba zone, consisting of infrastructure and services like leisure facilities, hotels,

---

324 Ibid.

325 "Angola, China Sign Memorandum for New General Hospital of Luanda," *Agência Angola Press ANGOP* 18 April 2012, Date Accessed: 16 August 2013 <http://www.portalangop.co.ao/angola/en_us/noticias/saude/2012/3/16/Angola-China-sign-memorandum-for-new-General-Hospital-Luanda,ea71cc03-64c9-4062-afec-d0ee306f2563.html>.

326 "Angola and China Sign Cooperation Agreement," *allAfrica* 18 December 2013, Date Accessed: 19 December 2013 http://allafrica.com/stories/201312190167.html.

327 "China's CITIC Builds 6,000 Homes in Angola," *Macauhub* 17 March 2014, Date Accessed: 18 March 2014 <http://www.macauhub.com.mo/en/2014/03/17/china%E2%80%99s-citic-builds-6000-homes-in-angola/>.

restaurants, tourist parks and scientific studies facilities.[328] The project was awarded to the China Far East Investment Group.

In May 2014, the construction of the parliament building with a distinctive dome reminiscent of Washington's Capitol Building was completed by the China International Fund and became "a new landmark for Luanda."[329] (See Appendix 2).

Recently, in November 2014, the Industrial and Commercial Bank of China has granted a loan of US$ 120 million to be used for urban renewal project of the Futunga de Belas area in Luanda.[330]

2.2.3.4 Construction of Power Plants

China has been particularly investing with its state company China Machine-Building International Corporation (CMIC) in construction of power stations in Angola for about ten years. In 2002, CMIC was awarded the project of rehabilitation and extension of the power system in Luanda. The first phase of the project was completed with a US$ 15 million loan from the China Exim Bank. In 2005, CMIC, alongside Angolan company Agua La Anda Electric Power Corporation, signed a second phase of the project. CMIC was not only obliged to the rehabilitation and construction of the power system in Luanda, but also to the transformation stations and provision of required materials.

In 2009, Chinese National Electronics Import and Export Corporation (CEIEC) and Angolan electricity distributor, Empresa de Distribuição de Electricidade (EDEL), agreed on a cooperation to reconstruct and expand Luanda's electrical grid. Progest, an Angolan consortium, would be subcontracted to the project as it is required under the agreed upon terms. All such Chinese-funded projects may allow a local participation of up to 30 % of the contract.[331]

---

328 "Environment Ministry Signs Zoo/Botanic Project Memo," *Agência Angola Press ANGOP* 4 December 2013, Date Accessed: 16 August 2013 <http://www.portalangop.co.ao/angola/en_us/noticias/ambiente/2013/11/49/Environment-Ministry-signs-Zoo-Botanic-Project-Memo,bbae0170-d211-43eb-9434-b411f7eca343.html>.

329 "Angola-China: Mutual Benefit," *Sonangol Universo* September 2013:13.

330 "Angola Takes on Loan from Chinese Bank for Real Estate Project," *Macauhub* 25 November 2014, Date Accessed: 25 November 2014 <http://www.macauhub.com.mo/en/2014/11/25/angola-takes-on-loan-from-chinese-bank-for-real-estate-project/>.

331 Ibid., 100.

In the construction of hydroelectric stations, Chinese Company Sinohydro Corporation Ltd. has made remarkable progress in Angola since 2003. Danielle Crisa, Sinohydro Consultant, noted that China's Sinohydro Corporation invested US$ 2.4 billion to rebuild infrastructure in Angola since the end of the country's civil war in 2002.[332] Sinohydro, contrary to common belief, is not only doing investments in hydro-sector but also in education, health care, construction of roads, airports and sports stadiums in Angola. One of the important projects awarded to the China's Sinohydro is the construction of the hydroelectric plant for the city of Kuito in the province of Bié. The investment which costs US$ 20 million, includes the construction of a water reservoir and a 4.5 km length water pipeline.[333] According to the Chinese Ministry of the Environment, the pipeline, which had been completed in 2009, provides 300 cubic meters of water per day, providing water for 400,000 people.[334] In April 2012, China's Sinohydro announced responsibility for the implementation of Luanda's 120 km length household water pipelines. It is expected that the Luanda Water Supply project would provide safe drinking water to more than 1 million people.[335] In July 2013, Sinohydro was awarded to a US$35 million contract extension for building new medium voltage sub-stations in the Angolan province of Kwanza Norte. It is anticipated that these two stations would improve the power supply to the municipalities of Cazengo and Cambambe.

In October 2013, the Angolan government revealed its intention to build fifteen hydroelectric plants in order to boost power generation in a bid attracting investment in other industries throughout the country.[336]

---

332 "Chinese Firm Invests $2.4 billion in Post War Angola," *Reuters Africa* 17 August 2009, Date Accessed: 25 November 2014 http://af.reuters.com/article/topNews/idAFJOE57G07P20090817.

333 Christiane Tholen, op.cit., 100.

334 Ibid., 100; "Angola-China: Mutual Benefits," *Sonangol Universo* September 2013:11.

335 Zhong Nan, "Power Giants Work on Local Touch," *China Daily* 20 December 2013, Date Accessed: 21 December 2013 <http://africa.chinadaily.com.cn/weekly/2013-12/20/content_17187099.htm>.

336 Colin McClelland, "Angola to Raise Power Output Fivefold to Attract Investors," *Bloomberg News* 4 October 2013, Date Accessed: 4 October 2013 <http://www.bloomberg.com/news/2013-10-03/angola-plans-to-raise-power-output-fivefold-to-attract-investors.html>.

According to the Director of Studies, Planning and Statistics at the Angolan Ministry of Energy and Water, José Salgueiro, Angola's goal is to have an installed capacity of 9,000 megawatts of generation capacity by 2025.[337] That number is five times more than today's capacity in Angola.[338] Ultimately, China's Xinjiang TBEA Group and Brazil's Odebrecht SA teamed up to build fifteen hydroelectric plants in Angola.

In May 2014, following the Chinese Premier Li Keqiang's visit to Angola, the Chinese Exim Bank announced the installation of US$ 170 million to be utilized for three important of projects[339]. Part of the money is reserved for the construction of Chiumbe-dala Dam and its power sub-station of Luena in the eastern Moxico Province.[340]

In January 2015, to boost socio-economic development and to diminish the energy deficit of Angola, Angola's Ministry of Finance paid out US$ 982 million (first installment: US$ 147.7 million) from the Strategic Financial Oil Reserve for Basic Infrastructure, and awarded the Chinese construction and engineering company, China Machinery Engineering Corporation (CMEC) to build an electricity generation plant in the north western city of Soyo.[341]

Just like other infrastructure projects, building power plants are a necessity for the Angolan government to enhance its growth rate and to open their land to the businesses. As José Salguiera noted: "Everything is planned

---

337 Ibid.

338 Ibid.

339 The projects namely: Chiumba-dala dam and its power sub-station of Luena in eastern Moxico province; Agro-industrial of Cuimba project in Zaire province; Economic and Commercial Training Institute of the African Portuguese Speaking Countries Community (PALOP).

340 "Eximbank Releases USD170 million for Projects in Angola," *Agência Angola Press ANGOP* 10 May 2014, Date Accessed: 10 May 2014 <http://www.portalangop.co.ao/angola/en_us/noticias/economia/2014/4/19/Eximbank-relases-Usd170-million-for-projects-Angola,42355548-b41a-4ab5-976f-7caf43bd251b.html>.

341 George Mpofu, "Angola to Boost Energy Output with $1bn Power Plant," *Ventures Africa* 12 January 2015, Date Accessed: 13 January 2015 <http://www.ventures-africa.com/2015/01/angola-to-boost-energy-output-with-1bn-power-plant/>.

to have the electricity there because it is the main way to say Angola is open for business."[342]

Conclusion of the Chapter

This chapter sheds light on the interdependent structure of the bilateral relations of China and Angola by addressing the reciprocal feature of the Chinese way of foreign aid 'Angola Mode', which refers to the idea of securing natural resources of recipient countries with low-interest loans and the projects linked to the construction of public facilities.

Findings in this chapter clearly demonstrate that the nature of China-Angola aid relations is mutually beneficial. Mutual beneficial relations stem from their mutual economic necessities. As Moravcsik assumes, national preferences of China and Angola are grounded in the constraints and opportunities imposed by economic interdependence. The lack of infrastructure and capital, which has been a critical obstacle to socio-economic growth of Angola, has matched China's increasing demand for energy resources and its foreign aid model, Angola Mode. As an old Chinese proverb says "To get rich, build roads first (要致富，先修路)". Angola has followed a rational strategy by benefiting from Chinese credits, used as a facilitation mechanism for the Angolan government to convert oil revenues into infrastructure projects. Those infrastructure projects have boosted the national capacity and brought enormous opportunities and potential for the continent's self-sufficiency and self-esteem. As mentioned above, there have been moments that decision preferences of the Angolan government have been transformed due to the changes in the priority rankings of their own needs and interests.

From this process, it is clear that the circumstances and mutual necessities affect the dimension of aid relations between China and Angola. Angola Mode, which has been the dominant aid model in China-Angola relations, has placed two unequal states over an equal platform. This confirms the idea that aid relations are characterized by reciprocal connections serving the interests of both China and Angola. It has not only become one of the major factors to challenge the dictates of Western countries and institutions, but also a facilitation mechanism to convert oil revenues into construction contracts.

342 Colin McClelland, ibid.

The three consequences of Angola Mode and its role in facilitating China's access to infrastructure projects, Angola's market and oil blocks, have also been closely examined. The first consequence of Angola Mode is that Angola Mode has given Chinese companies the opportunity to go global and develop themselves to compete in the international market. The second, under the terms of concessional loans, it was required by the Chinese government that Chinese enterprises were to be elected as contractors or exporters. According to the data retrieved from the Angolan Agência Nacional de Investimento Privado (ANIP), the number of Chinese contracts approved by the Angolan government increased steadily following the first oil-backed loan of China in 2004.[343] Correspondingly, under the terms of oil-backed credit lines, China has contributed money, labor and expertise quickly. The third is China's impact on the rebuilding of Angola went beyond just large-scale contracts. The presence of Chinese companies caused a fall of construction materials prices, which gave opportunity for the local people to build or renovate their own houses. The April 2011 article in The Economist magazine reinforced that by providing aid and infrastructure development to Africa, "China has boosted employment in Africa and made basic goods like shoes and radios more affordable."[344] This indicates the fact that the development of the country is needed to be understood not only through the infrastructure projects, but also via the opportunities that Chinese companies have opened for Angolan people.

More contracts for numerous infrastructure projects do not only imply the entrance of more Chinese companies into Angola, but also implies the introduction of Chinese businesses to the new Angolan market. To open Angola to the business and attract new business partners, reconstruction and rehabilitation of the country's infrastructures, from building roads to power plants, would be required. By the support of China through its Angola Mode strategy, Chinese companies, along with Angolan companies, found a common ground to grow their businesses together.

In the next chapter, business cooperation of Angolan and Chinese companies in various sectors will be under the magnifying glass of the author.

---

343 Agência Nacional de Investimento Privado (ANIP): <http://www.anip.co.ao/>.

344 Zhu Liangxiu, "The Chinese in Africa: Trying to Pull Together," *The Economist* 20 April 2011, Date Accessed: 17 August 2013 <http://www.economist.com/node/18586448>.

Chapter 3: Business Cooperation between China and Angola

China's business strategies in Angola have grown along with its growing investments in the infrastructure sector. Not only in investment (except the oil sector) but also in trade, has China overtaken Portugal and the US as the leading export-import partner of Angola, respectively.

The rapid increase in the volume of bilateral trade and Chinese investment in Angola strengthened bilateral ties and assisted the improvement of the business environment in the country. Following the improvement of the business environment, the Angolan government has taken additional steps to encourage trade and investment between Angola and China, and facilitate the entry of Chinese nationals (tourists, students, teachers, researchers, entrepreneurs, investors, and workers, etc.) into Angola. Today, 500 Chinese companies do business in Angola and 260,000 Chinese nationals are working and living in Angola.[345]

As it was stated in China's 2006 African Policy, the Chinese government supports the continued financing of Chinese companies' investment and business engagement in Africa. In 2007, the Angolan government took an important step to facilitate economic and commercial exchanges by organizing the Business Fair FILDA (Luanda International Fair). Many participants from China took part and demonstrated a keen interest in investing in Angola. FILDA's last meeting, which took place between the 16th and the 21st of July 2013, celebrated 30th years of the event, and China was invited as the guest country. In the opening ceremony of FILDA, China was awarded the best international representation and bigger international representation.[346]

345 "Angola and China Want to Boost Bilateral Ties," *Agência Angola Press ANGOP* 8 May 2014, Date Accessed: 9 May 2014 <http://www.portalangop.co.ao/angola/en_us/noticias/politica/2014/4/19/Angola-and-China-want-boost-bilateral-ties,5797cab0-cd72-4dec-ab60-b1fd530436f5.html>.

346 "FILDA 2013," *Welcome to Angola*, 2013, Date Accessed: 17 September 2013 <http://www.welcometoangola.co.ao/_filda_2013_3>.

The business meetings, organized through the economic and commercial cooperation between China and Portuguese-speaking countries[347] (Macau Forum) allow the Angolan government to take action in order to facilitate business transactions between China and Portuguese-speaking countries. In 2007, Angola became the first African country to establish a consulate-general in the Macau SAR. That decision was taken after a 30 % increase in the number of Chinese businessmen who applied for an Angolan visa over the 2006–2007 period.[348] In order to accelerate the visa-application process, right after the opening of the consulate-general in Macau SAR, Angola opened another consulate-general in Hong Kong. As the first Angolan consul in Macau SAR, Rodrigo Pedro Domingos stated:

> "There is a growing interest in Angola among businessmen and women based in Macau and mainland China. This can be seen by the number of visas that we issue and the number of businesspeople are looking for information and advice on how to do business with Angolan companies or in Angola."[349]

Due to the Macau connection, several economic agreements and investment projects are carried out. Geocapital,[350] which is an investment company linked to Macau, has invested in natural resources and investment banking in countries that share the same Portuguese heritage as Macau. In 2006, the Angolan Bank Banco de Fomento Angola (BFA), together with the Portugal's Banco Português de Investimento (BPI) and Macau's branch of the Bank of China extended a US$ 100 million credit line to support trade between China

347 Brazil, Portugal, Angola, Mozambique, Cape Verde, Guinea Bissau, Sao Tome and Principe, and East Timor.

348 "Milhares de Empresarios Chineses Pretendem Investir No Pais," *Jornal de Angola* 17 November 17 2007, Date Accessed: 17 September 2013 <http://jornaldeangola.sapo.ao/economia/milhares-de-empresarios-chineses-pretenden-investir-no-pais>.

349 José Carlos Matias, "Macao, China and Portuguese Speaking Countries," *Macao Magazine*, Issue: 4 (July 2010): 12, Date Accessed: 17 September 2013 <http://www.macaomagazine.net/index.php?option=com_content&view=article&id=90:macao-china-and-portuguese-speaking-countries&catid=39:issue-4>.

350 Geocapital owns 44 % of Guinea Bissau's Banco da África Ocidental (BAO).

and Angola.[351] By doing that, Angola not only paved the way for Chinese investments but also promoted the increase of bilateral trade.

In 2011, state-owned TAAG Angola Airlines (Linhas Aéreas de Angola) launched non-stop flights from Luanda to Beijing. In 2013, the air carrier TAAG added a second weekly flight to Beijing. The more than 400 passengers travelling from China to Angola and vice versa demonstrates TAAG's interest in increasing the number of flights to Beijing.[352]

In October 2012, the Angolan government signed an agreement with the Chinese government with the exemption of 95 % of tariffs in exporting Chinese products.[353] In 2013, the Angolan government took another important step to boost bilateral trade between China and Angola by selling oil to China with the Chinese currency Renminbi (人民币).

It is also possible to get some points from Angola's state-owned only daily paper, the Jornal de Angola,[354] which is in control of the Angolan government. In reports published by Jornal de Angola, China often comes to the forefront with news related to its economic and commercial activities rather than its cultural or political performances. In Angola's Jornal de Angola, every article mentioning the word 'China' in between 20 April - 20 May 2014 was reviewed in order to analyze the portrayal of China in the paper. The reviews resulted in a higher percentage of neutral reports, accounted for 58 % of mentionings; the percentage of positive reports (praising China and its activities) accounted for 38 %; the negative reports accounted for only 4 %. That small survey enables us to get an idea of the perception of Angola's political leaders and economic elite who control journalism in Angola. The positive and non-negative news published by the country's only daily

351 José Carlos Matias, "Macao, China and Portuguese Speaking Countries," *Macao Magazine*, Issue: 4 (July 2010): 13, Date Accessed: 17 September 2013 <http://www.macaomagazine.net/index.php?option=com_content&view=article&id=90:macao-china-and-portuguese-speaking-countries&catid=39:issue-4>.

352 "Taag com Dois Voos Semanais para China," *Portal de Angola* 24 September 2013, Date Accessed: 25 September 2013 <http://www.portaldeangola.com/2013/09/taag-com-dois-voos-semanais-para-china/>.

353 In the following month, November 2012, China has offered Zero Tariff Treatment to 95 % of Angolan goods exported to China.

354 Jornal de Angola is widely known as the "loyal mouthpiece" of the Presidency and MPLA.

newspaper is a confirmation of the satisfaction of the economic actors, which are known with their closeness with the government and its ruling party, MPLA.

It seems likely that China is using its financing activities to facilitate opportunities for Chinese companies to conduct business with local firms in various sectors. The most attractive sectors for Chinese investors in Angola are construction, agriculture, manufacturing and the extractive industries, particularly oil and diamonds.

3.1 Cooperation in Oil and Diamond Sector

The US is well known due to its large investments in the Angolan oil sector. As it is explained in the previous chapter, the US companies' investments in Angola have been predominantly in the oil sector. In several reports, it is shown that the US investments in Angola have greatly exceeded investments by China.[355] Today, US oil companies acted as operators for eleven of forty-nine Angolan oil blocks, and as non-operators in five Angolan oil blocks whereas Chinese oil companies are acting as non-operators in twelve Angolan oil blocks. (See Table 3.1).

Table 3.1: Comparison of numbers and types of Chinese and U.S Oil Companies' Investments in Oil Blocks in Angola, as of 2013

US Firms	⚙	⚙	⚙	⚙	⚙	⚙	⚙	⚙	⚙	⚙	⚙	◊	◊	◊
Chinese Firms	◊	◊	◊	◊	◊	◊	◊	◊	◊	◊	◊	◊	◊	

US: 11 operator roles, 3 non-operator roles
China: 0 operator roles, 13 non-operator roles

⚙: Operator role
◊: Non-operator role

Chinese oil companies' weakness is that Chinese oil companies generally lack the technology, capacity and experience to manage offshore oil

355 According to Deborah Brautigam, the reason behind the low figures of China investment is the non-existence of published data on its investments in Angola.

operations.[356] The weakness of US oil companies is that, contrary to the relationship between the US government and US companies, Chinese companies are mostly state-owned and are closely connected to the Chinese government. Connection between the government and companies eventually provides financial power to Chinese companies, and allow them not to consider the cost of the purchases. A representative from a large US oil company argues: "In some cases Chinese companies are willing to pay much higher prices than the US companies to purchase ownership interests, in part because Chinese firms are not answerable to shareholders and because they receive support, including financing, from the Chinese government."[357] Since 2002, Chinese loans to Angola account for US$ 14.5 billion while US loans, in that same period, remained at US$ 680 million. Another advantage China has over the US in Angola, is the local content requirements of the Angolan government. As explained in previous chapters, the Angolan government requires foreign countries to employ local workers and partnerships with domestic firms. In terms of employing local workers, Angolan labor laws limit the number of foreign employees to 30 % of the workforce. In other words, Angolans are required to constitute 70 % of the workforce. However, China is exempted from that law. The Chinese government and the Angolan government agreed that Chinese companies in Angola can use up to 70 % foreign labor and no less than 30 % Angolan labor. In terms of partnering with domestic firms, compared to US companies, Chinese companies are tend to engage more in partnerships with domestic companies, since US companies are very much concerned with the challenges raised from a partnerships with potentially corrupt entities. US companies have responsibilities under the US Foreign Corrupt Practices Act, which outlaws payments to foreign government officials to assist in securing business opportunities.[358] Thus,

356 "US GAO - Sub-Saharan Africa: Case Studies of U.S and Chinese Economic Engagement in Angola, Ghana, and Kenya; a Supplement to GAO-13-199," *United States Government Accountability Office*, (February 2013): 14 Date Accessed: 14 August 2013 <http://www.gao.gov/assets/660/652043.pdf>.

357 Ibid., 45.

358 Criminal Division of the US Department of Justice and the Enforcement Division of the U.S Securities and Exchange Commission, "A Resource Guide to the US Foreign Corrupt Practices Act," November 2012, *The United States*

close links between Angolan government and Angolan companies decrease the chance of a potential partnership between Angolan and the US companies. Contrary to US companies, Chinese companies do not have such responsibilities; partnering with domestic companies is largely supported by the Chinese government.

As Figure 3.1 illustrates, there is a strong connection between the Chinese and Angolan oil companies, as well as China's Hong Kong based fund, China International Fund (CIF). After the launch of several reports written by the US China Economic & Security Review Commission and British foreign policy think tank Chatham House, CIF's mysterious background and vast influence came onto the scene. According to reports written by the US China Economic & Security Review Commission and Chatham House, CIF makes up part of a network of Chinese private enterprises (more than thirty subsidiaries). The report calls these companies the "88 Queensway Group". These companies are managed and owned by some key individuals, who have no background before they established the 88 Queensway Group. Some of them include Veronica Feng (冯婉筠), Luo Fang Hong (罗方红) (whom owns 1 % of CIF), and Wu Yang (武洋与).[359] The 88 Queensway Group is under the suspicion of being a front company for the Chinese government, because "key personnel have ties to Chinese state-owned enterprises and government agencies."[360] The US China Economic & Security Review Commission's report argues, "by posing as a private firm, the Group creates numerous companies within a complicated organization structure to invest globally, thereby enabling the Group to acquire assets unnoticed."[361] Suspicions grew when in a company filing, CIF director Wu Yang's Beijing address matched an address associated with the Ministry of Public Safety (MPS).[362] Besides that, China's Ambassador to Angola, Zhang Bolun (张伯伦), asserted, that the "CIF enjoys a close

Department of Justice, Date Accessed: 17 September 2013 <http://www.justice.gov/criminal/fraud/fcpa/guidance/>.

359 Lee Levkovitz, Marta McLellan, J.R. Warner, op.cit., 8.

360 Ibid., i; "转载：武洋与"中国国际基金公司"、徐锦华（徐京华）、冯婉筠、罗方红的关系," 幻影世界，Date Accessed: 3 October 2012 <http://mirage-world.wordpress.com/>.

361 Lee Levkovitz, Marta McLellan, J.R. Warner, op.cit., ii.

362 Ibid., 7.

relationship with President dos Santos"[363]; clues in the connection between CIF and the Angolan government.

Figure 3.1: Partnership of Chinese and Angolan Oil Companies in Oil Sector

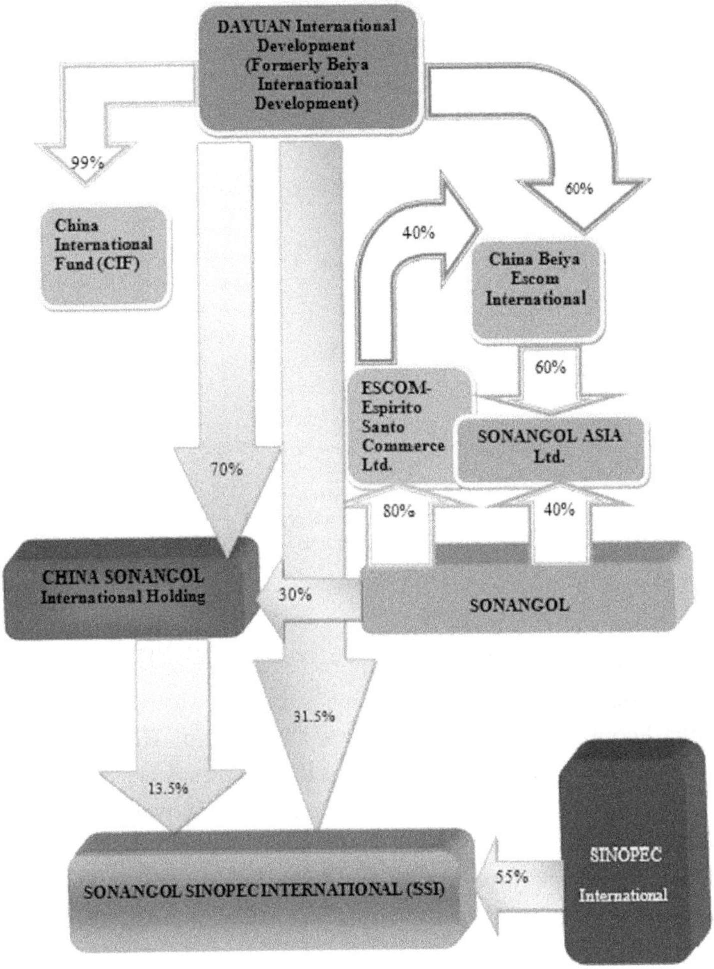

Source: Adopted from diagram in Marcus Power and Ana Cristina Alves eds. (2012).

---

363 Rafael Marques de Morais, "The New Imperialism: China in Angola," *World Affairs*, 2011, Date Accessed: 4 July 2014 <http://www.worldaffairsjournal.org/article/new-imperialism-china-angola>.

According to the reports, CIF is 99 % owned by a Hong-Kong based company Dayuan International Development Ltd. (大遠國際發展有限公司).[364] Therefore, when we talk about CIF, it also means we talk about Dayuan International Development Ltd. (from 2003 to 2006 called: Beiya International Development Ltd.) or vice versa. The company is 30 % owned by Wu Yang (武洋) and 70 % by New Bright International Development Ltd. which is 30 % owned by Luo Fang Hong (罗方红) and 70 % by Veronica Feng (冯婉筠). (See Figure 3.2).

Figure 3.2: Ownership Structure of 88 Queensway Group[365]

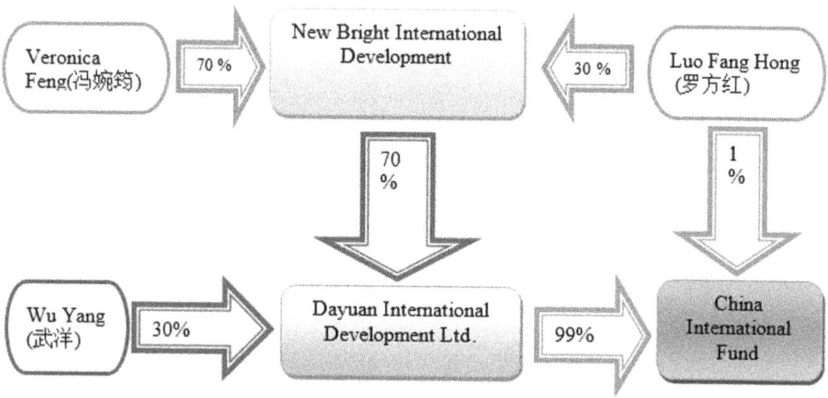

CIF was established in the beginning to fund large-scale national reconstruction projects in developing countries, but later it was revealed by the US China Economic & Security Review Commission Report, that under the name of another company, Dayuan International Development Ltd., CIF partnered with several companies. As director of over sixty CIF-linked companies worldwide, Luo Fang Hong's businessman husband Xu Jinghua (徐京華) has become the driving force behind CIF.[366] Furthermore, Xu Jinghua is known for his friendly ties with Angolan President José Eduardo dos Santos. Xu Jinghua's connections with Angolan President dos Santos date back to the Cold War. During his training in a Soviet

364 Lee Levkovitz, Marta McLellan, J.R. Warner, op.cit., 14.
365 Ibid., 14.
366 Vines et al. (2009), op.cit., 69.

academy in Baku, he met today's Angola's President Dos Santos and during the civil war (1975–2002) he provided arms to the MPLA on behalf of the Chinese government.[367]

In June 2004, Angola's state oil company Sonangol formally partnered with China International Fund, through Sonangol Asia Ltd., whose ownership shares comes from Sonangol (40 %) and China Beiya Escom International (60 %)[368], and is directed by Luo Fang Hong, Wu Yang and Manuel Vicente.[369] Right after that partnership, in 2004, China Sonangol International Holding Ltd. (CSIH) was constituted as a joint venture between Sonangol (30 %) and Dayuan International Development Ltd. (70 %). On paper, CSIH does not consist of any Mainland Chinese companies, but is creation of Angola's Sonangol and Hong Kong based Dayuan International Development Ltd. (CIF's parent company). However, the role of the China International Fund, which is almost entirely (99 %) owned by Dayuan International Development in the remarkable business expansion of Chinese government in Angola, is plain to see; despite denials of Chinese officials' link between CIF and the Chinese government.[370] Furthermore, the companies at 88 Queensway Group are assumed to act as 'fronts' to hide the personal interests of businessmen, such as Manuel Vicente.[371] In September 2004, China Sonangol, together with Dayuan International Development and Sinopec, set up a joint venture, Sonangol Sinopec International (SSI). In this joint venture, Sinopec succeeded in becoming the majority shareholder by owning a 55 % share, while Dayuan International Development owns 31.5 % and China Sonangol owns the remaining 13.5 % share. (See Figure 3.1).

---

367 Lucy Corkin (2013), op.cit., 135.

368 China Beiya Escom International is owned 40 % by Portuguese Espirito Santo Commerce Bank (ESCOM) and 60 % by Dayuan International Development Ltd.

369 Manuel Vicente, who has been the Vice President of Angola since September 2012, had served as the chairman of Angola's Sonangol from 1999 to 2012.

370 Markus Weimer and Alex Vines, "China's Angolan Oil Deals 2003-11," in eds. Marcus Power and Ana Cristina Alves, op.cit., 99.

371 It is believed that, Manuel Vicente and the 88 Queensway Group incorporated nine subsidiaries of China Sonangol, see Lee Levkovitz, Marta McLellan, J.R. Warner,op.cit., 19.

Table 3.2: Sonangol Sinopec International (SSI) Oil Assets in Angola

Name of Oil Block	Asset	Type of Oil Block	Acquisition Year	Consortium
Block 18	50 %	Deep water	2004	BP [OP] 50 %
Block 15/06	20 %	Deep water	2006	ENI [OP] 35 % Sonangol 15 % Total 15 % Falcon Oil 5 % Statoil 5 %
Block 17/06	27.5 %	Deep water	2006	Total [OP] 30 % Sonangol 20 % Somoil 10 % Falcon Oil 5 % Acrep 17 S.A. 5 % Partex 2.5 %
Block 18/06	40 %	Deep water	2006	Petrobras [OP] 30 % Sonangol 20 % Falcon Oil 5 % Geminas 5 %
Block 3/05A	25 %	Shallow water	2006	Sonangol [OP] 25 % Ajoco 20 % Eni 12 % Somoil 10 % Naftagas 4 % Ina-Nafta 4 %
Block 3/05	25 %	Shallow water	2006	Sonangol [OP] 20 % Ajoco 20 % Eni 12 % Somoil 10 % Naftagas 4 % Ina-Nafta 4 %
Block 31	10 %	Ultra deep water	2013	BP [OP] 26.67 % Sonangol 25 % Sonangol P&P 20 % Statoil 13.33 % China Sonangol 5 %

Sources: Sonangol Concession Map-2012, for Block 31 http://www.worldoil.com/Sinopec_JV_raises_stake_in_Angola_deepwater_block.html

Table 3.3: China Sonangol International Holding (CSIH) Oil Assets in Angola

Name of Oil Block	Asset	Type of Oil Block	Acquisiaion Year	Consortium
Block 31	5 %	Ultra-deep water	2010	BP [OP] 26.67 % Sonangol 25 % Sonangol P&P 20 % Statoil 13.33 % SSI 10 %
Block 32	20 %	Ultra-deep water	2010	Total [OP] 30 % Sonangol 20 % Esso 15 % Marathon 10 % Galp 5 %
Block 19/11	10 %	Pre-salt	2011	BP [OP] 50 % Sonangol P&P 40 %
Block 36/11	20 %	Pre-salt	2011	Conocophillips [OP] 30 % Sonangol P&P 50 %
Block 38/11	15 %	Pre-salt	2011	Statoil[OP] 55 % Sonangol 30 %

Source: Sonangol Concession Map-2012

In August 2004, China Sonangol established itself as a company that has right to export Angolan oil to China and act as a middleman between Sonangol and Sinopec.[372] It is believed that almost all of China's oil imports from Angola come from China Sonangol.[373] In 2006, China Sonangol was awarded 25 % of equity shares in each shallow Block 3/05A and Block 3/05, which were previously owned by TOTAL and known as Block 3/80.

In September 2004, one month after the establishment of China Sonangol, Sonangol Sinopec International, was set up between China Sonangol and Sinopec Overseas Oil and Gas (SOOG), a subsidiary of parent company Sinopec group. In March 2010, Sinopec (Hong Kong) International Ltd.[374]

372 "Queensway Syndicate and the Africa Trade," *The Economist* 13 August 2011, Date Accessed: 18 August 2013 <http://www.economist.com/node/21525847>.

373 Ibid.

374 Sinopec (Hong Kong) International Ltd. is 100 % owned by China Petroleum & Chemical Corporation. (Sinopec).

acquired 55 % of shares in SSI from the parent company Sinopec Group or China Petrochemical Corporation Group. In other words, Sinopec International replaced the Sinopec Overseas Oil and Gas (SOOG) by acquiring 55 % of shares in SSI for USD$ 2.457 billion. With this acquisition, Sinopec would hold 27.5 % of Block 18 in Angola through Sinopec (Hong Kong) International Ltd., after SSI bought a 50 % stake in deep-water oil Block 18. That acquisition of deep-water oil assets was Sinopec's first overseas success.[375] The assets are also the highest quality overseas assets that Sinopec ever had.[376] In Sinopec's website, the oil in Block 18 is described as "a world class deep-water oil asset in terms of output, with the highest reserves and production volume among projects of similar."[377]

In addition to that Sinopec via Sinopec (Hong Kong) International Ltd. has now equity stakes in Block 15/06, Block 17/06, Block 18/06 and Block 31. (See Table 3.2). SSI's success to win Block 17/06 (27 %) and Black 18/06 (40 %) by outbidding Western companies, ExxonMobil and BP, received a lot of attention. With the completion of this transaction, it was anticipated that Sinopec Corp.'s remaining proven reserves of crude oil would increase by 102 million barrels, up 3.6 %, and its daily crude oil production would increase by 72,520 bbl, up 8.8 %.[378]

After we check the tables above (Table 3.2 and Table 3.3), we cannot disregard the souring of relations between Sinopec and Sonangol. In between 2006 and 2011, the Angolan government altered its attitude towards SSI and became eager to decrease the chance of Sinopec's access to oil assets by promoting further opportunities to China Sonangol to outbid SSI. It could imply that as Angolan economy grows, Angolan preferences also change and tend to take more of its own interests into account. Here are a couple of examples: Following the acquisition of oil Block 15/06, Block 16/06 and

---

375 "Sinopec's First Acquisition of Overseas Upstream Assets," *News,* SINOPEC, 28 March 2010, Date Accessed: 13 August 2013 <http://english.sinopec.com/media_center/news/20100329/download/en-news100329d.pdf>.

376 "Sinopec Acquires Overseas Oil and Gas Assets for the First Time," *News,* SIONPEC, 26 March 2010 Date Accessed:18 august 2013 <http://sipc.sinopec.com/sipc/en/news/com_news/20100803/news_20100803_602117800000.shtml>.

377 Ibid.

378 Ibid.

Block 17/06 by SSI, both companies agreed to work on a new project of a new US$ 3 billion oil refinery in Lobito (Sonaref) with a capacity of 240,000 barrels per day; this was one of the pre-requisites for the acquisition of those blocks.[379] However, in early March 2007, the deal was cancelled due to the disagreements between Sinopec and Sonangol over which markets would be designated to receive Sonaref's refined petroleum products. It came to the forefront that China's demand of 80 % of Sonaref's production would be exported to foreign markets, and this was strictly rejected by Angola, which imports over 70 % of its refined oil.[380] Manuel Vicente, former chairman of Sonangol, had criticized the Chinese company in the Angolan media, claiming: "We cannot construct a refinery just to make products for China."[381] At the end of 2008, the technical implementation of the project was awarded to an American company, Kellogg Brown & Root (KBR). However, according to a report published by the US Energy Information Administration, in January 2013, "Sonangol [was] exploring [a] possible collaboration with a number of other international oil companies, but to date no agreements have been reached."[382] More news related to the souring relations of Sinopec and Sonangol was discussed just a few months after the collapse of the deal for the Sonaref project. In 2007, Sinopec participated alone in the tender round for new Angolan blocks opening up. However the round was frozen in the middle of 2008 due to the proximity of presidential elections in September 2008, and due to the economic crisis.[383] Sinopec didn't give up and at the end of 2008, made another attempt to acquire petroleum assets in Angola. Sinopec acted together with another Chinese petroleum company,

379 Ana Cristina Alves, "Taming the Dragon: China's Oil Interests in Angola," in eds. Marcus Power and Ana Cristina Alves, op.cit., 113.

380 "Sonangol 35 Year Milestone of Success Beckons," *Sonangol Universo* December 2010: 39, Date Accessed: 13 August 2013 <http://www.sonangol.co.uk/wps/wcm/connect/c4b95a00475d1922ac54fd7c37a37d2d/SU28-web.pdf?MOD=AJPERES>.

381 Indira Campos and Alex Vines, "Angola and China: A Pragmatic Partnership," *Centre for Strategic and International Studies* (March 2008): 17.

382 U.S Energy Information Administration. *A Report on Angola*. EIA, February 2014:4 Date Accessed: 20 April 2014. <http://www.eia.gov/countries/analysisbriefs/Angola/angola.pdf>.

383 Ana Cristina Alves, "Taming the Dragon: China's Oil Interests in Angola," in Marcus Power and Ana Cristina Alves eds., op.cit., 115.

China National Offshore Oil Company (CNOOC), to acquire Marathon's 20 % shareholding in ultra-deep water Block 32, which is operated by TOTAL. Sinopec and CNOOC's $1.3 billion offer outbid other companies such as Indian ONGC and Brazilian state owned oil company Petrobras, as well as the other Chinese oil company, China National Petroleum Corporation (CNPC). In July 2009, Sinopec, CNOOC and Marathon signed the agreement. However in September 2009, Sonangol announced its intention to exercise its preferential right to blocking access of Chinese companies to this asset. It is estimated that, Sonangol found Chinese Companies, Sinopec and CNOOC' s offer lower than its real value which is considered at US$ 1.4 billion-US$ 1.6 billion.[384]

Even during the era of economic crisis, Angola was able to say no to Chinese companies' sole attempt (without Sonangol) at entering the Angolan oil blocks. There is no definitive answer on why the Angolan government has taken such negative actions towards Sinopec, but it could be argued that Angola did so to avoid the drop in prices of its oil assets or lessen the possibility of depending on only one part, or both. But certainly, these are very significant examples that reaffirm that China-Angola relations are not always driven by China's interests.

Table 3.4: Comparison of Sinopec and Sonangol's Shares in Angolan Oil Blocks

Sinopec's shares in Angolan oil Blocks through SSI (SSI: 4.05 % Sonangol, 40.95 % Dayuan International, 55 % Sinopec.)		**Sonangol's shares in Angolan oil blocks through SSI and China Sonangol** (China Sonangol: 30 % Sonangol, 70 % Dayuan International.)	
		Through SSI	**Through China Sonangol**
11 %	Block 15/06	0.81 % Block 15/06	1.5 % Block 31
15 %	Block 17/06	1.1 % Block 17/06	6 % Block 32
22 %	Block 18/06	1.62 % Block 18/06	3 % Block 19/11
13.75 %	Block 3/05	1.01 % Block 3/05	6 % Block 36/11
13.75 %	Block 3/05 A	1.01 % Block 3/05 A	4.5 % Block 38/11
27.5 %	Block 18	2 % Block 18	
5.5 %	Block 31		

384 Ibid., 116.

Furthermore, as shown in Table 3.4, Sinopec, as the majority shareholder of SSI, owns more oil shares in Angolan blocks than that of Sonangol, which owns only 4.05 % share in SSI. However in China Sonangol, despite the largest share of Chinese Dayuan International Holding (70 %), Sonangol, which represents 30 % of the share in China Sonangol, owns more percentage of shares through China Sonangol than the shares it owns through SSI. A more favorable position of China Sonangol for the Angolan government can also clarify the question why in recent years SSI has been very often outbid by China Sonangol in acquisition of oil shares in Angolan oil blocks.

Refusals from the Angolan government did not discourage Sinopec, and its attempts for reconciliation finally worked in June 2013. Sinopec, through its joint venture Sonangol Sinopec International, once again seized an opportunity to acquire a 10 % stake of US' Marathon Oil Company in offshore Block 31.[385] Apart from that, in spite of the previous defeat of SSI against China Sonangol in terms of its attempts of acquisition of oil blocks, SSI still owns more shares of Angolan petroleum assets than China Sonangol.[386] Certainly, SSI's acquirement of a 50 % share in oil Block 18 in 2004, right after the extension of the first oil-backed China Exim Bank loans, played a crucial role in keeping SSI owning more shares than China Sonangol. However, neither SSI nor China Sonangol's assets in Angola are in operation phases. Having non-operator roles in Angolan oil assets can only be explained by a lack of technology and capacity to manage offshore oil operations. Therefore, Angola, which still needs operators, prefers a strategy not to depend on one party. As Lucy Corkin explains, Angola has differed itself from most oil states as encouraging Western business rather than fostering anti-Western sentiment.[387] The cooperative steps taken by Angola and the U.S in the natural gas sector confirm Corkin's statement. The US's Chevron and Angola's Sonangol came together to develop and commercialize Angola's enormous natural gas resources. According to US

385 "Marathon Oil Strikes $1.5 billion Deal," *BusinessWeek* 26 June 2013, Date Accessed: 27 June 2013 <http://www.businessweek.com/ap/2013-06-26/marathon-oil-strikes-1-dot-5-billion-deal>.

386 Ana Cristina Alves, "Taming the Dragon: China's Oil Interests in Angola," in Marcus Power and Ana Cristina Alves eds., op.cit., 119.

387 Lucy Corkin (2013), op.cit., 153.

Government Energy Information Administration's (EIA) recently released Angola Country Analysis Brief, Angola had 10.9 trillion cubic feet (Tcf) of natural gas reserves in 2011, up from an estimated 2 Tcf in 2007.[388] Angola currently flares the majority of its natural gas but the Angolan government has plans to convert natural gas into liquefied natural gas (LNG).[389] Chevron and Sonangol together with other shareholders, including Total, BP and Eni, built the country's first LNG plant near Soyo in northern Angola.[390] The factory has so far exported three LNG shipments to Brazil, China and Japan. US Company, Chevron, which operates the project, has a 36.4 % stake in it, whereas Angolan state company Sonangol owns 22.8 %, and Total, BP and Eni each own 13.6 %. China is not yet part of that project but rising domestic demand accelerated China's interest in securing LNG resources, as well. In August 2013, the China National Offshore Oil Corporation (CNOOC) acquired the first shipment of an estimated 155.000 cubic meters LNG from Angola.[391]

Apart from the oil sector, China has declared its intention to support Angolan diamond exports. In the last twenty years, the diamond sector in China has developed very fast. Today, China is anticipated to displace India as the leading diamond processor in the world. On the other hand, Angola has been the fourth largest diamond producer in the world by value after Botswana, Russia and Canada. But explored diamond percentage is only 40 %.[392] In order to double its diamond production, Angola had long searched for foreign investors, which did not arrive in the country

---

388 U.S Energy Information Administration. *A Report on Angola.* EIA, February 2014:9 Date Accessed: 20 April 2014. <http://www.eia.gov/countries/analysisbriefs/Angola/angola.pdf>.

389 Ibid., 9.

390 Ibid., 9.

391 "Angola LNG supplying liquid natural gas to China's CNOOC group," *Macauhub* 14 August 2013, Date Accessed: 15 August 2013 <http://www.macauhub.com.mo/en/2013/08/14/angola-lng-supplying-liquid-natural-gas-to-china%E2%80%99s-cnooc-group/>.

392 Denine Walters, "Diamond Mining in Angola: Enter China and South Africa," 18 July 2011, Consultancy Africa Intelligence, Date Accessed: 31 March 2013. <http://www.consultancyafrica.com/index.php?option=com_content&view=article&id=795:diamond-mining-in-angola-enter-china-and-south-africa&catid=82:african-industry-a-business&Itemid=266>.

because of its poor global rankings in human rights, its reputation for severe official corruption and diamond smuggling. China International Fund Ltd., however, on 6 April 2005, accepted a joint venture agreement with Angola's state-owned diamond company *Empresa Nacional de Diamantes* (Endiama). The Council also approved Endiama's participation in the creation of Endiama China International Holding Ltd. (中安鑽石國際控股有限公司) to produce and market Angolan diamonds. In late 2005, in order to provide Chinese diamond producers to reach rough diamonds, China offered Angola to enter in business relations by creating a trade platform between Shanghai Diamond Exchange and two Angolan, state-owned diamond companies, Endiama and *Sociedade de Comercialização de Diamantes de Angola* (Sodiam). "The platform would help ensure all diamond transactions run through the official channels at the exchange."[393] As of 2012, diamonds represent 2.8 % of Angolan export products. In 2009, China became the top buyer of Angolan diamond production, overtaking the United States.[394] According to Endiama, the Chinese market had accounted for up to 40 % of its exports annually, on average between the years 2009 and 2012.[395]

With China's entrance to the Angolan diamond sector, Angola also took political steps to hold up its regional ambitions. In 2006, Angola played a leading role in the establishment of the African Diamond Producers Association (ADPA) with 12 members[396]. According to Alex Vines, the establishment of that kind of association is nothing more than an attempt

393 Jeff Miller, "China Seeks Angola Rough Trade Exchange by 1Q06," *Rapaport* 13 December 2005, Date Accessed: 15 September 2013 <http://www.diamonds.net/News/NewsItem.aspx?ArticleID=13860>.

394 "Chinese Demand Helping Angolan Diamond Industry," *Macauhub* 24 May 2010, Date Accessed: 16 September 2013 <http://www.macauhub.com.mo/en/2010/05/24/9127/>.

395 "China's Diamond Demand Sparkles," *China Daily* 9 November 2011, Date Accessed: 16 September 2013 <http://www.chinadaily.com.cn/cndy/2011-11/09/content_14060784.htm>.

396 Angola, Botswana, Central African Republic, Democratic Republic of Congo, Ghana, Guinea, Namibia, Sierra Leone, South Africa, Tanzania, Togo, Zimbabwe.

to minimize fears of an OPEC-style cartel.[397] In addition, in 2014, China served as the Chair and Angola served as the Vice Chair of Kimberley Process.[398] Angola has been chairing the Kimberley Process since January 2015.

As mentioned before, Angola, as the fourth largest diamond producer in the world, possesses extensive diamond reserves, in particular within Northeastern and central regions of Angola, notably in Lunda Norte and Lunda Sui provinces. There are three big diamond mines in Angola: Catoca, Fucauma and Luarica. (See Map 3.1). The Catoca diamond mine (Sociedade Mineira de Catoca), established in 1993 in the Lund Sui Province, is the fourth largest diamond mine in the world and extracts diamonds from a kimberlite pipe.[399] The Catoca diamond mine accounts for more than 75 % of Angola's diamond production.[400]

Map 3.1: Diamond Mines in Angola

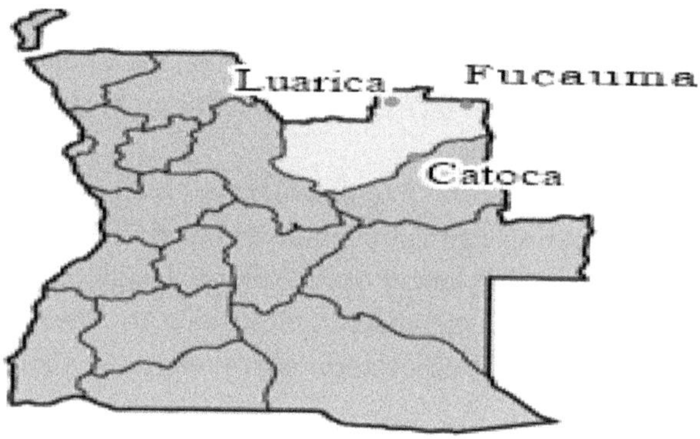

397 Alex Vines, "Angola: Looking Beyond Elections," *European Union Institute for Security Studies*, October 2008:4, Date Accessed: 19 September 2013 <http://www.iss.europa.eu/uploads/media/Angola_looking_beyond_elections.pdf>.

398 Kimberly Process is established to prevent conflict diamonds, by ensuring that all diamond shipments are conflict free. See: <http://www.kimberleyprocess.com/en/chair>.

399 Kimberlite pipes are the most important source of mined diamonds today and refer to the extraction of diamonds from volcanic pipes.

400 Keith Campbell, "Good News for Angolan gem Companies' Shareholders," *Mining Weekly* 9 August 2013, Date Accessed: 19 August 2013 <http://www.miningweekly.com/article/shareholders-in-two-diamond-companies-get-good-news-2013-08-09>.

The mining company, Sociedade Mineira de Catoca, is owned by Angola's state-owned diamond company Endiama EP, with a 32 % stake and a consortium of international mining companies, including Russia's Alrosa which owns 32.8 %, Brazilian Odebrecht Mining Services holds a 16.4 % stake and, since June 2011, China Sonangol, holds a 18 % stake. (See Figure 3.4). In June 2011, China Sonangol acquired Lev Leviev's[401] (Bukharian-Israeli Company) 18 % stake for US$ 400 million and became the first Chinese company that owned part of a diamond mine.[402] Furthermore, the company produced 6.78 million carats of rough diamonds in 2011, by leveling the sales up to US$ 611 million, a 16 % increase over 2010.[403] Overall Angola had exported 8.56 million carats (worth US$ 1.14 billion) diamonds to three major importers: United Arab Emirates (UAE), Israel and Switzerland. (See Figure 3.3).

Figure 3.3: Angola's Diamond Export Destinations, 2011

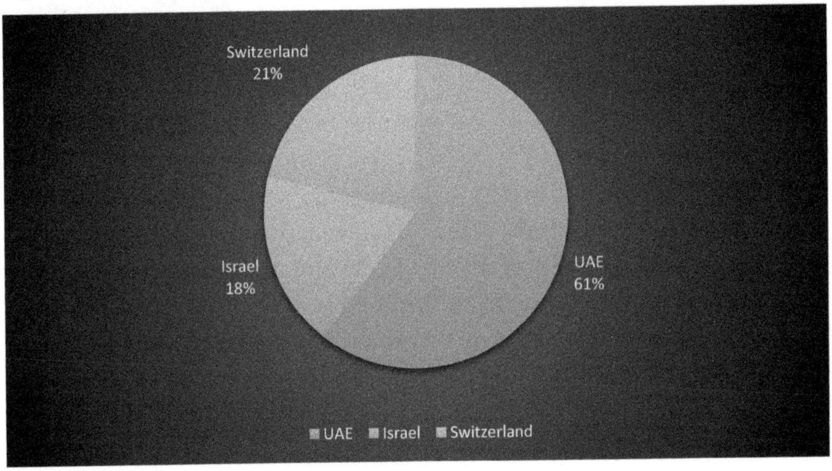

Source: IDEX Online

401 Leviev acquired the stake in the Angola mine in the 1990s for $20 million.

402 Tal Moise, "Leviev Sells Angola Diamond Mine Stake," *Globes* 29 May 2011, Date Accessed: 19 August 2013 <http://www.globes.co.il/en/article-1000649762>.

403 "Angola Diamond Profits Increased in 2011," *Diamond News,* The Israeli Diamond Industry, 12 August 2012, Date Accessed: 20 November 2013 <http://www.israelidiamond.co.il/english/news.aspx?boneid=918&objId=11594>.

In September 2011, in an attempt to attract more foreign investors, Angola made it possible for investors to take a majority stake in mining companies and to reduce their tax liability from 35 % to 25 %. In 2014, Hong Kong replaced Switzerland, and together with UAE and Israel became the main destinations of diamonds mined in Angola.[404]

Figure 3.4: The Shareholder of Catoca Mining Company (Sociedade Mineira de Catoca)

Furthermore, in November 2013, the Angolan news agency ANGOP reported that three foreign firms in Brazil, China and Spain agreed on carrying out a project to map the geology of Angola and determine which parts of the land are likely to contain major diamond reserves.[405] Chair of Endiama, Carlos Sumbula, noted that currently explored diamond reserves accounted for only 40 %.[406] Lack of technical capacity forced Angola to work with

404 "Diamonds Help Angola to Offset Drop in Oil Prices," *Macau Daily Times* 16 December 2014, Date Accessed: 16 December 2014 <http://macaudaily-times.com.mo/diamonds-help-angola-offset-drop-oil-prices.html>.

405 "País Terá Informações Precias Sobre Potencialidade Mineira," *Agência Angola Press ANGOP* 19 November 2013, Date Accessed: 20 November 2013 <http://www.portalangop.co.ao/angola/pt_pt/noticias/economia/2013/10/47/Pais-tera-informacoes-precisas-sobre-potencialidade-mineira,ede0b0ec-40dd-47bd-95af-f73f6459981f.html>.

406 "Angola to Host Diamond Conference in June," *Diamond News,* The Israeli Diamond Industry,17 April 2013, Date Accessed: 20 November 2013 <http://www.israelidiamond.co.il/english/news.aspx?boneid=918&objId=12861>.

foreign companies, among which Chinese companies CITIC and CRCC also play a role. According to a report by ANGOP, Brazilian firm Costa Negocios examine the Eastern region of the country, the Chinese firm CITIC examines the North of the country and Spanish firm Impulso examines the South of the country.[407] In June 2014, it is also announced by the African Media that Chinese Railway Construction Company (CRCC) and Endiama teamed up to work together in prospect of diamonds in Southern Angola.[408] The deal between Angola and these foreign companies was to allow each foreign company to be responsible for the organization of its own logistics. Therefore, each company was expected to spend more than US$ 10 million over a five year period.[409] The Geological Institute of Angola (IGA) Director-General Makenda Ambroise noted, "the main work needed to be carried out to foreign companies because there were no local firms that were capable of all of the conditions it had set."[410]

In short, besides being the second-largest diamond processing country (behind India), China is also the second-largest diamond consuming market (behind the US) that search for newly explored rough resources. Therefore, Angola, with its attractive (not yet explored) geological and mining resources, appeared to be China's investment destination in mining industry. Through the joint venture with Angolan state-owned company Sonangol, China has been strengthening its presence in Angolan oil and diamond reserves. By acquiring stakes in Angolan oil blocks and diamond mine, China is also winning political influence in Angola. As China gains more political influence, China's partnership with many companies in different sectors is

---

407 Ibid.

408 "China Railway Construction: to Prospect Diamond in Angola," *4-Traders* 3 June 2014, Date Accessed: 3 June 2014 <http://www.4-traders.com/CHINA-RAILWAY-CONSTRUCTIO-6500144/news/China-Railway-Construction--to-Prospect-Diamond-in-Angola-18536023/>.

409 "País Terá Informações Precias Sobre Potencialidade Mineira," *Agência Angola Press ANGOP* 19 November 2013, Date Accessed: 20 November 2013 <http://www.portalangop.co.ao/angola/pt_pt/noticias/economia/2013/10/47/Pais-tera-informacoes-precisas-sobre-potencialidade-mineira,ede0b0ec-40dd-47bd-95af-f73f6459981f.html>.

410 Ibid.

very welcoming and trusting. That encourages China to diversify its interests in Angola whilst helping Angola to diversify its oil-based economy.

3.2 Cooperation in the Automotive Sector

It was two years before the civil war in Angola came to an end when the China's People's Daily newspaper reported that China was planning to build the first motorcyle assembly line in Angola with a total investment of US$ 7.2 million.[411] Although the country was suffering from the consequences of civil conflict, the head of the Chinese Guangdong Overseas Construction Corporation (GOCC), Wang Zhenfeng (王振峰), had managed to present ten samples of motorcycles to the Angolan Industrial Ministry by highlighting the Angola's potential for the motorcycles market.[412] At the ceremony, Angolan Industrial Minister Albina Asis welcomed China's cooperation attempts by considering it as a good example in the development of Angolan economy.[413]

Another development associated with cooperation in automotive sector was released in January 2005, when the Angolan government signed a contract with the Chinese Chung Fong Holding Company (CFHC) to restart production at the National Steelworks Company. The Chinese company began installing equipment at the factory in 2005. CFHC would be the owner of 51 % of the project, while the Angolan government owned 49 %; the cost of the project was estimated to be US$ 28 million.[414]

In 2007, China's second biggest automaker company Dongfeng (东风汽车股份有限公司) and Japan's Nissan invested US$ 30 million to establish Angola's first car manufacturing plant, CSG Automovel-Zhengzhou Nissan (ZZNissan) plant, in the industrial zone of Viana (North of Luanda).

411 "China to Build Motorcycle Assembly Line in Angola," *People's Daily* 6 May 2000, Date Accessed: 19 September 2013 <http://english.people.com.cn/english/200005/06/eng20000506_40248.html>.

412 Ibid.

413 Ibid.

414 Omayra Bermúdez-Lugo, "The Mineral Industry of Angola," *2005 Minerals Yearbook Angola US Geological Survey (USGS)* August 2007:2, Date Accessed: 19 September 2013 <http://minerals.usgs.gov/minerals/pubs/country/2005/aomyb05.pdf>

Together with the Angolan company CSG Automovel, Dongfeng and Nissan, they established the joint venture CSG Automovel- ZZ Nissan with equal stakes. The joint venture plant was funded by China International Fund (US$ 30 million) and based on technology from Japan's Nissan Motor Co., production in the plant started in April 2008; the factory produces approximately 30,000 commercial vehicles yearly, including pickup trucks, small, medium and large buses, light trucks, multiuse passenger vehicles and the Nissan Paladin jeep.[415] Approximately 500 Angolan workers, trained by Chinese engineers, participate in the production of 'Made in Angola' automobiles.[416]

In the aviation sector, the first steps were taken in January 2008 when Angolan national airline TAAG agreed on buying Chinese manufactured the Modern Ark 60 (MA-60) aircrafts after a demonstration flight took place between Luanda and Lubango cities of Angola. According to Sun Zhiwei (孙志伟), Deputy Managing Director of China National Aero-Technology Import and Export Corporation (CATIC), "Luanda, the capital of Angola has the greatest potential to become a new air transportation hub in southern African region which calls for an effective regional transit network throughout the country and MA-60 could be the most suitable type of aircraft meeting the requirement."[417]

As the world's number one motor vehicle producer, China's investment in Angola is seen as a good example for its contribution to diversification of the economy, capacity building and technology transfer. China has also positive effects on the development of various industry sectors in Angola, by becoming a source of inspiration for the establishment of Special Economic Zones in Angola. In 2009, Angola established a Special Economic Zone (*Zona Económica Especial, ZEE)* in Viana, outside of Luanda with a principal objective of reducing Angola's dependence on imports and diversifying the economy. To that end, currently Viana Special Economic Zone (ZEE)

415 "First Cars Made in Angola to Go On Sale This Year," *Macauhub* 16 October 2007, Date Accessed: 19 September 2013 <http://www.macauhub.com.mo/en/2007/10/16/3893/>.

416 Ibid.

417 "China-Made MA60 Commuter Plane Debuts in Angola," *China.org.cn (中国网)* 25 January 2008, Date Accessed: 19 September 2013 <http://www.china.org.cn/english/business/240750.htm>.

offers services such as the production of automobiles, construction materials, plastics, ceramics, agricultural irrigation equipment, as well as fiber-optic cables. In the near future, it is expected that with its seventy-three factory units, the ZEE will produce poultry-based products, agricultural products, food, clothing and footwear, hygiene and cleaning products, electricity and telecommunications towers, electrical materials and equipment.[418]

3.3 Cooperation in Agricultural and Fishing Sector

The agricultural sector is another sector where China helps the diversification of Angolan economy. During the period of Portuguese administration, the agricultural sector was accounted for half of exports, employing 40 % of the working population. The country was the world's third largest coffee producer, as well as a significant producer of maize, cotton, sugar cane and sisal. However, during the Angola's twenty-seven years of civil war, the agriculture sector in Angola was badly damaged. According to the Macau news service Macauhub, a recent study mentioned, "Just 1 % of the 2000 farms in Benguela province appropriated by private owners in the last few years have been appropriately used."[419] In other words, Angola's agricultural potential was being used below the optimum level.

Angola, with its more than 35 million hectares arable land and favorable climate, is a potentially rich agricultural country. China, who is facing shrinking arable land due to an increasing rate of city migration, as well as worsening air pollution, has steadily advanced the cooperation in agricultural sector. Investment in the Angolan agricultural sector should be encouraged, not only because it can be used as a potential development strategy to shift the country from a single to a more diversified economy,

---

418 "Seventeen New Industrial Units to Start Operating in 2012 in Angola's Luanda/Benga Special Economic Zone," *Macauhub* 30 May 2011, Date Accessed: 19 September 2013 <http://www.macauhub.com.mo/en/2011/05/30/seventeen-new-industrial-units-to-start-operating-in-2012-in-angola%E2%80%99s-luandabenga-special-economic-zone/>.

419 "Angola Moves Ahead with New Agricultural Development Strategy," *Macauhub* 16 August 2013, Date Accessed: 19 September 2013 <http://www.macauhub.com.mo/en/2011/08/16/angola-moves-ahead-with-new-agricultural-development-strategy/>.

but also to benefit China itself by decreasing the possible strains on China's agricultural sector.

The first phase of US$ 2 billion credits given by the China Exim Bank in 2004, corresponds to fifty projects from energy to education sectors across the country; it involves a US$ 149 million project in agriculture sector. Chinese Exim Bank awarded US$ 149 million for the acquisition of new agricultural machinery as well as the rehabilitation of irrigation systems through China Hydropower Construction Group Corporation in the areas of Luena, Caxito, Grandjelas and Waco-Kungo. In June 2006, on the occasion of the Chinese Premier's visit to Angola, Angola asked the Chinese government to send Chinese agricultural experts to Angola. By doing that, Angola aimed to promote agricultural development in four provinces: Biè, Huíla, Moxico, and Kuando-Kubango. In November 2006, China declared its US$40 million assistance for a project which promotes more than a thousand Angolan family-based farmers in the province of Kwanza Sul to take part in a project to re-launch irrigated cotton production.[420] The re-launching of cotton production is essential for Angola to diversify its economy and to ensure independence, in terms of importing manufactured products by renovating its textile industry. As of August 2014, there are three restored textile factories in Benguela, Luanda and Kwanza Norte that are expected to be operating at the end of 2014.[421]

In 2009, The China Development Bank granted a US$ 1 billion loan to Angola for the development of its agricultural sector, particularly for increasing the rice production.[422] In 2011, Chinese government organized in Hunan Province a training course of hybrid rice technology for Portuguese-speaking countries, in which five officials of the Ministry of Agriculture of Angola were trained. That training project targeted agro-technicians and

---

420 "China finances cotton production project in Angola," *Macauhub* 8 November 2006, Date Accessed: 19 September 2013 <http://www.macauhub.com.mo/en/2006/11/08/2019/>.

421 "Resurgent Textile Industry Helps Diversify Angola's Economy," *Macauhub* 4 August 2014, Date Accessed: 4 August 2014 <http://www.macauhub.com.mo/en/2014/08/04/resurgent-textile-industry-helps-diversify-angola%E2%80%99s-economy/>.

422 However unlike the loans from CIF and China Exim Bank, this loan was not given as an oil-backed loan.

government officials to acquire China's world-leading hybrid-rice (super rice) cultivating technique, which China began to develop in the 1960s, after the invention of Dr. Yuan Longping (袁隆平). Dr. Yuan Longping invented the hybrid rice technique to solve the famine problem in the country; applying fertilizers to give rice enough nutrition and let them grow quickly. The company named after Yuan Longping, Yuan Longping High-tech Agriculture has large-scale programmes in Africa. In an interview, scientist Dr. Yuan Longping argued that, "If the acres under hybrid rice reached half of the total rice planting area, the world's total rice output could increase by 150 million tons a year, enough to feed 400 million more people."[423] In May 2014, it was reported by Angolan News Agency ANGOP that the market recorded a decrease in commodity goods prices, including rice. The price of 1 kg of rice fell 40 % to US$ 2.30 in 2014, from US$ 3.88 in 2012.[424]

Another Chinese company, The China CAMC Engineering Co., Ltd. (CAMCE) is also carrying out the $61.5 million Longa agro-industrial project in Angola's Kuando Kubango province. The project, funded by the China Development Bank as part of an agreement signed in 2010 with the Ministry for Agriculture and Rural Development, aimed to create 800 direct jobs and produce almost 15,000 tons of rice a year, using water from Longa River.[425] Other than rice production, the Longa agro-industrial project also involves the construction of a center for training local rural workers in agro-livestock techniques and building a weather station. In April 2013, the same company, CAMCE, signed a US$ 168 million agricultural cooperation contract with Angola's Ministry of Agriculture, Rural Development and Fisheries to cultivate 5,000 hectares with soya, maize, and also supplying

---

423 "China Launches Hybrid Rice Training Base for Foreign Agrotechnicians," *Xinhuanet*（新华网） *13* September 2009, Date Accessed: 19 September 2013 <http://news.xinhuanet.com/english/2009-09/13/content_12043011.htm>.

424 "Cost of Living in Luanda, Angola," *Cost of Living: Angola*, Numbeo, n.d., Date Accessed: 19 September 2013 <http://www.numbeo.com/cost-of living/city_result.jsp?country=Angola&city=Luanda>.

425 "China –Angola 30 Years On," *Macauhub* 16 August 2013, Date Accessed: 19 September 2013 <http://www.macauhub.com.mo/en/2013/08/16/china-angola-30-years-on-time-to-%E2%80%9Chave-no-doubts%E2%80%9D/>.

processing plants at Camacupa, Bié province at a cost of US$ 88 million.[426] In 2013, a Longa Agro-Industrial Farm in Kuito Kuanavale municipality, funded by China Development Bank, was inaugurated. In the period between 2013 and 2014, it produced 3,700 tons of rice, and created jobs for 270 Angolans.[427]

In November 2012, Angola and China signed a cooperation agreement for the construction of an agricultural research centre in Mazozo, approximately 40 kilometers from the centre of the Angolan capital, Luanda. Moreover, in the provinces of Uige and Malanje, CITIC set up an agricultural study and research centres. Besides that, CITIC has decided to provide two years of training services for twenty-eight Angolan technicians in China.[428]

Construction Company China Ferrovia (CR20) is also implementing agricultural projects in the Moxico Province of Angola. According to the Macau news service Macauhub, two technicians from the company travelled to the site of the future Camaiangala (70 km north of Luanda) agricultural project to collect soil samples, which will be analyzed in Chinese laboratories.[429] The project aims to produce rice, potatoes, beans and other products that are essential for the local population. In the context of the rehabilitation of the agriculture sector, between China Hydropower Construction Group Corporation and the Angolan Ministry of Agriculture, a US$ 54 million contract was signed. With this project, the Angolan government aimed to rehabilitate 9,240 hectares of farmland, which includes four areas: Caxito, Gandjelas, Luena, Wako-Kungo.

---

426 "Angola-China: Mutual Benefits," *Sonangol Universo* September 2013:11.

427 "Rice Production in Angola's Kuando Kubango Province Funded by Credit Line from China," *Macauhub* 5 June 2013, Date Accessed: 5 June 2014 <http://www.macauhub.com.mo/en/2014/06/05/rice-production-in-angola%E2%80%99s-kuando-kubango-province-funded-by-credit-line-from-china/>.

428 António Escobar and Ana Correia da Silva, "Three Decades of China-Angola Cooperation," *Macao Magazine* Issue 15, (August 2013): 82, Date Accessed: 19 September 2013 <http://www.macaomagazine.net/index.php?option=com_content&view=article&id=277:three-decades-of-china-angola-cooperation&catid=50:issue15>.

429 "China –Angola 30 Years On," *Macauhub* 16 August 2013, Date Accessed: 19 September 2013 <http://www.macauhub.com.mo/en/2013/08/16/china-angola-30-years-on-time-to-%E2%80%9Chave-no-doubts%E2%80%9D/>.

In May 2014, during the visit of Premier Li Keqiang to Angola, another agro-industrial project came to the forefront. The project, which was released along with the China Exim Bank's US$170 million loan, designated for development of agro-industry in northern Zaire province.

As a part of the Luanda project, which aims to bring true revolution to Angola's agriculture field, Chinese company, Sinotruck, delivered over 1,000 Sinotruk tractors to Angola in October 2014.[430] In November 2014, Angolan government contracted with the Chinese state company CITIC to invest US$5 billion in 2015 in an agricultural project in order to increase production of corn, soybeans and wheat and to help "rebuild the agricultural sector of the country."[431]

The fishing sector in Angola, just like the agricultural sector, was a major industry before independence from Portugal, including before the civil war, which began in 1975. In the early 1970s, Angola's annual catch was more than 300,000 tons.[432] Angola's rich fishing grounds concentrated on three provinces: Benguela, Luanda, Lobito and Moçamades. Global species database of fish species, Fish Base, estimated that more than 918 fish species exist in Angola waters.[433] In order to help Angola use its potential in fishing sector, Chinese company China National Machinery Equipment Import and Export Corporation (SINOMACH) financed the purchase of thirty-six fishing trawlers, 3,000 fishing boats and ten vessels to maintain the coast guard. This investment of US$ 267 million, which is the part of the second phase of US$ 2.4 billion credit lines from China Exim Bank in the year of 2004,

430 "Over 1000 Sinotruk Tractors Export to Angola," *ChinaTrucks.com* 13 October 2014, Date Accessed: 13 October 2014 <http://www.chinatrucks.com/news/2014/1013/article_5468.html>.

431 "Chinese State Company Invests in Agriculture in Angola," *Macauhub* 18 November 2014, Date Accessed: 18 November 2014 <http://www.macauhub.com.mo/en/2014/11/18/chinese-state-company-invests-in-agriculture-in-angola/>.

432 Sean Sheehan, *Cultures of the World: Angola,* (New York: Marshall Cavendish Benchmark, 2010) 53.

433 Fish Base. *Fish Species in Angola*. n.d., Date Accessed: 22 September 2013 <www.fishbase.us>.

forecasts the creation of the direct employment of 20,000 and a further 100,000 indirectly.[434]

In conclusion, Angola's enormous amount of arable land and rich fishing grounds created another platform for both countries to develop together. China, containing 19 % of the world's population but only 7 % of the world's arable land, is not able to feed its huge population. Additionally, according to Food and Agriculture Organization of the United Nations (FAO), 80 % of the major rivers in China are today so polluted that they no longer sustain fish life.[435] In the next years, it is expected that, because of land degradation, urbanization and worsening air pollution, China's ability to feed its 1.3 billion people will be even more difficult. As UN Expert, Olivier De Schutter noted: "The shrinking of arable land and the massive land degradation threatens the ability of the country to maintain current levels of agricultural production, while the widening gap between rural and urban is an important challenge to the right to food of the Chinese population."[436] On the other hand, Angola, maintains a great deal of potential, awaiting for investors to allow them to benefit from its expansive agricultural land, which makes up nearly half (46.2 %) of the total area. To achieve food sufficiency, Angola and China engaged in mutual beneficial interactions, by benefiting from China's great agricultural expertise and Angola's agricultural land. It leads to an interdependent relationship that each party requires the other for survival.

Conclusion of the Chapter

This chapter has given us an idea on how trade with 'Angola Mode' characterized the relations between China and Angola. China's business strategies

---

434 Garth Shelton and Claude Kabemba eds., *Win-Win Partnership: China, Southern Africa and the Extractive Industries,* (Johannesburg: Southern Africa Research Watch, 2012) 60.

435 Food and Agriculture Organization of the United Nations (FAO), *AQUASTAT Online Service* 2010, Date Accessed: 23 September 2013 <http://www.fao.org/nr/water/aquastat/countries_regions/china/index.stm>.

436 Jonathan Watts, "Chinese Ability to Feed Its People Questioned by UN Expert," *The Guardian* 23 December 2010, Date Accessed: 23 September 2013 <http://www.theguardian.com/environment/2010/dec/23/china-ability-to-feed-population-warning>.

in Angola have widened along with its growing investments in the infrastructure sector. Investment in infrastructure sectors assisted Angola to rebuild the destroyed country after a twenty-seven year civil war ended in 2002.

Better infrastructure conditions in the country facilitated the development of business interactions between China and Angola, which is overly reliant on oil production. The business cooperation between the two countries paved the way for the development of other sectors other than petroleum. In addition to that, these business interactions have resulted in mutual beneficial interactions and establishment of several joint ventures between the Chinese and Angolan state-owned companies in several sectors, from oil, to diamond, to automotive. According to Angola's Petroleum Minister José Maria Botelho de Vasconcelos the weight of oil production in Angola's Gross Domestic Product (GDP) declined from between 60 and 65 % in 2009 to between 41 and 43 % in 2014.[437] The decrease of the weight of oil production in Angola's GDP reflects the contribution of other sectors to the gross domestic product. According to a report published by the African Economic Outlook, Angola's GDP growth of 5.1 % in 2013 was driven strongly by non-oil activities, notably in energy (22 % expansion), fisheries (10 %), agriculture (9 %), manufacturing (8 %) and construction (8 %).[438]

Every step taken by the Chinese government toward a partnership with the Angolan government through cooperation or establishment of joint ventures would return to Chinese and Angolan governments not only as an economic but also political gain. In that context, the various impacts of the bilateral relationship on Angolan preferences will be key focus of the next chapter.

---

437 "Oil Accounts for Smaller Portion of Angola's GDP as Production in Other Sectors Increases," *Macauhub* 7 November 2014, Date Accessed: 7 November 2014 <http://www.macauhub.com.mo/en/2014/11/07/oil-accounts-for-smaller-portion-of-angolas-gdp-as-production-in-other-sectors-increases/>.

438 Joel Muzima & Domingos Mazivila, op.cit. 2.

Chapter 4: The Impacts of the Bilateral Economic Relations on Angola's Preferences

China's engagement in Africa with the principle of non-interference in internal affairs of other countries and credits given in the scope of Angola Mode has changed the general understanding of many concepts inherited from Western countries. China emerged in Africa as a country that does not play a traditional and conventional role of foreign countries, 'aid giver', but rather acts as an economic partner. China has been praised by African scholars such as Dambisa Moyo for seeing African countries not as an 'aid case' but as an investment destination and an economic partner to diversify and advance their economies together.[439]

China's influence in Angola surely is not limited with the mutations of the general understanding of a foreign country's role in the African continent. China's involvement in the Angolan economy resulted in widespread impacts on several areas, such as Angolan governing party, Angola's socio-economic development, its labor market, its financial institutions, the environment, Sonangol's global presence and the traditional economic partners of Angola.

4.1 The Impacts on the Angolan Governing Party MPLA

The Chinese Development Model, along with its way of engagement with Angola (through Angola Mode and no-strings attached principle) has been very much appealing for the Angolan government whose priorities are related more to the development of economy than improvements in human rights and democracy. China's non-interference principle can also be regarded as the justification of the idea that trade and economic preferences are above the good governance concerns. Under that principle, the bilateral economic relations between China and Angola have eventually strengthened

439 Andrew Moody, "More China, Less Bono is Prescription," *China Daily* 22 March 2013, Date Accessed: 23 March 2013 <http://africa.chinadaily.com.cn/weekly/2013-03/22/content_16335831.htm>.

the governing party MPLA's position, not only in the country but also in the world. An Angolan economist José Cerqueira once stated: "For IMF we should have ears, but no mouth."[440] However, today, with China's help, the Angolan government has learned to stand strong and speak out to object specific requirements of the traditional donors.

Moreover, the agreement between China and Angola in the frame of Angola Mode has enabled Angola to utilize the majority of credits sourced from the Chinese government for infrastructure development of its country. Increase of income (GDP) through oil exports and the flow of Chinese credits in connection with infrastructure projects were used by the ruling party, MPLA, in the 2008 and 2012 election campaigns.[441] Through the numerous infrastructure projects and visible new construction buildings throughout the country, the Angolan government found a chance to strengthen its hold on power and legitimatize its leadership among the Angolan population. It explains the fact that, the cooperation between China and Angola has been supporting the Angolan government not only materialistically, but also politically.

Undoubtedly, China has played a significant role in bringing about change in Angolan President José Eduardo dos Santos' approach to development conditions and processes. His famous quote "there is no magic wand that can resolve our problems. The solution rests with our work and discipline"[442] left today its place to another quote he said to declare his willingness to share Angola's success with other countries in a diplomatic meeting in January 2015 "we live in a world in which no country, be it big or small, can solve by its own all its problems. Man is gregarious by

440 "Never too Late to Scramble," *The Economist* 26 October 2006, Date Accessed: 23 March 2013 <http://www.economist.com/node/8089719>.

441 Both elections resulted in the sweeping victory of MPLA, in 2008 and 2012 elections MPLA won 82 % and 73 %, respectively, of the national votes.

442 "Jose Eduardo Dos Santos," *BrainyQuote.com. Xplore Inc,* 2015, Date Accessed: 18 January 2015 <http://www.brainyquote.com/quotes/quotes/j/joseeduard178683.html>.

nature and this characteristic is reflected within human communities and in relations amongst people and nations."[443]

Under China's shadow, the US President Obama's initial attempts to enhance bilateral ties with the Angolan government came to nothing. When Obama came power in 2009, he pointed out that Angola is among three strategic partners[444] of the US on the African continent. Afterwards, two partners had arranged a meeting to celebrate the twentieth anniversary of US-Angola relations. However the appointment was postponed by the Angolan Foreign Minister. Two important issues seemed to be at the root of the problems. First, China emerged as a political and economic-friend of Angola and provided a chance for Angola to engage in economic relationships with other nations. Second, Angola has been seen as a challenge for US businessmen as well as diplomats since the two most well-known indexes in the world, such as Reporters Without Borders' World Press Freedom Index and the Economist Intelligence Unit's Democracy Index rank Angola as 'not free' and 'authoritarian regime', respectively.[445] In addition, right after American business magazine, Forbes, named eldest daughter of President José Eduardo dos Santos, Isabel dos Santos, as Africa's first female billionaire[446], Transparency International ranked Angola 153th out of 177 countries in its corruption perceptions index.[447] Furthermore, according to the Doing Business 2014 Report, Angola ranks 179th out of 189 economies.[448]

443 "Angola Wants to Share Successes with Other Countries-President dos Santos," *Agência Angola Press ANGOP* 16 January 2015, Date Accessed: 17 January 2015 <http://www.portalangop.co.ao/angola/en_us/noticias/politica/2015/0/3/Angola-wants-share-successes-with-other-countries-President-dos-Santos,04bf1877-2c0c-4802-9b35-efde4f78a9d3.html>.

444 The other two countries are: South Africa and Nigeria.

445 Reporters without Borders, "World Press Freedom Index," 2014; the Economist Intelligence Unit, "Democracy Index," 2012.

446 "Isabel dos Santos, Daughter of Angola's President, is Africa's First Billionaire," *Forbes* 23 January 2013, Date Accesssed:23 April 2013 <http://www.forbes.com/sites/kerryadolan/2013/01/23/isabel-dos-santos-daughter-of-angolas-president-is-africas-first-woman-billionaire/>.

447 Transparency International, "Corruption Perceptions Index," 2013.

448 World Bank, *Doing Business Report 2014: Understanding Regulations for Small and Medium- Size Enterprises,*(Washington DC: World Bank Group, 2013) 3, Date Accessed: 15 May 2014 <http://www.doingbusiness.org/~/

This demonstrates that there are more challenges in the Angola-US relations than Angola's relationship to China. No matter what their interests are, the mechanism of the relations between Angola and China is based on cooperation and interdependence. This reciprocal nature of China-Angola relations has gradually increased China's popularity in the eyes of the governing party, MPLA. As former Ambassador, Ji Peiding who served in China's Foreign Service in Nigeria, Zimbabwe, Namibia and South Africa for forty-seven years, noted: "The difference between us and the Americans [in Africa]? It is very simple. The Americans sometimes behave like a teacher whereas we behave like a brother."[449]

Consequently, China, by obtaining large amount of loans, helped Angola not only to recover its economy and rebuild its war-torn country, but also gave Angola's governing party, MPLA, a chance to build its self-esteem, strengthen its position and learn to develop a more balanced foreign policy toward foreign countries and institutions.

4.2 The Impacts on Angola's Socio-Economic Development

Since China's initial involvement in Angola with oil-backed loans, the Angolan economy has begun its 'Golden Age' period. Between 2002 and 2008, Angola experienced some of its highest Real GDP growth in its history; in 2007 and 2008, it even saw an economic growth rate of 20 %. In April 2008, Angola surpassed Nigeria to become Africa's largest oil producer, and in the same year, oil prices, which were in the previous year an average of 52.6 dollar per barrel, raised and reached the value of 93.7 dollars per barrel. The expansion of Angolan oil exports with the engagement of China in the country assisted Angola's real GDP increase, which experienced an annual average growth of 17 % from 2003 to 2008.[450] In addition, the population

---

media/GIAWB/Doing%20Business/Documents/Annual-reports/English/DB14-Full-Report.pdf>.

449 Nicholas Kotch, "China 'like a brother' to Africa, says former envoy as US summit approaches," *Business Day Live* 30 April 2014, Date Accessed: 30 April 2014 <http://www.bdlive.co.za/africa/africanbusiness/2014/04/30/china-like-a-brother-to-africa-says-former-envoy-as-us-summit-approaches>.

450 Arne Wing and Ivar Kolstadt, "Opinion: Is Oil-Rich Angola a Development Success?," *CNN* 30 August 2012, Date Accessed: 23 September 2013

below the poverty line in Angola has decreased from 70 % in 2003 to 35 % in 2013. Through the rehabilitation of water systems and rebuilding of electricity and hydro-electricity networks throughout the country, today in Luanda, 60,000 people have access to electricity and clean water. In October 2014, the CIF Luanda plant, which was completed in October 2011, allowed Angola to reach the production of eight million tons per year, which would make Angola a self-sufficient country in terms of its production of cement.[451]

The reconstruction of streets, bridges, and railways facilitated transportation conditions in the country. Better conditions in transportation increased commercial activities. Elimination of tariffs on 95 % of exports from LDCs in Africa (at the 2009 FOCAC meeting) has also played a significant role in gaining momentum of commercial activities.[452] Besides that, through the reconstruction of hospitals and schools by the Chinese companies, many Angolans are able to access health care and education possibilities.[453]

Although the rehabilitation of education and health sectors remained a priority, in the past few years, China has broadened its investment in Angola's telecommunication sector. The low-cost technology from China decreased the prices in the country, and provided goods for affordable prices. The quality of goods has become the target of Western reports and articles. However, as one Nigerian foreign affairs official noted: "The Western world is never prepared to transfer technology- but the Chinese do, while Chinese technology may not be as sophisticated as some Western governments', it is better to have Chinese technology than to have none at all."[454]

<http://edition.cnn.com/2012/08/30/opinion/opinion-angola-development-elections/>.

451 "Chinese Plant Makes Angola Self-Sufficient in Cement," *Macauhub* 10 October 2014, Date Accessed: 10 October 2014 <http://www.macauhub.com.mo/en/2014/10/10/chinese-plant-makes-angola-self-sufficient-in-cement/>.

452 "An Interpretation of New Measures on Economic and Trade Cooperation from 4th Ministerial Conference," *FOCAC*, 24 May 2010, Date Accessed: 21 September 2013 <http://www.focac.org/eng/dsjbzjhy/t696509.htm>.

453 Indira Campos and Alex Vines, "Angola and China: A Pragmatic Partnership," *Centre for Strategic and International Studies* (March 2008): 19.

454 "Friend or Forager? How China is winning the Resources and the Loyalties of Africa," *Financial Times* 23 February 2006, Date Accessed: 23 September 2013 <http://www.ft.com/intl/cms/s/0/9678cdf4-a412-11da-83cc-0000779e2340.html#axzz32p1snTrA>.

In December 2014, Angolan economy has been impacted by the drop in oil prices. It is expected that the oil contribution toward GDP to fall by 3.5 % because of lower oil prices.[455] "Legislators are preparing a budget for 2015 that may post a deficit of 7.8 % of gross domestic product."[456] At such a difficult economic moment for Angola, China Development Bank granted $2 billion line of credit to Angola's state oil company Sonangol. According to the company's statement, this Chinese financing will support Sonangol's plans for expansion in oil and gas, including the project of a new refinery in Lobito.[457]

Therefore, it is possible to argue that China has been playing a central role in the development of the Angolan economy. As a confirmation of that, Angola's ambassador to China, João Garcia Bires, said: "The rhythm and the index of our growth shows signs that we are on the right path and that is why, within five or ten years, we believe we will have a modern Angola. This struggle is not easy, we are counting on collaboration with China."[458]

4.3 The Impacts on Angola's Labor Market

Following the civil war, China provided Angola with vital financial and economic opportunities. High inflation, rampant corruption and heavy trail of destruction left by the twenty-seven year struggle, caused a fear among Western countries. Angola failed to convince the West that they need their financial assistance in order to rebuild their land and economy.

---

455 Manuel Soque and Colin McClelland, "Angola Faces Budget Crunch on Falling Oil Price, Dos Santos Says," *Bloomberg News* 15 December 2014, Date Accessed: 15 December 2014 <http://www.bloomberg.com/news/2014-10-15/angola-faces-budget-crunch-on-falling-oil-price-dos-santos-says.html>.

456 Manuel Soque and Colin McClelland, "Angola May Cut Funding for HIV Prevention as Oil Prices Fall," *Bloomberg News* 9 December 2014, Date Accessed: 15 December 2014 <http://www.bloomberg.com/news/2014-12-08/angola-may-cut-funding-for-hiv-prevention-as-oil-prices-decline.html>.

457 "Angola Gets USD 2 Billion Credit From China," *Agência Angola Press ANGOP* 12 December 2014, Date Accessed: 12 December 2014 <http://www.portalangop.co.ao/angola/en_us/noticias/economia/2014/11/50/Angola-gets-Usd-billion-credit-from-China,db7b0e75-e943-4e16-a131-72dbc5b8f26d.html>.

458 "Angola-China: Mutual Benefits," *Sonangol Universo* September 2013:14.

When the Angolan economy's inflation reached over 100 %, China emerged as replacement to Western countries, and signed a deal with the Angolan government to provide what the West could not. In other words, they welcome the fact that China is willing to send large amounts of capital into the Angolan economy, in contrast to other investors who are not willing to run the risk of investing such capital.

With the help of the Chinese Angola Mode strategy, many of Chinese state-owned companies found the opportunity to invest abroad and the Angolan government could seize the chance to rebuilding its devastated economy. However, the deals between Chinese and Angolan governments, in the scope of Angola Mode, the oil for infrastructure loans provided an opportunity for Chinese workers to benefit from this engagement. The deals allowed Chinese companies to win 70 % of the contracts and to be exempted from the Angolan Labor Law. In other words, Chinese companies are allowed to hire as many Chinese workers as they wish on a contractual basis of infrastructure projects. In 2007, a survey of Chinese companies' projects in Angola determined the percentage of local labors in various sectors. According to that survey, the sectors requiring more technical expertise such as telecommunications and hydropower have the lowest rate of local employment (37.8 % and 42 %, respectively).[459] Agriculture, catering and trading are the sectors that are hiring the highest amount of local labors in Angola (81 %, 75.3 % and 73.8 %, respectively).[460] In the construction sector, in which China has been intensively investing, Angolan workers make up 30 % to 70 % of the total labors.[461] However, on the management level, local employment is very rare. Even in the Chinese company canteens, the only local staff consists of those who are responsible for washing dishes.[462] There are several reasons behind China's intention to hire more Chinese employees than local ones. The first reason is associated with the lack of skilled labor in the country caused by the civil war and a lack of education facilities. The

459 Xiaoyang Tang, "Bulldozer of Locomotive? The Impact of Chinese Enterprises on the Local Employment in Angola and the DRC," Journal of Asian and African Studies 45.3 (2010): 354.

460 Ibid., 354.

461 Ibid., 354.

462 Lucy Corkin, *Uncovering African Agency: Angola's Management of Credit Lines* (London: Ashgate Pub.Co., 2013) 110.

second reason may be related to the work habits and the language barrier; many Chinese workers can speak neither English nor Portuguese and there are none or a few Angolan workers who can speak Mandarin. Both reasons are related to the fact that the education possibilities and the number of educated people in Angola are limited. The gross enrollment ratio in primary, secondary, vocational, and in higher education is about 75 %, 27 %, 12.7 % and 2.3 %, respectively.[463]

From a narrow perspective, it could be concluded that China does not give many opportunities to local employees. However, what China is currently doing is nothing more than 'growing men instead of growing rice.' China's long-term plans could be seen as non-efficient from a narrow sight, but both China and Angola seem to agree that they need time to train skilled local labors. As Angola's ambassador to China, João Garcia Bires, said: "Little by little, the [Angolan] specialists of tomorrow will be able to handle the equipment coming from China and other countries, and at the same time be faithful spreaders of the Chinese language in Angola."[464] In short, in contrast to expanding concerns, Chinese efforts and scholarship opportunities provided by several Chinese state-owned companies demonstrate the fact that, at the moment, China and Angola both aware of necessity of Angolan local labor in the industry for the promotion of the sustainable development of the economy.

4.4 Impacts on the Financial Institutions of Angola

A decade ago, Angola found itself in a very difficult situation as a country who just got out of a twenty-seven year long civil war with a total of US$ 11 billion foreign debt. The IMF was the only option provided to the Angolan government. Embracing an IMF Structural Adjustment Programme (SAP) required reforms in Angola's government institutions, such as taking steps to combat corruption and more transparency in the management of oil sector. The Paris Club, through which Angola was planning to maintain

463 Africa Development Bank, "Angola: Country Gender Profile," (August 2008): 22, Date Accessed: 23 September 2013 <http://www.afdb.org/fileadmin/uploads/afdb/Documents/Project-and-Operations/ADB-BD-IF-2008-210-EN-ANGOLA-COUNTRY-GENDER-PROFILE.PDF>.

464 "Angola-China: Mutual Benefits" *Sonangol Universo* September 2013:14.

the reschedule of its US$ 11 billion debt, announced that they could move forward providing much needed debt relief only if the conditions of IMF were placed. It was precisely at this time that China stepped toward Angola by offering a series of billions dollar infrastructure projects that were effectively paid off with oil exports. The offer coincided with a moment that oil prices were climbing up. This put Angola in a position unable to return such a profitable offer. Angola turned its back on the IMF and its SAP, and it switched its face to the oil industry for infrastructure loans coming from China. Angola has, in a short time, become the largest African trading partner of China. The growth in oil production and oil export-led growth in GDP, as well as new investments coming from China not only opened up new business opportunities but also a growth in the banking sector. According to the African Business Magazine (October 2012), six Angolan Banks[465] earned a place among the top 100 largest banks on the African continent. As of 2012, there is an 18.3 % increase in the number of branches, a 9.2 % increase in the number of employees, a 20.6 % in assets and a 13.3 % increase in the banking income.[466] In October 2014, Africa's 49th largest Bank *Banco Espírito Santo Angola* (BESA) is replaced by *Banco Económico*, whose shareholders include Angola's oil company Sonangol, Portugal's Novo Banco and a Chinese-owned company Lektron Capital.[467] The biggest Angolan bank by branches, Banco BIC, is partly owned by Isabel dos Santos and already has 202 branches. The bank already has branches in

---

465 Banco Angolano de Investimentos (BAI), still called Banco Africano de Investimentos, is in 27th place with equity of US$ 708 million. In 28th place is Banco de Poupança e Crédito (US$ 705 million). In 32nd is Banco BIC (650 million). Banco Espírito Santo Angola (BESA) is ranked 49th with US$ 383 million-Banco Espirito Santo is replaced by Banco Económico in October 2014. In 86th place comes Banco Millennium Angola, with US$ 171 million. See: "Medium Banks Challenge South African Dominance," *African Business* 16 October 2012, Date Accessed: 21 September 2013 <http://africanbusinessmagazine.com/special-reports/medium-banks-challenge-south-african-dominance/>.

466 "Angola Banking Survey," KPMG, November 2012:32, Date Accessed: 23 September 2013 <https://www.kpmg.com/PT/en/IssuesAndInsights/Documents/kpmg-bank-ao-2012en.pdf>.

467 "Banco Económico replaces Banco Espírito Santo Angola," *Macauhub* 30 October 2014, Date Accessed: 4 November 2014 <http://www.macauhub.com.mo/en/2014/10/30/banco-economico-replaces-banco-espirito-santo-angola/>.

South Africa and Namibia; it was announced in April 2014 that Banco BIC is planning to enter China, as well.[468] Even Banco BIC acquired 10 % of Portugal's *Banco Português de Investimento* (BPI). Furthermore, Angola has already invested between US$ 10–15 billion in Portugal's banking sector, as well as media, construction and agriculture sectors.[469] The President of the Portuguese Institute for International Relations and Security, Pedro Seabra, commented on "the dynamics between colony and master have been so inverted. This is definitely a first for Africa."[470]

However, Angolan economy highly depends on oil exports to and investments from China. Angolan Central Bank has pursued an interest on rebuilding trust in the Angolan local currency (Kwanza) to keep the currency stable in case of a possible economic shock in China. For that reason, the Angolan government passed a new foreign exchange law requiring oil companies operating in Angola to make all payments through local banks, as opposed to normal procedures wherein money would be kept in overseas banks.[471] In May 2013, Angola passed another law that requires foreign oil companies to start using the local currency (Kwanza) to pay taxes. With this new law, the Angolan government seeks to increase capital flow in order to provide further resources for the economy and harmonize the exchange rate system in Angola.[472] Making payments in Kwanza strengthened Kwanza's value and led Angola to start a process to de-dollarize the economy, which will help to control inflation. In order to strengthen the central bank in

---

468 "Angolan Bank Banco BIC Plans to Enter Chinese Market," *Macauhub* 10 April 2014, Date Accessed: 10 April 2014 <http://www.macauhub.com.mo/en/2014/04/10/angolan-bank-banco-bic-plans-to-enter-chinese-market/>.

469 "Portugal Indebted Angola after Economic Reversal of Fortune," *The Guardian* 3 June 2014, Date Accessed: 4 June 2014 <http://www.theguardian.com/world/2014/jun/03/portugal-economy-bailout-angola-invests>.

470 "Angola and Portugal. Role reversal," *The Economist* 3 September 2011, Date Accessed: 21 September 2013 <http://www.economist.com/node/21528310>.

471 U.S State Department Bureau of Economic and Business Affairs, "2013 Investment Climate Statement-Angola," March 2013, Date Accessed: 21 September 2013 <http://www.state.gov/e/eb/rls/othr/ics/2013/204590.htm>.

472 Colin McClelland and Manuel Soque, "Angolan Law Compelling Kwanza Use to Boost Economy, Massano Says," *Bloomberg News* 4 July 2013, Date Accessed: 21 September 2013 <http://www.bloomberg.com/news/2013-07-04/angolan-law-compelling-kwanza-use-to-boost-economy-massano-says.html>.

Angola, the government announced its plan to sell two twenty-year bonds (valued at US$ 601 million) to meet its capital needs.[473]

Consequently, the exchange rate system has been harmonized and inflation has been restricted. The level of inflation decreased from 18.5 % in 2005 to a record low of 7.22 % as of April 2014.[474] Additionally, local banks, through new source of liquidity, has been strengthened and gained opportunity in funding private and public sector investments in areas outside of oil.

The reforms in the financial sector mainly points to the strengthening of the local currency, which seems to be a good start as a pull-factor for the potential foreign trade partners and investors (other than China) and the rebuilding of the Angolan economy. Therefore, it is possible to argue that China's opportunities and challenges has become an important factor in determining Angola's preferences on the path of development.

4.5 The Impacts on the Environment

In regards to the environmental consequences of Chinese engagement in Africa, China's environmental record in Africa is relative negative. There are already widespread concerns over the environmental impact of Chinese people and companies in Angola, as well as in Africa. Concerns are mainly focused on oil spills during the exploration of oil, as well as the legal and illegal import of timbers, raw ivory, rhino horns.

Angola, together with Cameroon, The Republic of Congo, Equatorial Guinea and Gabon, contains one of the largest tropical rainforest on the continent and are regarded as significant importers of timbers. Remarkable deforestation in the country attracted the attention of many Western environmental organizations. As Alden & Alves stated: "As the largest importer of logs from the region, China is under fire from Western environmental

473 Colin McClelland, "Angola Plans 20 Year Kwanza Bond Sales to Boost Central Bank," *Bloomberg News* 31 January 2014, Date Accessed: 31 January 2014 <http://www.bloomberg.com/news/2014-01-31/angola-plans-20-year-kwanza-bond-sales-to-boost-central-bank-1-.html>.

474 Isabel Felino, "Angola Inflation Rate," *Trading Economics* 16 April 2014, Date Accessed: 08 May 2014. <http://www.tradingeconomics.com/angola/inflation-cpi>.

organizations."[475] Concerns over China have increased due to its domestic environmental regulations and standards, which are yet to be significantly improved.

As an oil rich country, the exploration of oil by international oil companies resulted in a great deal of oil spills. These spills led to pressing issues in the country. The situation of Niger Delta, where hundreds of oil spills occur, proves that oil spills create major danger to the environment, including underwater habitats and human health. These spills create impacts that eventually lead to a huge risk on livelihoods security in the long term.

These major risks can be seen in the Cabinda Province of Angola. The Cabinda Province is well-known for its enormous oil resources. About 60 % of Angola's oil production comes from the Cabinda region. The exploration facilities of international oil companies threaten local fishing livelihoods. The fishermen in the region, interviewed by Directorate General for External Policies of the Union for a project requested by the European Parliament, claim that: "These underwater reefs and rock structures, which are essential for breeding fish, are destroyed by the use of dispersants that make spilled oil that floats on the surface of the sea sink to the sea floor."[476] The President of the *Associação dos Pescadores de Cabinda* (APESCAB – Association of Cabindan Fishermen representing over 1200 members in the northern province of Cabinda), verify the Fishermen's claims: "The whole of the sea space around Cabinda province is negatively affected by oil production. There is little physical space for fishing already and oil production further constrains this."[477]

According to the Angolan Minister of Environment, Fátima Jardim, in 2013, twenty oil spill cases were recorded, and the state would no longer

475 Chris Alden and Ana Cristina Alves, "China and Africa's Natural Resources: The Challenges and Implications for Development and Governance," *South African Institute of International Affairs (SAIIA),(*September 2009):19, Date Accessed: 23 September 2013 <http://www.voltairenet.org/IMG/pdf/China_and_Africa_s_Natural_Resources.pdf>.

476 Heike Baumüller et.al., "The Effects of Oil Companies' Activities on the Environment, Health and Development in Sub-Saharan Africa," (Brussels: European Parliament, 2011) 21, Date Accessed: 23 September 2013 <http://www.chathamhouse.org/sites/default/files/0811ep_report_0.pdf>.

477 Ibid., 20.

be based only on measures of environmental education and awareness but also enforce the law, strengthen their capacity to improve inspection and sanction all damages to the environment.[478]

Because the documentation of pollution by the oil industry in Angola is relative weak, it is hard to evaluate the Chinese oil companies' role in pollution at offshore and onshore. An interview conducted by the Chatham House states that: "The government and companies do not necessarily report all spills and there are examples where spillages were only reported by chance a month later."[479] However, it is possible to reach some media articles over Western oil companies' activities in Angolan oil blocks. According to the BBC News, in 2002, by fining the US oil company Chevron Texaco a total of US$ 2 million for causing environmental damage, Angola became the first African nation that imposed a fine on a company operating in its waters.[480] And, in 2013, the Italian oil company ENI paid the Angolan state a total of US$ 3.5 million in compensation due to an oil spill during exploration activities.[481]

According to an article cited by the Angolan news agency ANGOP, between 2013–2017, the Angolan Environment Industry plans to implement an environmental monitoring plan for the oil, gas and petrochemical sector.[482] The goal of the ministry is to be able to manage and eliminate oil spills.

---

478 "Environment Minister Pledges Greater Attention to Oil Spill," *Agência Angola Press ANGOP* 23 December 2013, Date Accessed: 24 December 2013 <http://www.portalangop.co.ao/angola/en_us/noticias/ambiente/2013/11/51/Environment-Minister-pledges-greater-attention-oil-spill,72a0a020-6f59-4ffd-b310-26a86b20bca4.html>.

479 "The Effects of Oil Companies' Activities on the Environment, Health and Development in Sub-Saharan Africa," Directorate-General for External Policies of the Union- A Project for European Parliament, (August 2011):18, Date Accessed: 23 September 2013 <http://www.chathamhouse.org/sites/default/files/0811ep_report_0.pdf>.

480 "Angola Fines Chevron for Pollution," *BBC News* 1 July 2002, Date Accessed: 23 September 2013 <http://news.bbc.co.uk/2/hi/business/2077836.stm>.

481 "Angolan Oil Sector to have Environmental Monitoring," *Macauhub* 3 January 2014, Date Accessed: 4 January 2014 <http://www.macauhub.com.mo/en/2014/01/03/angolan-oil-sector-to-have-environmental-monitoring/>.

482 "Oil Sector Gains Environmental Monitoring," *Agência Angola Press ANGOP* 2 January 2014, Date Accessed: 3 January 2014 <http://www.portalangop.co.ao/angola/en_us/noticias/ambiente/2014/0/1/Oil-sector-gains-environmental-monitoring,dafeec95-7eb0-4bd3-bcc6-56adba18f61b.html>.

Another threat to the African environment is the illegal ivory trade. Ivory trade or trade of 'white gold' has been the greatest danger for elephants. In particular, China has been accused of contributing to the illegal ivory trade. Although the international trade in ivory has been banned since 1983, the illegal trade of ivory has doubled since 2007 with China, the largest retail market for illegally acquired ivory. However China is not the only country contributing to the illegal trade of ivory, the US is a close second. It is reported that over 35,000 elephants are being killed each year for their tusks.[483]

In recent years, China has taken some measures to improve the environmental impact of China's overseas investments and to raise public awareness. The more China involves in overseas business activities, the more China faces challenges resulting from the lack of African government transparencies. During the last decade, China has shown some willingness "towards a number of international regulation initiatives to improve governance, transparency and sustainability of natural resources development in Africa."[484] China took its first step in 2004, by letting the China Exim Bank adopt its environmental policy, which urges Chinese companies to comply with host country policies. In November 2008, China's Industrial Bank became the first Chinese financial institution to adopt the Equator Principles. In addition, in August 2012, together with wildlife protecting group WildAid, former NBA player and newly elected member of Chinese People's Political Consultative Conference (CPPCC) of Shanghai Yao Ming and Chinese actress Li Bing Bing (李冰冰) teamed up to start a campaign with a slogan "When the buying stops, the killing can too", to reduce ivory demand and raise awareness of elephant and rhino poaching.

The campaign has begun to bear fruit. In May 2013, a court sentenced three Chinese dealers in Fujian Province to fifteen years in prison after they were found importing and selling illegal ivory products.[485] In January

483 "China's Ivory Crush Sends Message," *News,* Wildaid, 6 January 2014, Date Accessed: 6 January 2014 <http://www.wildaid.org/news/china%E2%80%99s-ivory-crush-sends-message>.

484 Chris Alden and Ana Cristina Alves, op.cit., 20.

485 "Three Men Jailed in China for Vast Ivory Smuggling Operation, *Wildlife Extra* May 2013, Date Accessed: 23 September 2013 <http://www.wildlifeextra.com/go/news/ivory-smuggling-arrest.html#cr>.

2014, China has destroyed about six tons of illegal ivory in its stockpile. This came soon after the US, which pulverized six tons of illegal ivory in November 2013.[486] Right after the destruction of illegal ivory products by China, a film on illegal wildlife products, focusing on reducing demand for rhino horn and elephants, made by Yao Ming, along with Duke of Cambridge Prince William and popular former football player David Beckham, began to be shown in a public service message broadcast on China's main television stations. Between December 30, 2013 and January 26, 2014, through a China-led operation, *codenamed Cobra II*, conducted by China, the United States, South Africa, the Lusaka Agreement Task Force, the ASEAN Wildlife Enforcement Network, and the South Asia Wildlife Enforcement Network, more than 3 tons of ivory and its products, over 1,000 hides, thirty-six rhino horns and a large number of other wildlife products have been captured, and over 400 suspects arrested.[487] In this operation, for the first time in its history, China sent overseas (to Kenya) enforcement staff to arrest a Chinese suspected ivory smuggler.[488] "China's authorities, including forestry, customs, police, judiciary and quarantine departments, put more than 100,000 staff on the operation and uncovered over 200 cases involving more than 250 suspects."[489]

Operation Cobra II was also supported by the World Customs Organization, Interpol and the Convention on International Trade in Endangered Species of Wild Fauna and Flora (CITES) in which China and Angola took part together after Angola joined the CITES in December 2013. In mid-March 2014, it was reported by Reuters that a state-owned Chinese

---

486 By destroying the ivory products in June 2013, the Philippines became the world's first ivory- consuming nation to destroy its national ivory. In February 2014, France joined China, US and the Philippines by destroying three tons of illegal ivory stocks.

487 "China Leads International Wildlife Crime Bust," *allAfrica* 10 February 2014, Date Accessed: 11 February 2014 <http://allafrica.com/stories/201402111485.html>.

488 "China, Africa Arrest Cross-Border Ivory Smuggler," *Xinhuanet*（新华网）10 February 2014, Date Accessed: 11 February 2014 <http://news.xinhuanet.com/english/africa/2014-02/10/c_126104674.htm>.

489 "China Leads International Wildlife Crime Bust," *allAfrica* 10 February 2014, Date Accessed: 11 February 2014 <http://allafrica.com/stories/201402111485.html>.

crafts chain had suspended sales of elephant ivory at its stores in China and Hong Kong.[490] Furthermore, in February 2014, famous actor Jackie Chan joined the fight against wildlife poaching as well and noted in an interview: "Chinese attitudes towards buying illegal wildlife products are undergoing a huge change."[491] One year after that interview, in February 2015, China, as the world's largest importer of smuggled tusks, imposed a one-year ban on ivory imports to protect elephants.[492]

Despite China's call for an international crackdown on wildlife crime in 2012 and leadership in the first and second Cobra operations involving twenty-two and twenty-eight countries, respectively, Angola did not participate in both China-led Cobra I and Cobra II operations. However, in December 2013, a remarkable decision and measure came from the Angolan government. Angola announced that it became the 179th party to join the Convention on International Trade in Endangered Species (CITES). Angola's decision to join the CITES, along with Chinese government's efforts to raise public awareness, give us a hope that with the intention of both countries, there will be decrease in the ivory trade between China and many African countries, including Angola.

4.6 The Impacts on Sonangol's Global Presence through the Joint Venture 'China Sonangol International Holding Ltd. (CSIH)'

The joint venture China Sonangol International Holding Ltd. (CSIH), which is owned by Sonangol (30 %) and Hong Kong based company Dayuan

---

490 Clare Baldwin, "China Government-Owned Crafts Chain Suspends Controversial Ivory Sales," *Reuters* 18 March 2014, Date Accessed: 19 March 2014 <http://in.reuters.com/article/2014/03/18/us-china-ivory-idINBREA2H1OZ20140318>.

491 Adam Vaughan, "Jackie Chan: Chinese Attitudes to Illegal Wildlife Products are Changing," *The Guardian* 13 February 2014, Date Accessed: 14 February 2014 <http://www.theguardian.com/environment/2014/feb/13/jackie-chan-chinese-attitudes-illegal-wildlife-products-change>.

492 Dan Levin, "China Bans Import of Ivory Carvings for One Year," *The New York Times* 26 February 2015, Date Accessed: 26 February 2015 <http://www.nytimes.com/2015/02/27/world/asia/china-bans-import-of-ivory-carvings-for-one-year.html?smid=tw-nytimes&_r=0>.

International Development (70 %) was established in 2004 for the purpose of implementing various projects in the Chinese and Angolan oil sectors. Eventually, the joint venture has expanded in other countries with different economic activities. Today, CSIH has offices in nine cities (Luanda, Conakry, Dubai, Jakarta, Singapore, Hong Kong, Hainan, Shanghai and Beijing) in six different countries. Besides that, CSIH invested in more than ten oil blocks in Africa and Cepu-Indonesia. In Africa, except Angola, CSIH gained access to offshore oil blocks of Guinea. In 2008, CSIH overtook ultra-deepwater blocks at the Nigerian Coast from the US oil company Devon.

In recent years, CSIH began to diversify into other businesses outside oil and gas sector. For instance, the transportation sector, which includes shipping and aviation, has emerged as a new business sector that CSIH is increasingly investing in. Currently, CSIH has a vessel fleet consisting of panamax, bulk carriers, large scale barges and tug boats. The company is also planning to invest in the oil tanker shipping business.[493] China took important steps in the aviation sector as well. After long negotiations with the Tanzanian government to take over 49 % shares in the near-bankrupt Tanzanian national airline, Air Tanzania (TC), CSIH succeeded in acquiring 49 % of Air Tanzania in exchange for oil-exploration rights in two oilfields in the Lake Rukwa basin in South-West Tanzania.[494] In addition, in February 2007, CSIH purchased three Airbus Corporate Jetliners and two Legacy Embraer 600 Executive Jets from a Brazilian aircraft manufacturer.[495] CSIH owns a fleet of more than ten airbus planes, which are either used as corporate jets or leased out to third parties.[496]

In Mozambique, through CIF, the CSIH entered in other business sectors, such as agriculture, construction, manufacturing, mining, tourism and trade. CIF, which is owned by Dayuan International Development (formerly known

493 China Sonangol, List of Projects: Shipping <http://www.chinasonangol.com/transportation.html>.

494 Beibei Yin, "Chinese Investment in Tanzania Bears Bitter Fruit," *The Guardian* 2 March 2012, Date Accessed: 23 September 2013 <http://www.theguardian.com/global-development/2012/mar/02/chinese-investment-tanzania-airport-eviction>.

495 Lee Levkovitz, Marta McLellan, J.R. Warner, op.cit., 27.

496 China Sonangol, List of Projects: Shipping <http://www.chinasonangol.com/transportation.html>.

as Beiya International), established a joint venture CIF-MOZ with the holding company of the ruling Frelimo Party, SPI Gestão e Investimentos SARL. 80 % of the joint venture CIF-MOZ is owned by CIF and 20 % of it is owned by SPI Gestão e Investimentos SARL[497].

In Zimbabwe, in November 2009, the IHS Global Insight stated that the CSIH signed an US$ 8 billion investment deal with Zimbabwe's government. The financial package, which includes five agreements targeting gold and platinum refining, oil and gas exploration, fuel purchase and distribution, as well as construction of houses and roads.

In late 2008, CSIH purchased the JP Morgan Building from Africa, Israel and the US for US$ 150 million. It was considerably more than the building was worth at that time, according to a former Africa-Israel executive.[498] Months later, CIF purchased 49 % of the former New York Times Building, and 49 % of the Clock Tower in Manhattan for US$ 710 million.[499] In 2009, CSIH acquired a US$ 200 million stake in the oil and gas field in Indonesia. In 2011, it was announced that 9.23 % of major construction and civil engineering firm OKP Holdings Limited (胡金标控股有限公司) in Singapore are purchased by the CSIH.[500] Following this transaction, CSIH's stake in OKP increased to 14.15 % and CSIH involved itself in a construction project of a luxury condominium at Anguilla Park. In December 2013, CSIH made headlines in a Singapore newspaper, *The Edge Singapore,* with its 'flagship' project, Twenty One Angullia Park.[501] In September 2013,

497 Markus Weimer and Alex Vines, "China's Angolan Oil Deals 2003-11," in eds. Marcus Power and Ana Cristina Alves, op.cit., 97.

498 Laura Rena Murray, et.al., African Safari: CIF's Grab for Oil and Minerals, *Caixin Online* 17 October 2011, Date Accessed: 23 September 2013 <http://english.caixin.com/2011-10-17/100314766.html>.

499 Lee Levkovitz, Marta McLellan, J.R. Warner, op.cit., ii.

500 "Global Conglomerate China Sonangol Buys 15 million OKP Holdings Shares; Move Prepares Ground for Future Business Collaboration," *Joint Press Release by OKP Holdings Limited and China Sonangol*, 19 August 2011, Date Accessed: 23 September 2013 <http://okp.listedcompany.com/newsroom/20110819_171529_5CF_85E51C02E7F7CB44482578F00030FE16.1.pdf>.

501 Cecilia, Chow, "Top Condo Deals of 2013," *The Edge Singapore* 30 December 2013:8.

CSIH signed a memorandum of understanding to build, own and operate a crude oil refinery in Dubai, the United Arab Emirates.

As is seen with a joint venture with a Chinese company, an Angolan company seized an opportunity to encourage an expansion overseas to diversify its business operations in different countries.

4.7 The Impacts on the Traditional Economic Partners of Angola

> "Hence to fight and conquer in all your battles is not supreme excellence; supreme excellence consists in breaking the enemy's resistance without fighting."
> *Sun Tzu*

China's entrance into Angola as an alternative economic partner altered the positions of traditional economic partners of Angola, in particular Portugal and the US. Through the approaches such as the Angola Mode and the principle of non-interference of internal affairs of sovereign states, China and Chinese companies have gained competitive advantage against Western countries and their companies. It is today so clear that, European countries, with the exception of Portugal, play a very small role in Angola. In the US, the former largest trade partner of Angola of the 21st century is losing its place to China.

As shown in Figure 2.4, China overtook the US for the first time in 2007 as the largest importer of Angolan products. Beginning from 2008, Chinese exports to Angola exceeded that of the US. By late 2012, China overtook Portugal as the leading source of Angolan imports.[502] Chinese attractive loans tied to trade in oil promoted increases in the annual bilateral trade as Angola's bilateral trade to the US decline.

From 2005 to 2012, China's imports from Angola increased 390 %, while during the same period US imports from Angola increased only 15 %. In 2012, US imports from Angola were worth US$ 9.8 billion; a 27.7 % fall from the previous year. (See Figure 2.4). The 27.7 % fall of US imports in 2012 could be a result of an increase in its domestic oil and natural production from shale resources. According to the US Government Energy Information

---

502 John Grobler, "Chinese Infrastructure Lubricates Outflow of Angolan and DRC Resources, *Pambazuka News* 10 April 2014, Date Accessed: 11 April 2014 <http://www.pambazuka.org/en/category/features/91304>.

Administration (EIA), in October 2013 the US domestic crude oil production exceeded oil imports for the first time since 1995.[503] (See Figure 4.1). However, US imports from Angola (except a sharp decline in 2009) experienced a sustained increase through 2012. (See Figure 2.4). Despite the steady increase during the period of 2009 to 2012, the US imports from Angola consistently remained lower than that of China. In 2012, it was reported by EIA that, whilst 13 % of Angolan oil went to the US, China imported nearly half (46 %) of it.[504] Thus, these numbers are reflecting the shift in Angola's trade from West to East.

Figure 4.1: U.S. Monthly Crude Oil Production and Crude Oil Net Imports, Jan 2010- Jan 2014

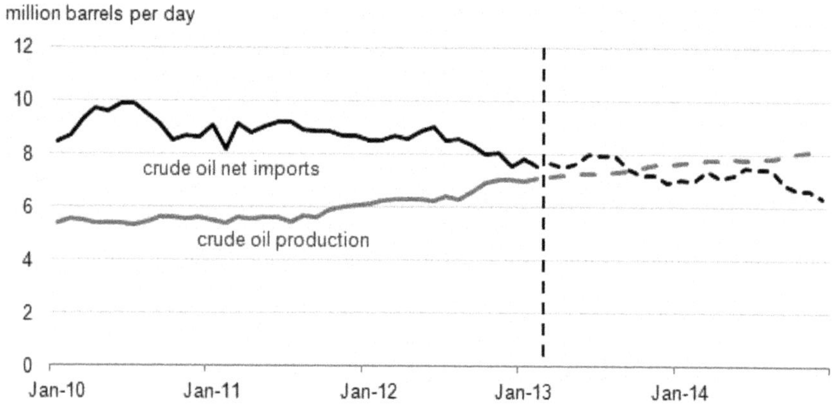

Source: U.S. Energy Information Administration, March 2013 Short-Term Energy Outlook

As mentioned in the previous chapters, Angola Mode has given the opportunity for Chinese companies to go global and develop themselves to compete in the international market. Under the terms of oil-backed credit lines, it is required that the Angolan government reserves 70 % of its contracts for

503 U.S Energy Information Administration. *US Crude Oil Production on Track to Surpass Imports for First Time Since 1995*, EIA, 20 March 2013, Date Accessed 21 March 2013 <http://www.eia.gov/todayinenergy/detail.cfm?id=10451>.

504 U.S Energy Information Administration. *A Report on Angola*. EIA, February 2014:9 Date Accessed: 20 April 2014. <http://www.eia.gov/countries/analysisbriefs/Angola/angola.pdf>.

Chinese companies. As a consequence of the deal between Chinese and Angolan government, the construction sector in Angola has become a leading investment destination of China. On the other hand, US companies have lead in investments in the Angolan petroleum sector. Figure 4.2 illustrates the number of US and Chinese projects approved by the Angolan government. It's important to note that the graph does not include the contracts financed by China Exim Bank and US oil companies. This is because oil-backed loans are not classified as investments and the ANIP is involved with promoting economic diversification through investment in the non-oil industries. Therefore, Chinese companies that are supported by China Exim Bank's oil-backed credit lines do not have to register with the Angolan National Agency for Private Investment (ANIP). According to the Angolan Ministry of Finance, the projects financed by the loan fall under a Program of Public Investments (PIP) as these companies are classified as national companies.[505] Therefore, the graph (Figure 4.2) illustrates private Chinese companies are investing more than the private US companies. According to ANIP, China is at the top of the list of countries with private investment contracts, mainly in sectors such as industry, telecommunication and construction. The US takes first place with its investments in the oil sector, which is not registered at ANIP.[506] It explains that the US companies are not willing to invest in Angola outside the oil sector. US based companies seem to be less inclined, in comparison to Chinese companies, to risk investments in sectors other than oil and gas. US companies, compared to Chinese companies, are very much concerned about risks associated with conducting business in the region, such as corruption and a lack of economic and political stability. Furthermore, Angola's strict requirements of foreign companies, which include hiring local employees and

505 Lucy Corkin, China's Contribution to the Development of African Infrastructure through Investment in the Extractive Industries, *Afrodad Occasional Papers* Issue 8 (2007):2.

506 "China is Biggest Foreign Investor in Angola in 1st Semester," *Macauhub* 30 July 2012, Date Accessed: 21 March 2013 <http://www.macauhub.com.mo/en/2012/07/30/china-is-biggest-foreign-investor-in-angola-in-1st-half/>; *"US GAO - Sub-Saharan Africa: Case Studies of U.S and Chinese Economic Engagement in Angola, Ghana, and Kenya; a Supplement to GAO-13-199," United States Government Accountability Office*, 14 May 2014. <http://www.gao.gov/assets/660/652043.pdf>.

partnering with domestic firms, increased US' hesitation in this regard. A US official explains the reasons of that hesitation in following words:

> "...given the intertwining of Angolan private and government interests, complying with Angola's local content requirements could put US companies in a position of having to partner with unknown, and potentially corrupt, entities. For instance, in one case a US firm reported its partnership with an Angolan firm to US officials after the US firm became aware of links between the local firm and a senior Angolan government official."[507]

US' reluctance to invest in other sectors, other than the oil industry, paves the way for more contracts with Chinese private companies and provides them more opportunities to work with the Angolan companies.

*Figure 4.2: Comparison of the Number of U.S. and Chinese Projects Approved by the Angolan Government**

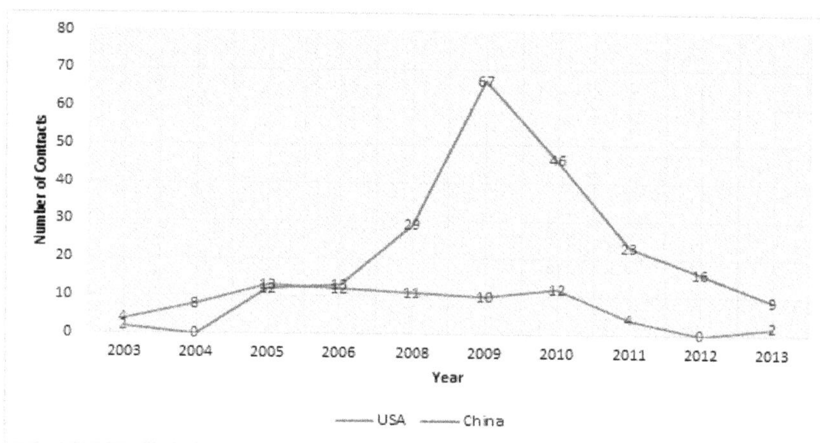

Source: ANIP
*Projects financed by China Exim Bank and oil companies (Chinese and U.S.) are not recorded in ANIP

507 "*US GAO - Sub-Saharan Africa: Case Studies of U.S and Chinese Economic Engagement in Angola, Ghana, and Kenya; a Supplement to GAO-13-199,*" *United States Government Accountability Office*, 14 May 2014. <http://www.gao.gov/assets/660/652043.pdf>.

The US consistently did not contribute to other sectors rather than oil, particularly medium to large factories that would create jobs for local people. In the oil sector, however, the US' leading role has also been diminished after the formation of China-Angola joint ventures, such as CSIH and SSI. Data on the purchase of ownership interests in oil blocks in Angola indicate that, as of January 2014, Chinese oil companies are gaining foothold, despite the ongoing supremacy of US oil companies in Angola's oil blocks. (See Figure 4.3). As illustrated below, from 2009 to 2013, CSIH gained access to five more oil blocks by owning 5 %, 20 %, 10 %, 20 %, 15 % shares in blocks 31, 32, 19/11, 36/11 and 38/11, respectively. Moreover, SSI increased its investment in Angola's oil blocks, by purchasing Marathon's 10 % interest in oil block 31 in 2013.[508]

Figure 4.3: Comparison of Numbers of U.S. and Chinese Firms' Investments in Angolan Oil Blocks (2009 & 2014)

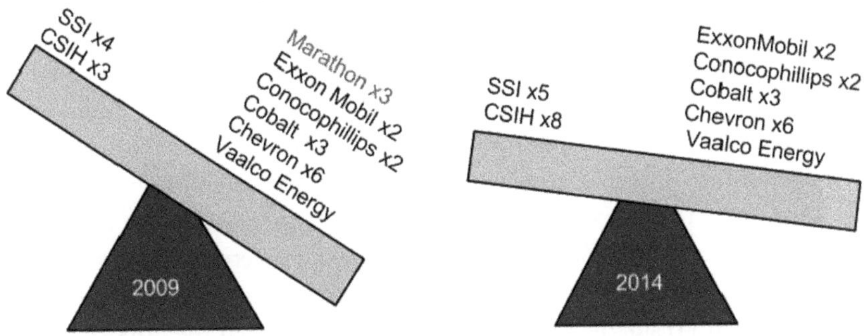

In September 2013, Marathon announced its exit from Angola by selling its remaining 10 % interest in oil block 32 to Sonangol E.P.[509] Marathon's shares of three blocks, in five years (between 2009 and 2014), were purchased by

508 "Marathon Oil Announces US$1.5 Billion Sale of Interest in Angola Block 31," Marathon Oil Corporation 25 June 2013, Date Accessed: 23 September 2013 <http://ir.marathonoil.com/releasedetail.cfm?ReleaseID=773689>.

509 "Marathon Oil Announces Share Repurchases, Asset Divestiture and Acquisition Update," Marathon Oil Corporation 10 September 2013, Date Accessed: 23 September 2013 <http://ir.marathonoil.com/releasedetail.cfm?ReleaseID=789804>.

CSIH, SSI and Sonangol E.P.[510] Thereby, Chinese companies have increased their ownership interests in oil blocks in Angola, while there has been simultaneous, noticeable decrease in the ownership interests of the US companies.

Over the last few years, these developments highlight the shift of economic relations from top-down (West) to the reciprocal (East). While China lies in the heart of Angola's economic development, what lies in the heart of China-Angola relations is basically the political trust between two countries. As China's ambassador to Angola, Gao Kexiang (高克祥) said: "Co-operation has reached its best point because there is mutual political trust."[511] That political trust is rooted in China's principle of non-interference in other countries' internal affairs and carried on through today. Today, however, the political trust between China and Angola, indirectly serves another purpose, such as altering Angola's position in front of the developed countries. To put it another way, Chinese economic engagement in the context of mutual political trust has enabled other foreign countries to change their attitudes and languages when interacting with African leaders. The concepts, Mutuality, Common Development, and Equal Partnership, are more frequently used to describe the relations of China with African countries, rather than describing the North-South relations. Thus, the term 'mutual' was used only to refer to 'mutual accountability' in the documents of the Paris Declaration on aid effectiveness, and in the Accra Agenda for Action.[512] However, in recent official meetings, there has been a remarkable change in the languages used by official leaders. In October 2008, French President Sarkozy's visit to Angola noted the importance of "turning over a new leaf after the misunderstanding of the past and sealing an economic and political partnership 'between equals.'"[513] Besides that, the attitudes and languages of the officials from the US and Japan are also going through changes. The US sees Angola no longer as an aid case, but a

---

510 CSIH purchased 20 % stake of Marathon in oil block 32 in 2010, SSI purchased 10 % stake in oil block 31 in 2013 and Sonangol purchased Marathon's 10 % stake in oil block 32 in 2013.

511 "Angola-China: Mutual Benefits," *Sonangol Universo* September 2013:11.

512 Kenneth King, op.cit., 6.

513 Marie Sophie Joubert, "Sarkozy in Angola to Mend Ties," *France 24* 24 October 2008, Date Accessed 23 September 2013 <http://www.france24.com/en/20080523-sarkozy-angola-mend-ties-angola-france/?quicktabs_1=1>.

place of numerous opportunities. The Executive Director of the US-Angola Chamber of Commerce, Edmund De Jarnette once stated:

> "No Southern African country more than Angola has the potential to emulate the explosive economic growth of the Asian 'Tigers.' US companies have and will continue to excel in Angola's expansive oil and extractive minerals sector. In the coming years, increasing numbers of US companies will employ their comparative advantages in other promising Angolan sectors such as telecommunications, agriculture and infrastructure development. They will help Angola assume the vanguard of the young African 'Lions.'"[514]

Similarly, the US Secretary of State, John Kerry in his visit to Angola in May 2014, described Angola as "an important US partner within a cooperation recording a rising trend."[515] At the US-Africa Business Forum in Washington in August 2014, the US President Barack Obama defined African countries as "an equal, long-term partner which works toward development, investment and trade, and moves away from focusing on aid."[516] In May 2008, the Japanese government organized the Fourth Tokyo International Conference on African Development (TICAD), in order to shed light on importance of working together for African and global development; they welcomed African leaders under the campaign, "Towards a Vibrant Africa: A Continent of Hope and Opportunity."[517] As Angola's middle class continued to grow, it began to attract the attention of developed countries. Middle class countries have often been perceived to contain a great deal of potential due to their new, emerging and rising middle class population. They are expected to consume at greater levels, and ultimately increase the demand for local products. A German industry representative in Angola, Ricardo Gerigk, has called for the attention of German enterprisers, encouraging

---

514 Ibp USA, *Angola Jose Eduardo Dos Santos Handbook,* (Washington DC: International Business, Publications, 2013) 272.

515 "Angola, US Cooperation might Cover Agriculture and Energy," *Agência Angola Press ANGOP* 5 May 2014, Date Accessed: 5 May 2014 <http://www.portalangop.co.ao/angola/en_us/noticias/economia/2014/4/19/Angola-cooperation-might-cover-agriculture-and-energy,80fc9c5f-f6df-42d6-80c5-ef35caa88d99.html>.

516 "Obama Looks for Partnership with Africa," *The BRICS Post* 6 August 2014, Date Accessed: 6 August 2014 <http://thebricspost.com/obama-looks-for-partnership-with-africa/>.

517 "Japan Summit Promotes 'Vibrant Africa'," *UN Africa Renewal*, July 2008:6.

them not to miss the opportunity that Angola and other African countries offer. He offered advice to German businesses, "... But that [Germany still has warm relations with countries like Angola, which used to send students to communist East Germany during the Cold War] will all have changed in five to ten years' time, we will have to learn Mandarin to talk to the decision-makers in Angola."[518] Furthermore, despite Angola's disapproval of subscribing to the principles of the Extractive Industries Transparency Initiative (EITI), and its limited improvements in governance transparency, in May 2014, Angola managed to receive US$1 billion loan from the World Bank without any additional conditions to be used in rebuilding infrastructure and developing its agriculture; an institution which in 2005 had described the no-strings attached Chinese oil-backed credits as the core obstacle to Angola's development.[519]

From that perspective, it is apparent that China's involvement in Angola and throughout Africa has been challenging both Western hegemony and the behavior of Western countries and organizations towards Angola and the African continent. Therefore, through China's engagement in Angola, it created a competitive atmosphere, which ultimately provides various alternatives for Angola to gain beyond their initial restrictions. As noted by an Angolan minister: "Our relations with China not only allowed us to obtain large loans, but most important it forced the West to treat us with more respect and in a less patronizing way. For that we are grateful."[520]

---

518 "Stephen Brown, "Insight: Better Late than Never, Germany Joins New Scramble for Africa," *Reuters* 28 May 2014, Date Accessed: 28 May 2014 <http://www.reuters.com/article/2014/05/28/germany-africa-trade-idUSL6N0O53XS20140528>.

519 Ann Brown, "World Bank to Lend Angola $1Billion to Rebuild," *AFKinsider* 31 May 2014, Date Accessed: 31 May 2014 <http://afkinsider.com/58473/world-bank-lend-angola-1b-rebuild/>; "Angola: Public Expenditure Management and Financial Accountability," Document of the World Bank, 16 February 2005, Date Accessed: 31 May 2014 <http://www-wds.worldbank.org/external/default/WDSContentServer/WDSP/IB/2005/03/10/000090341_20050310101310/Rendered/PDF/290360AO.pdf>.

520 Loro Horta, "Angola and the Paradox of Chinese Power," *Diplomatic Courier* 17 August 2011, Date Accessed: 31 May 2014 <http://www.diplomaticourier.com/news/regions/africa/237-angola-and-the-paradox-of-chinese-power>.

Chapter 5: Conclusion

This dissertation set to answer a central question "How and to what extent has China gained an influence over the economic development of Angola since the end of the civil war in 2002?" In the context of this question it is intended to shed light on the controversial and complex economic relations of China-Angola, and to understand the existing relations through Moravcsik's IR theory of Commercial Liberalism. In consideration of both the theoretical approach and the research question, there were three distinct hypotheses that were derived. The three Commercial Liberalist hypotheses have been tested through an empirical examination.

In order to judge the validity of these hypothetical predictions, it is important to keep them in mind:

Hypothesis 1: Cooperation of China and Angola in the core economic areas would lead to a relationship based on interdependency in which both sides stand on mutual economic and political necessities.

Contrary to popular belief, the relations between China and Angola do not serve only Chinese interests but also Angolan interests. As is demonstrated in this study, regarding aid principles, China has advocated and applied key terms and concepts such as 'partnership,' 'developing together,' 'co-operation,' 'mutual benefits', versus concepts formerly and traditionally associated with 'aid', which tends to refer more specifically to 'charity.' The top-down foreign aid flow increases the dependency ratio of recipient countries to the cycle of development aid. These aid agreements, in which African countries are subject to the several terms and conditions, were seen ideal on paper. However, in practice, these agreements were unable to create the desirable circumstance associated with traditional development aid terms. Dambisa Moyo argues: "Aid [from Western Countries or Organizations] has been and continues to be, an unmitigated political, economic and humanitarian disaster for most parts of the developing world."[521] A World Bank study illustrates

521 Dambisa Moyo, op.cit., 12.

that more than 85 % of funds given by Western countries were used for other purposes.[522] Austrian Economist, Paul Rosenstein–Rodan, explained the situation in 1947: "The bank thought it financed an electric power station, but in fact financed a brothel"[523]

China emerged in a moment in which no Western countries were willing confront the challenges associated with investing in Angola and other African countries. As South African Diplomat stated, "Before China became interested in Africa, we used to try to talk to Western governments about infrastructure or agriculture and their eyes would simply glaze over."[524] Huge investment necessities in Angola matched China's aid priorities, seeking to promote the development of economic infrastructure with the instrument: Angola Mode.

Angola Mode, which reflects the idea of a series of oil-for-infrastructure loans with 'no political strings attached' and 'lower interest rates', created an interdependent relationship between China and Angola; similar to the oil-for-infrastructure model Japan used in China in early 1980s. China was aware of the necessity to modernize its infrastructure in order to utilize its own resources and capacity, and Japan held these opportunities. "China planned to use foreign funds primarily to boost production and exploit its own natural resources."[525] Today, when we examine China's Angola policy, we conclude that China took over the Japanese role of the 1980s. Whilst China secured energy supplies and natural resources, Angola enjoyed a period of stability with numerous projects to improve the infrastructure and economy of the country. Despite the fact that China and Angola are asymmetric powers, the interaction between the two states is based on mutual political and economic necessities. In an article written together by Vachudova and Moravcsik, they note: "Those countries that gain the most through more intense interstate cooperation—more precisely, those for whom cooperation is most attractive relative to unilateral (or minilateral) policy-making—have the most intense preferences for agreement

522 Ibid., 74.
523 Ibid., 74.
524 Sarah Raine, op.cit., 199.
525 "Bu Ming on Banking Contacts with Abroad," *Xinhuanet*（新华网）6 February 1980, quoted in Deborah Brautigam, op.cit., 48.

and thus are willing to compromise the most on the margin to further it."[526] Increasing the amount of oil exports has made this relationship significant for both countries. Increasing the growth rate of the average annual GDP, and decreasing inflation rates from over 100 % to one digit numbers, resulted in an increase of the annual average rate of GDP per capita. These developments allowed Angola to be the fastest growing African economy. In July 2012, the World Bank Report classified Angola as an 'upper middle income' country, a change from its former classification as a 'low income country' with a per capita income below US$ 1,000 merely ten years ago. Angola has become the third largest Sub-Saharan financial market behind Nigeria and South Africa.[527] The Angolan capital city, Luanda, has become the third-largest Portuguese-speaking city in the world (behind the two Brazilian cities of Rio de Janeiro and Sao Paolo).[528]

Moreover, progress within the Angolan economy and co-operation with China helped Angola build its self-esteem and self-confidence. Increasing self-confidence has created a platform for Angola defending its own interests. An example of which took place in March 2007, in which the deal between Sinopec and Sonangol to build a new US$ 3 billion oil refinery in Lobito (Sonaref) was called off and China's demand of 80 % of Angola oil refinery Sonaref's production was strictly rejected by Angola. Another example is related to Sonangol's decision to block access of Chinese companies to assets, which were already given to the two Chinese companies, Sinopec and CNOOC by the former owner, Marathon. It is assumed that Sinopec and CNOOC's offers were lower than the assets' real value, which caused an objection from Angola side.

By focusing on several areas of economic cooperation, China's goal has become to follow the fundamental principles of China's 2006 African Policy, which is based upon the enhancement of mutual economic gains.

---

526 Andrew Moravcsik and Milada Anna Vachudova, "Preferences, Power and Equilibrium. The causes and consequences of EU enlargement" in: Frank Schimmelfennig and Ulrich Sedelmeier, eds. *The Politics of European Union Enlargement. Theoretical Approaches*, (London:Routledge, 2005) 198–212.

527 "Angola is the Third-Largest Sub-Saharan Financial Market," *Macauhub* 23 July 2014, Date Accessed: 23 July 2014 <http://www.macauhub.com.mo/en/2014/07/23/angola-is-the-third-largest-sub-saharan-financial-market/>.

528 Luanda's population has grown from 400.000 in 1975 to 5 million in 2014.

The reluctance of Western companies to become involved in major investments, allowed the opportunity for China to gain competitive advantages in strengthening its relations with Angola by promoting its economic development through investments in infrastructure and creating business cooperation, while accessing oil and diamonds in return. Differing from Western countries, China's investments are related to the desires of the Angolan government, since it ultimately decides which infrastructure projects should be built. As Brant noted: "Chinese foreign aid emphasizes the importance of stimulating economic growth and implementing a development model based on each country's specific requirements and circumstances."[529] It is worth to note that, the investments related to internet and communication networks, as well as the construction of roads and railways would promote development not only in Angola, but also in neighboring countries. Improved access to transport, technology and energy, increased overall productivity, which boosts commercial activities in the region.

Viewing Angola as a business opportunity and trade partner, rather than an exploitative subject, increased China's popularity in the country and facilitated China's rapid entry into the country. As Kim pointed out, "China's good image as a donor is coupled with the attractiveness of its development model."[530] Since China became interested in Angola, Angola has taken very impressive economic steps. Moreover, China's mutual complementary or interdependent relationship with Angola, during a period in which Angola lacked the capital necessary to make investments in infrastructure and natural resource extraction, lies at the heart of progress. Angola's ambassador to China, João Garcia Bires, confirmed in an interview: "The help China has given our country has served as a starting point, so that Angola might occupy a leading position in various areas ... this help has marked and opened stages of development and that is why China is today our strategic partner."[531] Therefore, the relations between China and Angola

529 Philippa Brant, "Is China Challenging Traditional Donors' Development Policy?" *Whydev.org*, 14 October 2011, Date Accessed: 10 March 2013 <http://www.whydev.org/is-china-challenging-traditional-donors-development-policy/>.

530 Samuel S. Kim, "China and Globalization: Confronting Myriad Challenges and Opportunities," *Asian Perspective* 33.3 (2009): 43.

531 "Angola-China: Mutual Benefits", *Sonangol Universo* September 2013: 14.

fit Moravcsik's argument in an article written together with Kalypso Nicolaidis: "Governments with attractive and effective unilateral policies tend to be skeptical of co-operation, while governments able to achieve policy goals only by altering the pattern of externalities imposed by the policies of foreign government policy tend to favour it."[532]

Hypothesis 2: China's business cooperation with Angola's domestic companies would increase their incentive to press the Angolan government to facilitate economic transactions.

As a consequence of his definition of the commercial liberalism, Moravcsik argued that "the greater the economic benefits for dominant private actors, the greater their incentive to press governments to facilitate such transactions; the more costly the adjustment imposed by economic interchange, the more opposition is likely to arise." According to Moravcsik, because governments seek to stay in power, they require the support of domestic actors. However, in countries like Angola, domestic companies are not fully independent on the government. Therefore, in that aspect, the question of whether the Angolan government is coming under pressure from domestic companies that have achieved favorable/unfavorable outcomes in their economic cooperation with China, leads to an another question: How likely is it that government officials in Angola are holding positions in private companies alongside their official missions? As explained in Chapter 3, there are allegations about Manuel Vicente, who has been the Vice President of Angola since September 2012, after serving as Chief Executive Officer of Sonangol (1999-January 2012) and as the Minister of State for Economic Coordination (January 2012-September 2012). It was claimed that he owns stakes in nine subsidiaries of China Sonangol.[533] Furthermore, an April 2012 article published by the Financial Times confirmed these allegations, by claiming that three top Angolan officials: Manuel Vicente, Manuel Hélder Vieira Dias Júnio (the head of the President's Military Bureau), and General Fragoso do Nascimento (the President's former Head

532 Andrew Moravcsik and Kalypso Nicolaidis, "Explaining the Treaty of Amsterdam: Interests, Influence, Institutions," *Journal of Common Market Studies* 37.1 (1999):61.

533 Lee Levkovitz, Marta McLellan, J.R. Warner, op.cit., 19.

of Communications) are secretly holding shares in an Angola-based private oil company, Nazaki Oil and Gaz.[534] Consequently, in Angola, the fact is, domestic companies and the Angolan government are very much interconnected. Therefore, in Angola there are several findings that demonstrate the efforts of the Angolan government to facilitate economic and commercial transactions between two countries. The Business Fair FILDA (Luanda International Fair) organization is an example of one. In 2007, Angola organized an International Fair in which many participants from China showed a keen interest in investing in Angola. In 2013, the Angolan government invited China as the guest country of the year. Another development, in terms of facilitating commercial transactions between China and Angola, took place in 2012. The state-owned Angola Airlines TAAG, which started flying to Beijing in 2008, increased the number of its non-stop flights from Luanda to Beijing to two times per week.[535] In addition, in 2013, in order to strengthen commercial ties with China, Angola decided to sell its oil to China in the Chinese national currency of Renminbi.[536]

In conclusion, looking at these efforts taken by the Angolan government, it is possible to argue that the Angolan government has pursued its foreign economic policy in accordance with the economic interests of dominant domestic actors, which benefit from close ties with China. Therefore, it confirms the Moravcsik's argument, that "Government policy is therefore constrained by the underlying identities, interests, and power of individuals

---

534 Tom Burgis and Cynthia O'Murchu, "Angolan Officials Held Hidden Oil Stakes," *Financial Times* 15 April 2012, Date Accessed: 23 March 2014 <.http://www.ft.com/intl/cms/s/0/effd6a98-854c-11e1-a394-00144feab49a.html#axzz331ZQBzlx>.

535 "Taag com Dois Voos Semanais para China," *Portal de Angola* 24 September 2013, Date Accessed: 25 September 2013 <http://www.portaldeangola.com/2013/09/taag-com-dois-voos-semanais-para-china/>.

536 Today, not only Angola, but also Russia, Iran, Sudan and Venezuela are selling their oil to China in Chinese Renminbi. It is expected that more than 5 million barrels per day are traded in Chinese national currency Renminbi. See Russ Winter, "China Maneuvers to Take Away US' Dominant Reserve Currency Status," Seeking Alpha 27 July 2013, Date Accessed: 23 March 2014 <http://seekingalpha.com/article/1578602-china-maneuvers-to-take-away-u-s-dominant-reserve-currency-status>.

and groups ... who constantly pressure the central decision makers to pursue politics consistent with their preferences"[537]

Hypothesis 3: Through the concepts such as Angola Mode and the principle of non-interference in the internal affairs of other sovereign countries, China has gained competitive advantage against the US and US companies.

In order to measure the extension of China's economic influence in Angola, it was necessary to compare their role to Angola's traditional economic partners. Therefore, the United States was selected as a dependent variable to evaluate how Chinese engagement in Angola affected Angola's relations with the US.

Concepts such as Angola Mode and the principle of non-interference in internal affairs of other countries, promoted opportunities to Chinese companies to go global and compete in the international market. Different from the US, China's investment in Angola does not concentrate solely on the oil sector. Chinese companies, under the terms of Angola Mode, are building high speed internet/communication networks, hospitals, schools, major highways and railways, airports, power plants, agriculture fields, and other areas of economic development that are far more extensive than what the US has done in Angola thus far.

As explained in Chapter 3, through the concessional loans, which were given at below market rates and in return for natural resources, China has surpassed the US by becoming the leading consumer of Angola's petroleum products. The relations between Angola and the US, which are mainly driven by oil trade and investment in Angolan oil blocks has been challenging by China. In the oil sector, US oil companies are still the largest investors and shareowners; however, it is worth nothing that they are losing their shares in Angolan blocks to China. In 2009, US oil companies had ownership interests in six oil blocks as non-operators, acting as operators for eleven oil blocks, whereas Chinese companies had ownership interests in only seven oil blocks as non-operators. From 2009 to 2013, however, CSIH gained access to five more oil blocks, and SSI increased its investment by gaining access to one more oil block, which was formerly owned by the US oil

537 Andrew Moravcsik (1997), op.cit., 518.

company, Marathon. Marathon Oil Company, which formerly held three oil shares in Angolan oil blocks, today has no shares in Angolan oil blocks. (See Table 3.2). As a result of this, from 2009 to 2013, Chinese companies gradually increased their interest in Angolan oil blocks, while US companies decreased, yet still remained the largest investors in the oil sector.

Angola while letting China increase its leverage, does not want to remain solely dependent on Chinese firms, which generally lack the technology, capacity and experience to manage offshore oil operations. However outside the oil sector, China is at the top of the list of countries with private investment contracts in sectors such as telecommunication and construction.

The US' reluctance to invest in other sectors other than the oil industry, is compatible with China's plan, which is based on going global through attractive loan offers and principles of non-interference in domestic politics. In the oil sector, China needs more time to gain experience, and the development of its technological capacity to overtake US companies' operator roles in Angolan oil blocks, but in other sectors, China has been filling the vacuum that Western companies left, by following a strategy to strengthen Chinese companies' relations with Angolans.

In conclusion, it is possible to argue that the theoretical arguments have parallels with the practical implications of this dissertation, despite the limited explanatory power of the Western theories, which are unfortunately not universally applicable. Considering our observations of China's relations with Angola, it is possible to argue an interdependent relationship results in mutual benefits for both sides. China emerged as an alternative partner for Angola who altered the Western mentality of seeing African countries as inferior, rather than an equal partner. In an interview with Time Magazine in 2007, Rwanda's President Paul Kagame said:

> "Many times they [the donors] have assumed they are the ones who know what countries in Africa need. They want to be the ones to choose where to put this money, to be the ones to run it, without any accountability. In other cases, they have simply associated with the wrong people and money gets lost and ends up in people's pockets. We should correct that. We should be working together, and agreeing where to put money, so that we know it will make a difference and are able to monitor that."[538]

538 Alex Perry, "A Conversation with Rwandan President Paul Kagame," *Time* 27 September 2007, Date Accessed: 20 February 2014 <http://content.time.com/time/magazine/article/0,9171,1666064,00.html.>.

China's method of not providing cash money and collecting oil revenues in an escrow account has targeted to mitigate the risks of corruption. Under the motto of 'win-win cooperation' or 'Angola Mode', China and Angola have seized a chance to extend their relations in various economic areas. First, China gave attention to the building of infrastructure, which had priority over other sectors, especially in terms of enabling growth of Angolan economy. Lacking infrastructure hindered Angola's ability to start the 'engine', or in other words, its business activities. After promoting investment for development in the infrastructure sector, the diversification of the Angolan economy and the education of local people has become the second target of Chinese and Angolan officials. These developments have become necessary in order to start the 'engine' of growth, but there has still been another significant sector yet to be developed; labor intensive manufacturing sector. It is expected, in the near future, China will lose 100 million jobs due to a decade of nearly 20 % annual wage increases.[539] Some manufacturing companies have already landed in developing Asian countries, such as India, Vietnam, and Cambodia. Angola, with its young labor force, which makes up 20 % of Angolan population, could be the next plan of both countries officials' in order to enable the 'engine' to keep on working.

In light of this dissertation, it is possible to argue that China's business interactions based on mutual benefits and close relations with local companies strengthened its position in Angola. The US' sole desire not to depend on foreign energy reserves in recent years (by peaking its domestic reserves through its recent success in exploiting shale oil and gas reserves in its own territories), coupled with China's increasing energy demand, matched well with Angola's supply of abundant oil reserves and national priorities. In just a short time, China has become Angola's largest trading partner. Becoming Angola's largest trading partner, along with opportunities, has also brought challenges. The challenges in China-Angola relations

539 Kathy Chu, "China Manufacturers Survive By Moving to Asian Neighbors," *The Wall Street Journal* 1 May 2013, Date Accessed: 23 March 2014 <http://online.wsj.com/news/articles/SB100014241278873237981045784530731035 66416>; Goutam Das, "Made in India," *Business Today* 2 March 2014, Date Accessed:23 March 2014 <http://businesstoday.intoday.in/story/india-benefits-china-begins-to-lose-manufacturing-edge/1/203040.html>.

are mainly related to China's economic performance and to the plunge in oil prices. Yet, both countries are attempting to mitigate the possible risks with several measures, such as trading beyond mineral resources and the strengthening of Angola's local currency through several financial reforms.

Today, Angola has become an African powerhouse that has managed to achieve economic growth while maintaining stability inside the country. As becoming one of the few most stable and peaceful African countries, Angola could be a model to promote growth and stability in neighboring countries. Angola, as the only African candidate country on the list, has been elected non-permanent member of the UN Security Council for the 2015–2016 period. Along with China, Angola's participation in the UN Security Council will undoubtedly give Luanda greater leverage within the international community to promote Angola's interests, as well as those of the region and the continent.

This study has made an effort to see if there is a remarkable Chinese influence in Angolan economy by taking account the actors' interests, their strategies, and the resulting outcomes on a bilateral and global level. In the scope of Moravcsik's Commercial Liberalism and the three hypotheses stated above, this dissertation 'China's Economic Engagement in Africa: A Case Study of Angola' could contribute to the continuous discussion of the shift of economic power from West to the East in Angola.

Bibliography

"4,000 Related Jobs in Angola." *Railways Africa,* 14 August 2012. 15 August 2013. <http://www.railwaysafrica.com/blog/2012/08/14/4000-rail-related-jobs-in-angola/>.

African Development Bank (AFDB). *Angola: Country Gender Profile. AFDB,* 2008. 13 April 2014. <http://www.afdb.org/fileadmin/uploads/afdb/Documents/Project-and-Operations/ADB-BD-IF-2008-210-EN-ANGOLA-COUNTRY-GENDER-PROFILE.PDF>.

African Development Bank (AFDB). *2011 Annual Report.* AFDB, 1 June 2012. 31 March 2013. <www.afdb.org>.

Alden, Chris. *China in Africa.* London: Zed Books, 2007.

–. "China and Africa: A Distant Mirror of Latin America." *Colombia Internacional* 75 (June 2012): 19–47.

Alden, Chris, Dan Large and Ricardo Soares de Oliveira. "China Returns to Africa Anatomy of an Expansive Engagement." *Real Instituto Elcano* (2008):1–19.

Alden, Chris and Ana Cristina Alves. "China and Africa's Natural Resources: The Challenges and Implications for Development and Governance." *South African Institute of International Affairs (SAIIA)*, 2009. 23 September 2013. <http://www.voltairenet.org/IMG/pdf/China_and_Africa_s_Natural_Resources.pdf>.

Alves, Ana Cristina. "China's Oil Diplomacy: Comparing Chinese Economic Statecraft in Angola and Brazil." A PhD Thesis for International Relations Department of London School of Economics, June 2011. 13 August 2013. <http://etheses.lse.ac.uk/206/1/Alves_China%E2%80%99s_Oil_Diplomacy.pdf>.

–."Taming the Dragon: China's Oil Interests in Angola." Power, Marcus and Ana Cristina Alves. *China and Angola: A Marriage of Convenience.* Cape Town, Dakar, Nairobi and Oxford: Pambazuka Press, 2012. 105–123.

–. "The Oil Factor in Sino-Angolan Relations at the Start of the 21st Century." *SAIIA Occasional Paper,* February 2010. 12 January 2012.

"Ambassador Praises Cooperation with China." *Agência Angola Press ANGOP* 11 April 2014. 12 April 2014. <http://www.portalangop.co.ao/

angola/en_us/noticias/politica/2014/3/15/Ambassador-praises-cooperation-with-China,83e5422e-3811-4ac6-aad3-b73c4e700681.htm>.

Forum on China And Africa Cooperation (FOCAC). *An Interpretation of New Measures on Econoimc and Trade Cooperation from 4th Ministerial Conference.* FOCAC, 24 May 2010. 21 September 2013. <http://www.focac.org/eng/dsjbzjhy/t696509.htm>.

"Angola and China Want to Boost Bilateral Ties." *Agência Angola Press ANGOP* 8 May 2014. 9 May 2014. <http://www.portalangop.co.ao/angola/en_us/noticias/politica/2014/4/19/Angola-and-China-want-boost-bilateral-ties,5797cab0-cd72-4dec-ab60-b1fd530436f5.html>.

"Angola and Portugal: Role Reversal." *The Economist* 3 September 2011. 21 September 2013. <http://www.economist.com/node/21528310>.

"Angola Banking Survey." *KPMG,* November 2012. 23 September 2013. <https://www.kpmg.com/PT/en/IssuesAndInsights/Documents/kpmg-bank-ao-2012en.pdf>.

"Angola Diamond Profits Increased in 2011." *Diamond News.* The Israeli Diamond Industry, 12 August 2012. 20 November 2013. <http://www.israelidiamond.co.il/english/news.aspx?boneid=918&objId=11594>.

"Angola Fines Chevron for Pollution." *BBC News* 1 July 2002. 23 September 2013. <http://news.bbc.co.uk/2/hi/business/2077836.stm>.

"Angola Gets USD 2 Billion Credit From China." *ANGOP* 12 December 2014. 12 December 2014. <http://www.portalangop.co.ao/angola/en_us/noticias/economica/2014/11/50/Angola-gets-Usd-billion-credit-from-China,db7b0e75-e943-4e16-a131-72dbc5b8f26d.html>.

"Angola is the Third-Largest Sub-Saharan Financial Market." *Macauhub* 23 July 2014. 24 July 2014. <http://www.macauhub.com.mo/en/2014/07/23/angola-is-the-third-largest-sub-saharan-financial-market>.

"Angola LNG Supplying Liquid Natural Gas to China's CNOOC Group." *Macauhub* 14 August 2013. 15 August 2013. <http://www.macauhub.com.mo/en/2013/08/14/angola-lng-supplying-liquid-natural-gas-to-china%E2%80%99s-cnooc-group/>.

"Angola Moves Ahead with New Agricultural Development Strategy." *Macauhub* 16 August 2013. 19 September 2013. <http://www.macauhub.com.mo/en/2011/08/16/angola-moves-ahead-with-new-agricultural-development-strategy/>.

"Angola Takes on Loan from Chinese Bank for Real Estate Project." *Macauhub* 25 November 2014. 25 November 2014. <http://www.macauhub.com.mo/en/2014/11/25/angola-takes-on-loan-from-chinese-bank-for-real-estate-project/>.

"Angola Takes out US$ 500 Million in Loans from China Exim Bank." *Macauhub* 9 July 2013. 20 April 2013. <http://www.macauhub.com.mo/en/2012/07/09/angola-takes-out-us500-million-in-loans-from-china-exim-bank/>.

"Angola, China Sign Memorandum for New General Hospital of Luanda." *Agência Angola Press ANGOP* 18 April 2012. 16 August 2013. <http://www.portalangop.co.ao/angola/en_us/noticias/saude/2012/3/16/Angola-China-sign-memorandum-for-new-General-Hospital-Luanda,ea71cc03-64c9-4062-afec-d0ee306f2563.html>.

"Angola, US Cooperation Might Cover Agriculture and Energy." *Agência Angola Press ANGOP* 5 May 2014. 5 May 2014. <http://www.portalangop.co.ao/angola/en_us/noticias/economia/2014/4/19/Angola-cooperation-might-cover-agriculture-and-energy,80fc9c5f-f6df-42d6-80c5-ef35caa88d99.html>.

"Angola: Education Ministry, Unitel, Huawei Create Joint Internet Project." *allAfrica* 5 June 2012. 15 August 2013. <http://allafrica.com/stories/201206060708.html?utm_source=twitterfeed&utm_medium=twitter>.

"Angola: Huambo-Angola/China Friendship School Shows Government Commitment." *allAfrica* 24 February 2014. 25 February 2014. <http://allafrica.com/stories/201402250252.html>.

"Angola: Rehabilitation of Kifangondo/Caxito/Uije Road Complete by 2008." *Agência Angola Press ANGOP* 26 June 2006. 15 August 2013. <http://www.portalangop.co.ao/angola/en_us/noticias/economia/2006/5/26/Rehabilitation-Kifangondo-Caxito-Uije-Road-Complete-2008,2fed05ff-5309-4eef-aab3-2194c897e018.html>.

"Angola-China: Mutual Benefits." *Sonangol Universo*, 2013: 6–15.

"Angolan Bank Banco BIC Plans to Enter Chinese Market." *Macauhub* 10 April 2014.10 April 2014. <http://www.macauhub.com.mo/en/2014/04/10/angolan-bank-banco-bic-plans-to-enter-chinese-market/>.

Angolan Ministry of Petroleum. "Relatòrio de actividades do sector petrolìfero, referente ao ano de 2009." 2010.

"Angolan Oil Sector to Have Environmental Monitoring." *Macauhub* January 2014. 4 January 2014. <http://www.macauhub.com.mo/en/2014/01/03/angolan-oil-sector-to-have-environmental-monitoring/>.

"Angola's Ghost Town: A New Town, with Few Residents." *CNN* 5 December 2012. 16 August 2013. <http://edition.cnn.com/video/data/2.0/video/international/2012/12/05/angola-ghost-town.cnn.html>.

Baldwin, Clare. "China Government -Owned Crafts Chain Suspends Controversial Ivory Sales." *Reuters* 18 March 2014. 19 March 2014. <http://in.reuters.com/article/2014/03/18/us-china-ivory-idINBREA2H1OZ20140318>.

"Banco Económico replaces Banco Espírito Santo Angola." *Macauhub* 30 October 2014. 4 November 2014. <http://www.macauhub.com.mo/en/2014/10/30/banco-economico-replaces-banco-espirito-santo-angola/>.

Baumüller, Heike et. al. *The Effects of Oil Companies' Activities on the Environment, Health and Development in Sub-Saharan Africa*. Brussels: European Parliament, 2011.

Beech, Hannah. "The 2013 Time 100." *Time* 18 April 2013. 21 June 2013. <http://time100.time.com/2013/04/18/time-100/slide/peng-liyuan/>.

"Benguela Railway to Offer 3,000 New Jobs." *Agência Angola Press ANGOP* 22 August 2012. 15 August 2013. <http://www.portalangop.co.ao/angola/en_us/noticias/transporte/2012/7/34/Benguela-Railway-offer-000-new-jobs,00b35b49-d4c9-418c-b259-7044f047fddb.html>.

Bermúdez-Lugo, Omayra. "The Mineral Industry of Angola." *2005 Minerals Yearbook Angola US Geological Survey (USGS)*, 2007. 19 September 2013. <http://minerals.usgs.gov/minerals/pubs/country/2005/aomyb05.pdf>.

Berthelemy, Jean Claude. "China's Engagement and Aid Efferctiveness in Africa." *African Development Bank Working Paper Series* 129 (2011): 4–35.

Bhola, Gaurav. "China and India Battle for Influence in Africa: Part 4." 15 October 2007. 1 July 2014 <http://www.gimmiethescoop.com/china-and-india-battle-for-influence-in-africa-part-4>.

Bingfei, Wang. "Interview: China Plays Active, Responsible Role in Angola's Post War Reconstruction." *Xinhua News* 19 August 2012. 15 August 2013. <http://news.xinhuanet.com/english2010/world/2011-08/19/c_131062120.htm>.

Blanchard, Ben. "China to Extend over $12 bn in Aid to Africa." *Reuters* 9 May 2014. 12 May 2014. <http://www.reuters.com/article/2014/05/09/us-china-africa-idUSBREA4802320140509>.

Brant, Philippa. "Is China Challenging Traditional Donors' Development Policy?" *Whydev.org* 14 October 2011. 10 March 2013. <http://www.whydev.org/is-china-challenging-traditional-donors-development-policy/>.

Brautigam, Deborah and Adama Gaye. "Is Chinese Investment Good for Africa." *Council on Foreign Relations,* 20 February 2007. 13 April 2013. <http://www.cfr.org/china/chinese-investment-good-africa/p12622>.

Brautigam, Deborah. "Chinese Aid and Luanda General Hospital in Angola: Still Falling Down?" *China in Africa Real Story.* 16 August 2013. <http://www.chinaafricarealstory.com/2011/04/chinese-aid-and-luanda-general-hospital.html>.

–. "China in Africa: Seven Myths." *ARI,* 2011. 4 July 2014. <http://www.realinstitutoelcano.org/wps/wcm/connect/07b4c88045b474b89aa7*df5e7489e10f/ARI239*e10f/ARI232011_Brautigam_ChinaAfrica_Seven_Myths.pdf?MOD=AJPERES&CACHEID=07b4c88045b474b89aa7df5e7489e10f>.

–. *The Dragon's Gift: The Real Story of China in Africa.* New York: Oxford University Press, 2009.

Brown, Ann. "World Bank to Lend Angola $1 Billion to Rebuild." *AFKinsider* 31 May 2014. 31 May 2014. <http://afkinsider.com/58473/world-bank-lend-angola-1b-rebuild/>.

Brown, Stephen. "Insight: Better Late Than Never, Germany Joins New Scramble for Africa." *Reuters* 28 May 2014. 28 May 2014. <http://www.reuters.com/article/2014/05/28/germany-africa-trade-idUSL6N0O53XS20140528>.

Burgis, Tom and Cynthia O'Murchu. "Angolan Officials Held Hidden Oil Stakes." *Financial Times* 15 April 2012. 23 March 2014. <http://www.ft.com/intl/cms/s/0/effd6a98-854c-11e1-a394-00144feab49a.html#axzz331ZQBzlx>.

Campbell, Keith. "Good News for Angolan Gem Companies' Shareholders." *Mining Weekly* 9 August 2013. 19 August 2013. <http://www.miningweekly.com/article/shareholders-in-two-diamond-companies-get-good-news-2013-08-09>.

Chang, Anita. "China: Media, Organizations Distorting Darfur." *US Today* 26 June 2008. 13 May 2013. <http://UStoday30.UStoday.com/news/world/2008-06-26-1059955913_x.htm>.

Chantelle, Benjamin. "Africa is not a Big Bull in China's Shop." *Mail & Guardian* 21 June 2013. 21 June 2013. <http://mg.co.za/article/2013-06-21-00-africa-isnt-a-big-bull-in-chinas-shop>.

Charbonneau, Louis and Michelle Nichols. "Exclusive: Russia, China Block Central African Republic Blacklist at U.N." *Reuters* 23 April 2014. 24 April 2014. <http://www.reuters.com/article/2014/04/23/us-centralafrica-un-sanctions-idUSBREA3M1GA20140423>.

Chen, Chuan, Pi-Chu Chiu, Ryan J. Orr and Andrea Goldstein. "An Empirical Analysis of Chinese Construction Firm's Entry into Africa." *CRIOCM 2007 International Symposium.* 2007.

Cheru, Fantu and Cyril Obi, Eds. *The Rise of China and India in Africa.* London: Zedbooks, 2010.

–. "De-Coding China-Africa Relations:Partnership for Development or Neo-Colonialism by Invitation." *World Financial Review.* September-October 2011: 72–75.

"China and Darfur." *The Washington Post* 14 December 2006. 13 May 2013. <http://www.washingtonpost.com/wp-dyn/content/article/2006/12/13/AR2006121302008.html>.

"China finances cotton production project in Angola." *Macauhub* 8 November 2006. 19 September 2013. <http://www.macauhub.com.mo/en/2006/11/08/2019/>.

"China is Biggest Foreign Investor in Angola in 1st Semester." *Macauhub* 30 July 2012. 21 March 2013. <http://www.macauhub.com.mo/en/2012/07/30/china-is-biggest-foreign-investor-in-angola-in-1st-half/>.

"China Keen to Play Role in Ending Darfur Crisis-UN." *Sudan Tribune* 10 September 2007.13 May 2013. <http://www.sudantribune.com/spip.php?article23688>.

"China Launches Hybrid Rice Training Base for Foreign Agrotechnicians." *Xinhua News* 13 September 2009. 19 September 2013. <http://news.xinhuanet.com/english/2009-09/13/content_12043011.htm>.

"China Outperforms Europe, Completes Fastest Angolan Railway." *People's Daily Online* 15 August 2014. 16 August 2014. <http://english.peopledaily.com.cn/n/2014/0815/c98649-8770415.html>.

"Chinese Plant Makes Angola Self-Sufficient in Cement." *Macauhub* 10 October 2014.10 October 2014. <http://www.macauhub.com.mo/en/2014/10/10/chinese-plant-makes-angola-self-sufficient-in-cement/>.

"China Provides Angola with US$ 10 Billion Between 2009 and 2010, Expansão Reports." *Macauhub* 8 February 2011. 13 August 2013. <http://www.macauhub.com.mo/en/2011/02/08/china-provides-angola-with-us10-billion-between-2009-and-2010-expansao-reports/>.

"China Railway Construction: to Prospect Diamond in Angola." *4-Traders* 3 June 2014. 3 June 2014. <http://www.4-traders.com/CHINA-RAILWAY-CONSTRUCTIO-6500144/news/China-Railway-Construction--to-Prospect-Diamond-in-Angola-18536023/>.

China Road Bridge Corporation. *A Project of CRBC in Angola Wins the Silver Award of 2012 CACEM National High-Quality Project.* CRBC, 4 January 2013. 15 August 2013. <http://www.crbc.com/site/crbcEN/achievenments/info/2013/1579.html>.

"China to Build Motorcycle Assembly Line in Angola." *People's Daily* 6 May 2000. 19 September 2013. <http://english.people.com.cn/english/200005/06/eng20000506_40248.html>.

"China vai investir USD 400 milhões em telecomunicaçoes." *Angonoticias* 24 February 2005. 15 August 2013. <http://www.angonoticias.com/Artigos/item/3944/china-vai-investir-usd-400-milhoes-em-telecomunicacoes>.

"China-Africa Economic and Trade Cooperation." Chinese Government's Official Web Portal. December 2010. 21 June 2013. <http://www.gov.cn/english/official/2010-12/23/content_1771603.htm>.

"China-Angola 30 Years On." *Macauhub* 2013 August 2013. 19 September 2013. <http://www.macauhub.com.mo/en/2013/08/16/china-angola-30-years-on-time-to-%E2%80%9Chave-no-doubts%E2%80%9D/>.

"China-Made MA60 Commuter Plane Debuts in Angola." *China.org.cn (中国网)* 25 January 2008. 19 September 2013. <http://www.china.org.cn/english/business/240750.htm>.

"China's CITIC Builds 6,000 Homes in Angola." *Macauhub* 17 March 2014. 18 March 2014. <http://www.macauhub.com.mo/en/2014/03/17/china%E2%80%99s-citic-builds-6000-homes-in-angola/>.

"China's Diamond Demand Sparkles." *China Daily* 9 November 2011. 16 September 2013. <http://www.chinadaily.com.cn/cndy/2011-11/09/content_14060784.htm>.

"China's Huawei Group Trains 800 Technicians in Angola." *Macauhub* 21 January 2015. 21 January 2015. <http://www.macauhub.com.mo/en/2015/01/21/chinas-huawei-group-trains-800-technicians-in-angola/>.

"China Hyway due to Deliver Angola's Moçâmedes Railroad in October." *Macauhub* 5 September 2014. 5 September 2014. <http://www.macauhub.com.mo/en/2014/09/05/china-hyway-due-to-deliver-angolas-mocamedes-railroad-in-october/>.

"China's People Daily Online Launches Portuguese-Language Portal." *The Portugal News Online* 8 January 2015. 8 January 2015. <http://theportugalnews.com/news/chinas-peoples-daily-online-launches-portuguese-language-portal/33633>.

"China's Sinopec Buys Marathon's Angola Oil Fields for $ 1.52 billion." *Reuters* 23 June 2013. 14 August 2013. <http://uk.reuters.com/article/2013/06/23/uk-china-cnpc-idUKBRE95M07B20130623>.

"China's Ivory Crush Sends Message." *News.* Wildaid, 6 January 2014. 6 January 2014. <http://www.wildaid.org/news/china%E2%80%99s-ivory-crush-sends-message>.

"Chinese Company Completes Massive Angolan Railway." *Shanghai Daily* 13 August 2014. 14 August 2014. <http://www.shanghaidaily.com/article/article_xinhua.aspx?id=235113>.

"Chinese Demand Helping Angolan Diamond Industry." *Macauhub* 24 May 2010. 16 September 2013. <http://www.macauhub.com.mo/en/2010/05/24/9127/>.

"Chinese Demand Helping Angolan Industry." *Macauhub* 24 April 2010. 11 August 2013. <http://www.macauhub.com.mo/en/2010/05/24/9127/>.

"Chinese Dream is for a Better World." *Mail & Guardian* 20 September 2013. 20 September 2013. <http://mg.co.za/article/2013-09-20-00-chinese-dream-is-for-a-better-world>.

„Chinese Firm Invests $2.4 billion in Post War Angola." *Reuters Africa* 17 August 2009. 25 November 2014. http://af.reuters.com/article/topNews/idAFJOE57G07P20090817.

"Chinese Group Huawei has 42 pct of Angola's Mobile Phone Market." *Macauhub* 17 December 2014. 17 December 2014. <http://www.macauhub.com.mo/en/2014/12/17/chinese-group-huawei-has-42-pct-of-angolas-mobile-phone-market/>.

"Chinese State Company Invests in Agriculture in Angola." *Macauhub* 18 November 2014. 18 November 2014. <http://www.macauhub.com.mo/en/2014/11/18/chinese-state-company-invests-in-agriculture-in-angola/>.

Chorbonneau, Louis and Michelle Nichols. "Exclusive:Russia, China Block Central African Republic Blacklist at UN." *Reuters* 23 April 2014. 24 April 2014. <http://www.reuters.com/article/2014/04/23/us-centralafrica-un-sanctions-idUSBREA3M1GA20140423>.

Chow, Cecilia. "Top Condo Deals of 2013." *The Edge Singapore*, 30 December 2013.

"Chronology for Cabinda in Angola." *University of Maryland Centre for International Development and Conflict Management,* 16 July 2010. 11 August 2013. <http://www.cidcm.umd.edu/mar/chronology.asp?groupId=54003>.

Chu, Kathy. "China Manufacturers Survive By Moving to Asian Neighbors." *The Wall Street Journal* 1 May 2013. 23 March 2014. <http://online.wsj.com/news/articles/SB10001424127887323798104578453073103566416>.

"Clinton Warns against New Colonialism in Africa." *Reuters* 11 June 2011. 13 May 2013. <http://www.reuters.com/article/2011/06/11/us-clinton-africa-idUSTRE75A0RI20110611>.

"Confucius Institute Headquarters Signs Agreements with Agostinho Neto University and CITIC Construction." *Hanban News* 28 March 2014. 5 May 2014. <http://english.hanban.org/article/2014-03/28/content_530183.htm>.

"Contractor to Start Lobito Port Reconstruction." *Dredging Today* 26 November 2012. 15 August 2013. <http://www.dredgingtoday.com/2012/11/26/contractor-to-start-lobito-port-reconstruction-angola/>.

Corkin, Lucy. "All's Fair in Loans and War: The Development of China-Angola Relations." In eds. Kweku Ampiah and Sanusha Naidu.*In Crouching Tiger, Hidden Dragon? Africa and China.* Scottsville: University of KwaZulu-Natal Press, 2008: 108–123.

–. "China and the Macau Forum." *Pambazuka News* 7 May 2009. 15 August 2013. <http://www.pambazuka.org/en/category/africa_china/56116/print>.

–. "China's Contribution to the Development of African Infrastructure through Investment in the Extractive Industries." *AFRODAD Occasional Papers* 8 (2007). 20 April 2013. <http://www.ccs.org.za/downloads/China%20Occasional%20Paper.pdf>.

–. *Uncovering African Agency: Angola's Management of Credit Lines.* London: Ashgate Pub. Co., 2013.

Cossou, Ergon. "Angola's Businesses Beat Most of Europe to 4G Mobile Services." *BBC News* 30 April 2012. 15 August 2013. <http://www.bbc.com/news/business-17898861>.

"Cost of Living in Luanda." *Cost of Living: Angola.* Numbeo, n.d. 19 September 2013. <http://www.numbeo.com/cost-of-living/city_result.jsp?country=Angola&city=Luanda>.

"Cost of Living Survey." *Newsroom: Cost of Living Survey.* Mercer, 23 July 2013. 24 July 2013. <http://www.mercer.com/newsroom/cost-of-living-survey-2013.html>.

"Country Profile: Angola." *Country Profile.* New Agriculturist, July 2009. 21 April 2013. <http://www.newag.info/en/country/profile.php?a=781>.

Criminal Division of the US Department of Justice and the Enforcement Division of the US Securities and Exchange Commission. "A Resource Guide to the US Foreign Corrupt Practices Act." *The United States Department of Justice,* November 2012. 17 September 2013. <http://www.justice.gov/criminal/fraud/fcpa/guidance/>.

Crouigneau, Francoise and Richard Hiault. "Wolfowitz Slams China Banks on Africa Lending." *Financial Times* 23 October 2006. 22 June 2011. <http://www.ft.com/intl/cms/s/0/45e594e0-62fc-11db-8faa 0000779e2340.html#axzz311VCmAUd>.

Das, Goutam. "Made in India." *Business Today* 2 March 2014. 23 March 2014. <http://businesstoday.intoday.in/story/india-benefits-china-begins-to-lose-manufacturing-edge/1/203040.html>.

Dliwayo, Rutendo. "A Continent vs. A Country: China putting strain on Africa's Clothing and Textile Industries." *Consultancy African Intelligence.* 2012.

"Diamond News: Angola to Host Diamond Conference in June." 17 April 2013. *The Israeli Diamond Industry.* 20 November 2013. <http://www.israelidiamond.co.il/english/news.aspx?boneid=918&objId=1286>.

"Diamonds Help Angola to Offset Drop in Oil Prices." *Macau Daily Times* 16 December 2014. 16 December 2014. <http://macaudailytimes.com.mo/diamonds-help-angola-offset-drop-oil-prices.html>.

"Diaoyu Islands Belong to China." *New York Times* 28 September 2012. A:16–17.

Dolan, Kerry. "Daddy's Girl: How an African 'Princess' Bankes $ 3 Billion in a Country Living on $2 a Day." *Forbes* 14 August 2013. 13 October 2013. <http://www.forbes.com/sites/kerryadolan/2013/08/14/how-isabel-dos-santos-took-the-short-route-to-become-africas-richest-woman/2/>.

Dr. Davies, Martyn, et al. *How China Delivers Development Assistance to Africa*. Stellenbosch: Centre for Chinese Studies, 2008.

Dreher, Alex and Andreas Fuchs. "Rogue Aid? The Determinants of China's Aid Allocation." *Working Papers CEB 11-035*, ULB – Universite Libre de Bruxelle,2011.

Drommond, Paulo and Estelle Xue Liu. "If China Sneezes, Africa Can Now Catch a Cold." *IMFdirect* 24 March 2014. 25 Marh 2014. <http://blog-imfdirect.imf.org/2014/03/20/if-china-sneezes-africa-can-now-catch-a-cold/>.

Duyvendak, J. J. L. *China's Discovery of Africa*. Arthur Probsthain: London, 1949.

Edwards, Lawrence and and Rhys Jenkins. "Chinese Competition and the Restructuring of South African Manufacturing." *Dev Research Briefing*, 4 August 2012.

Emmanuel, Vete Willy. "Chinese Investments in Angola." Jauch, Anthony Yaw Baah and Herbert. *Chinese Investments in Africa: A Labour Perspective*. African Labour Research Network, 2009. 366–383.

Enav, Peter. "Gambia Breaks Relations with Surprised Taiwan." *The Associated Press* 15 November 2013. 5 December 2013. <http://bigstory.ap.org/article/gambia-breaks-relations-taiwan>.

Enuka, Chuka. "Aid in Sino-Africa Relations: An Analysis of the Promptings, Pluses and Problems of China's Aid to Africa." *IUP* 55 (2011): 41–53.

"Environment Minister Pledges Greater Attention to Oil Spill." *Agência Angola Press ANGOP* 23 December 2013. 24 December 2013. <http://www.portalangop.co.ao/angola/en_us/noticias/ambiente/2013/11/51/Environment-Minister-pledges-greater-attention-oil-spill,72a0a020-6f59-4ffd-b310-26a86b20bca4.htm>.

"Envirornment Ministry Signs Zoo/Botanic Poject Memo." *Agência Angola Press ANGOP* 4 December 2013. 16 August 2013. <http://www.portalangop.co.ao/angola/en_us/noticias/ambiente/2013/11/49/Environment-Ministry-signs-Zoo-Botanic-Project-Memo,bbae0170-d211-43eb-9434-b411f7eca343.html>.

Escobar, Antonio and Ana Correia da Silva. "Three Decades of China-Angola Cooperation." *Macao Magazine* 15 (2013): 72–85. 19 September 2013. <http://www.macaomagazine.net/index.php?option=com_content&view=article&id=277:three-decades-of-china-angola-cooperation&catid=50:issue15>.

"Evaluating China's FOCAC Commitments to Africa and Mapping the Way Ahead." *Centre for Chinese Studies* (2010). 14 April 2013. <http://www.ccs.org.za/wp-content/uploads/2010/03/ENGLISH-Evaluating-Chinas-FOCAC-commitments-to-Africa-2010.pdf>.

Executive Research Associates (ERA). *China in Africa: A Strategic Overview.* ERA, October 2009. 1 May 2013. <http://www.ide.go.jp/English/Data/Africa_file/Manualreport/pdf/china_all.pdf>.

"Exim Bank Releases USD170 Million for Projects in Angola." *Agência Angola Press ANGOP* 10 May 2014. 10 May 2014. <http://www.portalangop.co.ao/angola/en_us/noticias/economia/2014/4/19/Eximbank-relases-Usd170-million-for-projects-Angola,42355548-b41a-4ab5-976f-7caf43bd251b.html>.

"Feature: Angolan Student Realizing Chinese Dream." *Xinhuanet* 5 May 2014. 5 May 2014. <http://news.xinhuanet.com/english/china/2014-05/05/c_133311725.htm>.

Felino, Isabel. "Angola Inflation Rate." *Trading Economics,* 16 April 2014. 8 May 2014. <http://www.tradingeconomics.com/angola/inflation-cpi>.

Fernandes, Sofia. "China and Angola: A Strategic Partnership." In eds. Marcus Power and Ana Cristina Alves *China and Angola: A Marriage of Convenience?* Cape Town, Dakar, Nairobi and Oxford: Pambazuka Press, 2012. 68–84.

"FILDA 2013." *Welcome to Angola,* 2013. 17 September 2013. <http://www.welcometoangola.co.ao/_filda_2013_3>.

"First Cars Made in Angola to Go On Sale This Year." *Macauhub* 16 October 2007. 19 September 2013. <http://www.macauhub.com.mo/en/2007/10/16/3893>.

Fish Base. *Fish Species in Angola*. n.d. 22 September 2013. <www.fishbase.us>.

Fishel, Michelle Chan. "Environment Impact: More of the Same." In eds. Firoze Manji and Stephen Marks. *The Sinosphere: China in Africa*. London: Institute for Public Policy Research IPPR, 2006. 5–11.

Fishel, Michelle Chan and Roxanne Lawson. "Quid Pro Quo? China's Investment for Resource Swaps in Africa." *Development* 50 (2007):63–68.

Fisher, H.J. "The Cambridge History of Africa c.1050-c.1600." Vol. 3. 1977.

"FM Spokesman: China Continue Offering Aid to Poor African Countries." *People's Daily* 7 July 2005. 11 May 2011. <http://english.people.com.cn/200507/07/eng20050707_194733.html>.

Food and Agriculture Organization of the United Nations (FAO), *AQUASTAT Online Service* 2010. 23 September 2013. <http://www.fao.org/nr/water/aquastat/countries_regions/china/index.stm>.

Forum on China and Africa Cooperation (FOCAC). *China's African Policy*. FOCAC, 12 January 2006. 11 May 2011.

Forum on China and Africa Cooperation. "Fifth Ministerial Conference of the Forum on China-Africa Cooperation Beijing Action Plan (2013–2015)." FOCAC, 2012. 23 May 2013. <http://www.focac.org/eng/zxxx/t954620.htm>.

"Friend or Forager? How China is Winning the Resources and the Loyalties of Africa." *Financial Times* 23 February 2006. 23 September 2013. <http://www.ft.com/intl/cms/s/0/9678cdf4-a412-11da-83cc-0000779e2340.html#axzz32p1snTrA>.

"Full Text of President Jiang's Speech at China-Africa Forum." *People's Daily* 11 October 2000.11 May 2011. <http://english.people.com.cn/english/200010/10/eng20001010_52238.html>.

Gagliardone, Iginio, Maria Repnikova, Nicole Sremlau. "China in Africa: A New Approach to Media Development?" *University of Oxford Programme in Comparative Media Law and Policy*, 2010. 21 June 2013.

Gao, Jinyuan. "China and Africa: The Development of Relations over Many Centuries." *African Affairs* 83:331 (1984): 241–250.

"Global Conglomerate China Sonangol Buys 15 Million OKP Holdings Shares; Move Prepares Groung for Future Business Collaboration." *Joint Press Release by OKP Holdings Limited and China Sonangol*, 2011.

23 September 2013. <http://okp.listedcompany.com/newsroom/20110819_171529_5CF_85E51C02E7F7CB44482578F00030FE16.1.pdf>.

Grobler, John. "Chinese Infrastructure Lubricates Outflow of Angolan and DRC Resources." *Pambazuka News* 10 April 2014. 11 April 2014. <http://www.pambazuka.org/en/category/features/91304>.

Gu, Xuewu. *Theorien der internationalen Beziehungen: Einführung*. München: Oldenbourg, 2010.

"Half of Angola's Exports are Sent to China." *Macauhub* 12 November 2012. 1 June 2013. <http://www.macauhub.com.mo/en/2012/11/12/half-of-angola%E2%80%99s-exports-are-sent-to-china/>.

"Head of State Inaugurates Moçâmedes Railway Station in Menongue." *Agência Angola Press ANGOP* 26 August 2012. 15 August 2013. <http://www.portalangop.co.ao/angola/en_us/noticias/politica/2012/7/34/Head-State-inaugurates-Mocamedes-Railway-station-Menongue,f2621ea8-d13d-42d4-ad85-f97f8cc732ac.html>.

Hilsum, Lindsey. "China and Africa and the G8-or Why Bob Geldord Needs to Wake up." In eds. Leni Wild and David Mepham. *The Sinosphere: China in Africa*. London: Institute for Public Policy Research IPPR, 2006. 5–11.

Hirth, Friedrich. *China and the Roman Orient: Researches into their Ancient and Medieval Relations*. Shanghai, 1885.

Hon et al. "Evaluating China's FOCAC commitments to Africa and Mapping the Way Ahead." *Report by the Centre for Chinese studies at Stellenbosch University*. 2010.

"Hub Role for Angola." *Sonangol Universo*, 2013.

Ibp US. *Angola Jose Eduardo Dos Santos Handbook*. Washington DC: International Business Publications, 2013.

"Isabel dos Santos, Daughter of Angola's President, is Africa's First Billionaire." *Forbes* 23 January 2013. 23 April 2013. <http://www.forbes.com/sites/kerryadolan/2013/01/23/isabel-dos-santos-daughter-of-angolas-president-is-africas-first-woman-billionaire/>.

Jansson, Johanna. "Chinese Investment in Gabon's Extractive Industries." *Pambazuka News* 2010. 1 July 2014. <http://www.pambazuka.org/en/category/africa_china/65779>.

"Japan Summit Promotes 'Vibrant Africa'." *UN Africa Renewal*,2008.

Jiali, Guo. "China Refutes Ghost City Allegation." *China.org.cn.* 4 July 2012. 5 September 2013. <http://www.china.org.cn/business/2012-07/04/content_25808562.htm>.

Jing, Li. "Changing the Face of Real Estate in Angola." *China Daily* 17 November 2014. 17 November 2014. <http://usa.chinadaily.com.cn/business/2014-11/17/content_18926287.htm>.

"Jose Eduardo Dos Santos." *BrainyQuote.com. Xplore Inc,* 2015. 18 January 2015. <http://www.brainyquote.com/quotes/quotes/j/joseeduard178683.html>.

Joubert, Marie Sophie. "Sarkozy in Angola to Mend Ties." *France 24* 24 October 2008. 23 September 2013. <http://www.france24.com/en/20080523-sarkozy-angola-mend-ties-angola-france/?quicktabs_1=1>.

Kagan, Robert. "What China Knows and We Don't: The Case for a New Strategy of Containment," *The Weekly Standard,* 20 January 1997: 22–27.

Kane, Alan. "Angola." *Centre for Affordable Housing Finance in Africa,* 2014. 21 August 2014 <http://www.housingfinanceafrica.org/country/angola/>.

Kaplinsky, Raphael, Dorothy McCormick and Mike Morris. "China and Sub Saharan Africa: Impacts and Challenges of a Growing Relationship." *SAIS Working Papers in African Studies,* 2008.

Karl, Terry L. *The Paradox of Plenty: Oil Boom and Petro States.* Berkeley: University of California Press, 1997.

Kelkar, Mugdha S. "Reopening of Benguela Railway Brings Economic Hope to Angola." *The National Law Review* 29 January 2015. 30 January 2015. <http://www.natlareview.com/article/reopening-benguela-railway-brings-economic-hope-to-angola>.

"Kenyan Girl Offered Chance to Go to College in China." *Xinhua News Agency* 20 March 2005. 11 May 2011. <http://news.xinhuanet.com/english/2005-03/20/content_2719001.htm>.

"Kilamba City Flats Sold Out." *Agência Angola Press (ANGOP)* 4 September 2013. 5 September 2013. <http://www.portalangop.co.ao/angola/en_us/noticias/sociedade/2013/8/36/Kilamba-City-flats-sold-out,9a874ce7-f6fa-4f25-b35a-9d888d4c07d4.html>.

Kim, Samuel S. "China and Globalization: Confronting Myriad Challenges and Opportunities." *Asian Perspective* 33.3 (2009): 41–80.

King, Kenneth. *China's Aid and Soft Power in Africa: In Case of Education and Training*. New York: James Currey, 2013.

Klare, Michael and Daniel Volman. "The African Oil Rush and American National Security." *Third World Quarterly* 27.4 (2006): 609–628.

Kobayashi, Takaaki. "Evolution of China's Aid Policy." *JBIC Institute (JBICI)* 27 (2008): 1–56.

Kopinski, Dominik, Andrej Polus and Ian Taylor. *China's Rise in Africa: Perspectives on a Developing Connection*. Routledge: New York. 2013.

Kotch, Nicholas. "China 'Like a Brother' to Africa, Says Former Envoy as US Summit Approaches." *Business Day Live* 30 April 2014. 30 April 2014. <http://www.bdlive.co.za/africa/africanbusiness/2014/04/30/china-like-a-brother-to-africa-says-former-envoy-as-us-summit-approaches>.

"Learn More about Trade in Angola." *Profile*. The Observatory of Economic Complexity (Harvard HKS/CDI –MIT Media Lab),2012.1 June 2014. <http://atlas.media.mit.edu/profile/country/ago/>.

Lee Levkovitz, Marta McLellan, J.R. Warner. "The 88 Queensway Group: A Case Study in Chinese Investors' Operations in Angola and Beyond." 2009.

Lee, Yvonne. "Sinopec to Acquire Angolan Oil Assets." *The Wall Street Journal* 29 March 2013. 13 August 2013. <http://online.wsj.com/news/articles/SB10001424052702303429804575149714050757630>.

Levin, Dan. "China Bans Import of Ivory Carvings for One Year." The New York Times 26 February 2015. 26 February 2015. <http://www.nytimes.com/2015/02/27/world/asia/china-bans-import-of-ivory-carvings-for-one-year.html?smid=tw-nytimes&_r=0>.

Liangxiu, Zhu. "The Chinese in Africa: Trying to Pull Together." *The Economist* 20 April 2011. 17 August 2013. <http://www.economist.com/node/18586448>.

"List of Projects: Shipping." n.d. *China Sonangol*. <http://www.chinasonangol.com/transportation.html>.

"Loan from China Development Bank to Sonangol is Sign of the Close Relationship Between Angola and China." *Macauhub* 11 March 2013. 20 April 2013. <http://www.macauhub.com.mo/en/2013/03/11/loan-from-china-development-bank-to-sonangol-is-a-sign-of-the-%E2%80%9Cclose-relationship%E2%80%9D-between-angola-and-china/>.

Lum, Thomas. "China's Assistance and Government-Sponsored Investment Activities in Africa, Latin America and Southeast Asia." *FAS Congressional Research Service Reports*, 25 November 2009. 11 May 2011.

Lyman, Princeton. "China's Rising Role in Africa." *Council on Foreign Relations,* 21 June 2005. 4 July 2014. <http://www.cfr.org/china/chinas-rising-role-africa/p8436>.

Malaquias, Assis. "China is Angola's New Best Friend-for Now." In eds. Marcus Power and Ana Cristina Alves. *China and Angola: A Marriage of Convenience.* Cape Town, Dakar, Nairobi and Oxford: Pambazuka Press, 2012. 26–44.

"Marathon Oil Announces US$1.5 Billion Sale of Interest in Angola Block 31." *Press Releases.* Marathon Oil Corporation, 25 June 2013. 23 September 2013. <http://ir.marathonoil.com/releasedetail.cfm?ReleaseID=773689>.

"Marathon Oil Strikes $1.5 Billion Deal." *Businessweek* 26 June 2013. 27 June 2013. <http://www.businessweek.com/ap/2013-06-26/marathon-oil-strikes-1-dot-5-billion-deal>.

Marks, Stephan. Introduction. *African Perspectives on China in Africa.* In eds. Firoze Manji and Stephan Marks. Nairobi and Oxford: Fahamu/Pambazuka News, 2007. 1–14.

Matias, José Carlos. "Macao, China and Portuguese Speaking Countries." *Macao Magazine* 4 (2010): 6–20. 17 September 2013. <http://www.macaomagazine.net/index.php?option=com_content&view=article&id=90:macao-china-and-portuguese-speaking-countries&catid=39:issue-4>.

McClelland, Colin and Manuel Soque. "Angolan Law Compelling Kwanza Use to Boost Economy, Massano Says." *Bloomberg News* 4 July 2013. 21 September 2013. <http://www.bloomberg.com/news/2013-07-04/angolan-law-compelling-kwanza-use-to-boost-economy-massano-says.html>.

–. "Angola Faces Budget Crunch on Falling Oil Price, Dos Santos Says." *Bloomberg News* 15 December 2014.15 December 2014. <http://www.bloomberg.com/news/2014-10-15/angola-faces-budget-crunch-on-falling-oil-price-dos-santos-says.html>.

–. "Angola May Cut Funding for HIV Prevention As Oil Prices Fall." *Bloomberg News* 9 December 2014, Date Accessed: 15 December

2014. <http://www.bloomberg.com/news/2014-12-08/angola-may-cut-funding-for-hiv-prevention-as-oil-prices-decline.html>.

McClelland, Colin. "Angola Plans 20 Year Kwanza Bond Sales to Boost Central Bank." *Bloomberg News* 31 January 2014. 31 July 2014. <http://www.bloomberg.com/news/2014-01-31/angola-plans-20-year-kwanza-bond-sales-to-boost-central-bank-1-.html>.

–. "Angola to Raise Power Output Fivefold to Attract Investors." *Bloomberg News* 4 October 2013. 5 October 2013. <http://www.bloomberg.com/news/2013-10-03/angola-plans-to-raise-power-output-fivefold-to-attract-investors.html>.

"Media Minister Ends Visit to China." *Agência Angola Press ANGOP* 23 June 2014. 23 June 2014. <http://www.portalangop.co.ao/angola/en_us/noticias/sociedade/2014/5/26/Media-Minister-ends-visit-China,31407300-f367-47cf-b3f0-98e99020e77d.html>.

"Medium Banks Challenge South African Dominance." *African Business* 16 October 2012. 21 September 2013. <http://africanbusinessmagazine.com/special-reports/medium-banks-challenge-south-african-dominance/>.

"Meet China's Folk Star First Lady in Waiting." *The Wall Street Journal* 13 February 2012. 21 June 2013. <http://blogs.wsj.com/chinarealtime/2012/02/13/peng-liyuan-meet-chinas-folk-song-singing-first-lady-in-waiting>.

Mensah, Paul Opoku. "China and the International Aid System: Transformation or Cooptation." Li Xing ed. *The Rise of China and the Capitalist World Order*. Burlington: Ashgate Publishing Ltd., 2010. 71–86.

"Milhares de Empresarios Chineses Pretenden Investir No Pais." *Jornal de Angola* 17 November 2007. 17 September 2013. <http://jornaldeangola.sapo.ao/economia/milhares-de-empresarios-chineses-pretenden-investir-no-pais>.

Miller, Jeff. "China Seeks Angola Rough Trade Exchange by 1Q06." *Rapaport* 13 December 2005. 15 September 2013. <http://www.diamonds.net/News/NewsItem.aspx?ArticleID=13860>.

"Mobile Phone Users Reach 14 Million in 2017." *Agência Angola Press ANGOP* 31 October 2013. 15 August 2013. <http://www.portalangop.co.ao/angola/en_us/noticias/ciencia-e-tecnologia/2013/9/44/Mobile-phone-users-reach-million-2017,585c0a1c-fb27-4fe7-addb-43b37718f5aa.html>.

"Moçâmedes Railway Project." *Subordinate Corporate*. China Hyway Group (中国浩远), n.d. 15 August 2013. <http://www.hyway-china.com/En_aboutHY.asp?lm=45&newsid=37>.

Moise, Tal. "Leviev Sells Angola Diamond Mine Stake." *Globes* 29 May 2011. 19 August 2013. <http://www.globes.co.il/en/article-1000649762>.

Montesqieu, Charles de Secondat Baron de. *Montesqieu: The Sprit of Laws*. Cambridge: Cambridge University Press,1989.

Moody, Andrew. "More China, Less Bono is Prescription." *China Daily* 22 March 2013. 23 March 2013. <http://africa.chinadaily.com.cn/weekly/2013-03/22/content_16335831.htm>.

Morais, Rafael Marques de. "The New Imperialism: China in Angola." *World Affairs,* 2011.4 July 2014. <http://www.worldaffairsjournal.org/article/new-imperialism-china-angola>.

Moravcsik, Andrew and Kalypso Nicolaidis. "Explaining the Treaty of Amsterdam: Interests, Influence, Institutions." *Journal of Common Market Studies* 37.1 (1999): 59–85.

Moravcsik, Andrew and Milada Anna Vachudova. "Preferences, Power and ...Equilibrium. The Causes and Consequences of EU enlargement." In eds. Frank Schimmelfennig and Ulrich Sedelmeier. *The Politics of European Union Enlargement. Theoretical Approaches*. London: Routledge, 2005. 198–212.

Moravcsik, Andrew. "Taking Preferences Seriously:A Liberal Theory of International Politics." *International Organization* 51.4 (1997): 513–553.

–. "Liberal International Relations Theory: A Scientific Asessment." In eds. Colin Elman and Miriam Fendius Elman. *Progress in International Relations Theory: Appraising the Field*. Cambridge: MIT Press, 2003: 159–204.

–. "The New Liberalism." In eds. Reus-Smit, Christian and Duncan Snidal. *The Oxford Handbook of International Relations*. Oxford: Oxford University Press, 2010: 234–254.

Moyo, Dambisa. *Dead Aid: Warum Entwicklungshilfe nicht funktioniert und was Afrika besser machen kann*. Berlin: Haffmans&Tolkemitt, 2011.

Mpofu, George. "Angola to Boost Energy Output with $1bn Power Plant." *Ventures Africa* 12 January 2015. 13 January 2015. <http://www.ventures-africa.com/2015/01/angola-to-boost-energy-output-with-1bn-power-plant/>.

Murray, Laura Rena, et. al. "African Safari: CIF's Grab for Oil and Minerals." *Caixin Online* 17 October 2011. 23 September 2013. <http://english.caixin.com/2011-10-17/100314766.html>.

Muzima, Joel & Domingos Mazivila. "Angola 2014." *African Economic Outlook*. 2014

"MWC: Huawei Wins Movicel LTE Contract." *CommsMEA* 27 February 2012. 15 August 2013. <http://www.commsmea.com/11957-mwc-huawei-wins-movicel-lte contract/?utm_source=twitterfeed&utm_medium=twitter#.UpUlm8Q2bRs>.

Nan, Zhong. "Power Giants work on Local Touch." *China Daily* 20 December 2013. 21 December 2013. <http://africa.chinadaily.com.cn/weekly/2013-12/20/content_17187099.htm>.

"Never too Late to Scramble." *The Economist* 26 October 2006. 23 March 2013. <http://www.economist.com/node/8089719>.

"Obama Looks for Partnership with Africa." *The BRICS Post* 6 August 2014. 6 August 2014 <http://thebricspost.com/obama-looks-for-partnership-with-africa>.

"Oil Accounts for Smaller Portion of Angola's GDP as Production in Other Sectors Increases." *Macauhub* 7 November 2014.7 November 2014. <http://www.macauhub.com.mo/en/2014/11/07/oil-accounts-for-smaller-portion-of-angolas-gdp-as-production-in-other-sectors-increases/>.

"Oil Sector Gains Environmental Monitoring." *Agência Angola Press ANGOP* 2 January 2014. 3 January 2014. <http://www.portalangop.co.ao/angola/en_us/noticias/ambiente/2014/0/1/Oil-sector-gains-environmental-monitoring,dafeec95-7eb0-4bd3-bcc6-56adba18f61b.html>.

Oliveira, Ricardo Soares de. "Business Success, Angola-Style:Postcolonial Politics and the Rise of Sonangol." *F. of Modern African Studies* 45.4 (2007): 595–619.

Onjala, Joseph. "A Scoping Study on China-Africa Economic Relations: The Case of Kenya." *African Economic Research Consortium (AERC)*. 5 March 2008.

Osava, Mario. "Building the New Angola: How Chinese and Brazilian Firms Rise Up to the Challenge." *Newstime Africa* 30 November 2012. 15 August 2013. <http://www.newstimeafrica.com/archives/29924>.

"Over 1000 Sinotruk Tractors Export to Angola." *ChinaTrucks.com* 13 October 2014. 13 October 2014 <http://www.chinatrucks.com/news/2014/1013/article_5468.html>.

Page, Jeremy. "China Swoons over New First Lady." *The Wall Street Journal* 22 March 2013. 21 June 2013. <http://online.wsj.com/news/articles/SB10001424127887324103504578376201701604218>.

"País Terá Informações Precias Sobre Potencialidade Mineira." *Agência Angola Press ANGOP* 19 November 2013. 20 November 2013. <http://www.portalangop.co.ao/angola/pt_pt/noticias/economia/2013/10/47/Pais-tera-informacoes-precisas-sobre-potencialidade-mineira,ede0b0ec-40dd-47bd-95af-f73f6459981f.html>.

Peng, Cui. "China Now Africa's Largest Trading Partner." *People's Daily Online* 18 November 2011. 27 November 2011. <http://english.peopledaily.com.cn/90778/7649195.html>.

Penhelt, Gernot. "The Political Economy of China's Aid Policy in Africa." *Jena Economic Research Paper n°2007-05*. 2007.

Perry, Alex. "A Conversation with Rwandan President Paul Kagame." *Time* 27 September 2007. 20 February 2014. <http://content.time.com/time/magazine/article/0,9171,1666064,00.html>.

"Portugal Indebted Angola after Economic Reversal of Fortune." *The Guardian* 3 June 2014. 4 June 2014. <http://www.theguardian.com/world/2014/jun/03/portugal-economy-bailout-angola-invests>.

Power, Marcus and Giles Mohan."Towards a Critical Geopolitics of China's Engagement with African Development." *Geopolitics* 15.3 (2010): 462–495.

"President Opens USD 8 Million Luanda General Hospital." *Agência Angola Press ANGOP* 3 February 2006. 5 September 2013. <http://www.portalangop.co.ao/angola/en_us/noticias/sociedade/President-Opens-USD-Million-Luanda-General-Hospital,42eba8a0-3295-4017-8785-c03e78d049b3.html>.

Qichen, Qian. *Ten Episodes in China's Diplomacy*. New York: HarperCollins, 2005.

"Queensway Syndicate and the Africa Trade." *The Economist* 13 August 2011. 18 August 2013. <http://www.economist.com/node/21525847>.

"Racing Abroad: While China Remains a Major Recipient of Foreign Investments, Its Firms are Making an Increasing Number of Big Acquisitions Abroad." *New York Times* 26 August 2011. Section A: 16–17. (Advertisement).

Raine, Sarah. *China's African Challenges*. New York: Routledge, 2009.

Redvers, Louise. "Angola's Chinese-Built Ghost Town." *BBC News* 2 July 2012. 15 August 2013. <http://www.bbc.co.uk/news/world-africa-18646243>.

–. "Angola's Trophy City a 'Ghost Town'." *Mail & Guardian* 23 November 2012. 16 August 2013. <http://mg.co.za/print/2012-11-23-00-angolan-trophy-city-a-ghost town%E2%80%8E>.

"Realize Your Potential: Annual Report 2006." *Annual Reports*. Huawei Technologies Co., Ltd., 2006. 15 August 2013. <http://www.huawei.com/ucmf/groups/public/documents/annual_report/092583.pdf>.

"Resurgent Textile Industry Helps Diversify Angola's Economy." *Macauhub* 4 August 2014. 4 August 2014. <http://www.macauhub.com.mo/en/2014/08/04/resurgent-textile-industry-helps-diversify-angola%E2%80%99s-economy/>.

Ribeiro, Jose. "Casas do Kilamba: A Bolha e as Cataratas." *Jornal de Angola* 10 November 2012. 16 August 2013. <http://jornaldeangola.sapo.ao/-127638>.

"Rice Production in Angola's Kuando Kubango Province Funded by Credit Line from China." *Macauhub* 5 June 2014. 5 June 2014. <http://www.macauhub.com.mo/en/2014/06/05/rice-production-in-angola%E2%80%99s-kuando-kubango-province-funded-by-credit-line-from-china/>.

Robertberg, Robert I. ed. *China into Africa: Trade, Aid and Influence*. Baltimore: Brookings Institution Press, 2008.

Rongxia, Li. "Significance of Zheng He's Voyages." *Beijing Review* 28 May 2005. 11 June 2012 <http://www.bjreview.cn/EN/En-2005/05-28-e/china-2.htm>.

Roth, Kenneth. "China's Silence Boost Tyrants." *International Herald Tribune*, 19 April 2006. 1 July 2014. <http://www.iht.com/articles/2006/04/19/opinion/edroth.php>.

"Route to Riches: The Lobito Corridor." *Sonangol Universo* (2013): 24–31.

Salvaterra, Neanda. "Angola Looks to China as Oil Sales to US Decline." *The Wall Street Journal* 13 May 2013. 13 August 2013. <http://online.wsj.com/news/articles/SB10001424127887323716304578481402547990718>.

Sautman, Barry and Yan Hairong. "Friends and Interests: China's Distinctive Links Friends and Interests: China's Distinctive Links with Africa." *African Studies Review* 50.3 (2007):75–114.

"Seventeen New Industrial Units to Start Operating in 2012 in Angola's Luanda/Benga Special Economic Zone." *Macauhub* 30 May 2011. 19 September 2013. <http://www.macauhub.com.mo/en/2011/05/30/seventeen-new-industrial-units-to-start-operating-in-2012-in-angola%E2%80%99s-luandabenga-special-economic-zone/>.

Sheehan, Sean. *Cultures of the World: Angola*. New York: Marshall Cavendish Benchmark, 2010.

Sheltin, Garth and Claude Kabemba, eds. *Win-Win Partnership: China, Southern Africa and the Extractive Industries*. Johannesburg: Southern Africa Research Watch, 2012.

"Sinopec Acquires Overseas Oil and Gas Assets for the First Time." *News*. SIONPEC, 26 March 2010. 18 August 2013. <http://sipc.sinopec.com/sipc/en/news/com_news/20100803/news_20100803_602117800000.shtml>.

"Sinopec's First Acquisition of Overseas Upstream Assets." *News*. SINOPEC, 28 March 2010. 13 August 2013. <http://english.sinopec.com/media_center/news/20100329/download/en-news100329d.pdf>.

Snow, Philip. *The Star Raft: China's Encounter with Africa*. New York: Weidenfeld&Nicolson, 1988.

"Sonangol 35 Year Milestone of Success Beckons." *Sonangol Universo* (2010): 36–39. 13 August 2013. <http://www.sonangol.co.uk/wps/wcm/connect/c4b95a00475d1922ac54fd7c37a37d2d/SU28-web.pdf?MOD=AJPERES>.

"Sonangol Rubrica Acordo Para Desenvolvimento de Refinaria do Lobito." *Agência Angola Press ANGOP* 16 March 2006. 30 August 2013. <http://www.portalangop.co.ao/angola/pt_pt/noticias/economia/2006/2/11/Sonangol-rubrica-acordo-para-desenvolvimento-refinaria-Lobito,4fd78bb4-05cd-47c7-a212-b184d8efb6b2.html>.

Sous, Manuel de. "Novo Aeroporto Orgulha África." *Jornal de Angola* 17 May 2012. 15 August 2013. <http://jornaldeangola.sapo.ao/politica/novo_aeroporto_orgulha_africa>.

Steiler, Ilona. *The European Union and China in Africa: Explaining Conflict and Cooperation with International Relations Theory*. Hamburg: Verlag Dr. Kovač, 2009.

"Taag com Dois Voos Semanais para China." *Portal de Angola* 24 September 2013. 25 September 2013. <http://www.portaldeangola.com/2013/09/taag-com-dois-voos-semanais-para-china/>.

Tang, Xiaoyang. "Bulldozer of Locomotive? The Impact of Chinese Enterprises on the Local Employment in Angola and the DRC." *Journal of Asian and African Studies* 45.3 (2010): 350–368.

Taylor, Ian. *China and Africa: Engagement and Compromise.* London: Routledge, xxxxxx2006.

–. *China's New Role in Africa.* London: Lynne Rienner Publishers, 2009.

"The World Bank: Classification of Countries." *The World Bank Data,* July 2012. 8 May 2014. <http://data.worldbank.org/about/country-classifications/country-and-lending-groups>.

"Three Men Jailed in China Vast Ivory Smuggling Operation." *Wildlife Extra,* May 2013. 23 September 2013. <http://www.wildlifeextra.com/go/news/ivory-smuggling-arrest.html#cr>.

Tran, Mark. "China Pulls Out Of Aid Partnership." *The Guardian* 29 November 2011. 1 June 2013. <http://www.theguardian.com/world/2011/nov/29/china-pulls-out-aid-partnership-bUSn?intcmp=239>.

"Transparency and Accountability in Angola." *Human Rights Watch,* 2010. 13 February 2014. <http://www.hrw.org/sites/default/files/reports/angola0410webwcover_1.pdf>.

"Two Projects of CRBC in Cambodia and Angola Win 2012 CCCC High Quality Project Awards." *China Road and Bridge Corporation (中国路桥工程有限责任公司),* 9 January 2013. 15 August 2013. <http://www.crbc.com/site/crbcEN/achievenments/info/2013/1571.html>.

U.S Energy Information Administration. *US Crude Oil Production on Track to Surpass Imports for First Time Since 1995.* EIA, 20 March 2013. 21 March 2013. <http://www.eia.gov/todayinenergy/detail.cfm?id=10451>.

U.S Energy Information Administration. *A Report on Angola.* EIA, February 2014. 20 April 2014. <http://www.eia.gov/countries/analysisbriefs/Angola/angola.pdf>.

US Energy Information Administration. *U.S Imports of Angola of Crude Oil.* EIA, 29 April 2014. 30 April 2014. <http://www.eia.gov/dnav/pet/hist/LeafHandler.ashx?n=PET&s=MCRIMUSO1&f=M>.

"US GAO-Sub-Saharan Africa: Case Studies of U.S and Chinese Economic Engagement in Angola, Ghana, and Kenya; a Supplement to GAO-13-199." *United States Government Accountability Office,* February 2013. 14 May 2014. <http://www.gao.gov/assets/660/652043.pdf>.

U.S Geological Survey (USGS). "Copper Data 2013." USGS Mineral Commodity Summaries, February 2014: 48–49. <http://minerals.usgs.gov/minerals/pubs/commodity/copper/mcs-2014-coppe.pdf>.

U.S State Department Bureau of Economic and Business Affairs. *2013 Investment Climate Statement-Angola*. 2013. 21 September 2013 <http://www.state.gov/e/eb/rls/othr/ics/2013/204590.htm>.

"UN Report: China Becoming Major Investor Abroad." *People Daily* 7 January 2014. 12 April 2014. <http://english.peopledaily.com.cn/200401/07/eng20040107_132003.shtml>.

"US: China Lacks Morals in Africa." *AlJazeera* 9 December 2010. 30 June 2013. <http://www.aljazeera.com/news/africa/2010/12/201012981346664660.html>.

Vaughan, Adam. "Jacki Chan: Chinese Attitudes to Illegal Wildlife Products are Changing." *The Guardian* 13 February 2014. 14 February 2014. <http://www.theguardian.com/environment/2014/feb/13/jackie-chan-chinese-attitudes-illegal-wildlife-products-change>.

Vines, Alex & Campos, Indira. "Angola and China: A Pragmatic Partnership." *Centre for Strategic and International Studies* (2008).

Vines, Alex. "Angola: Looking Beyond Elections." *European Union Institute for Security Studies*, October 2008. 19 September 2013. <http://www.iss.europa.eu/uploads/media/Angola_looking_beyond_elections.pdf.>.

–. "China in Africa: A Mixed Blessing." *Current History* (2007): 213–219.

Weimar, Markus and Alex Vines. "China's Angolan Oil Deals." In eds. Marcus Power and Ana Cristina Alves. *China and Angola: A Marriage of Convenience*. Cape Town, Dakar, Nairobi and Oxford: Pambazuka Press, 2012.

Walters, Denine. "Diamond Mining in Angola: Enter China and South Africa." *Consultancy Africa Intelligence,* 18 July 2011.31 March 2013. <http://www.consultancyafrica.com/index.php?option=com_content&view=article&id=795:diamond-mining-in-angola-enter-china-and-south-africa&catid=82:african-industry-a-business&Itemid=266>.

Watts, Jonathan. "Chinese Ability to Feed Its People Questioned by UN Expert." *The Guardian* 23 December 2010. 23 September 2013.

Weimar, Markus and Alex Vines. "China's Angola Oil Deals 2003-11." In eds. Marcus, Power and Ana Cristina Alves. *China and Angola: A Marriage of Convenience*. Cape Town, Dakar, Nairobi and Oxford, 2012. 85–104.

"Who is Afraid of Huawei." *The Economist* 3 August 2012. 15 August 2013. <http://www.economist.com/node/21559922>.

"Who is Benefiting from Trade Liberalization in Angola?: A Gender Perspective." *Publications*. UNCTAD, 2013. 13 February 2014. <http://unctad.org/en/PublicationsLibrary/ditc2013d3_en.pdf>.

Wild, Leni and Mepham David, eds. *The New Sinosphere: China in Africa*. London: Institute for Public Policy research-IPPR, 2006.

Wing, Arne and Ivar Kolstadt. "Opinion: Is Oil-Rich Angola a Development Success?" *CNN* 30 August 2012. 23 September 2013. <http://edition.cnn.com/2012/08/30/opinion/opinion-angola-development-elections/>.

Winter, Russ. "China Maneuvers to Take Away US' Dominant Reserve Currency Status." *Seeking Alpha* 27 July 2013. 23 March 2014. <http://seekingalpha.com/article/1578602-china-maneuvers-to-take-away-u-s-dominant-reserve-currency-status>.

World Bank. *Angola: Public Expenditure Management and Financial Accountability*. 16 February 2005. 31 May 2014. <http://www-wds.worldbank.org/external/default/WDSContentServer/WDSP/IB/2005/03/10/000090341_20050310101310/Rendered/PDF/290360AO.pdf>

World Bank. *Doing Business Report 2014:Understanding Regulation for Small and Medium-Size Enterprises*. Washington DC: World Bank Group, 2013.

Wu, Yuan. *China and Africa (1956–2006)*. Beijing: China Intercontinental Press, 2008.

Xing, Li. *The Rise of China and the Capitalist World Order*. Burlington: Ashgate Publishing Ltd., 2010.

Yin, Beibei. "Chinese Investment in Tanzania Bears Bitter Fruit." *The Guardian* 2 March 2012. 23 September 2013. <http://www.theguardian.com/global-development/2012/mar/02/chinese-investment-tanzania-airport-eviction>.

York, Geoffrey. "Why China is Making a Big Play to Control Africa's Media." *The Globe and Mail* 11 September 2013. 13 September 2013. <http://www.theglobeandmail.com/news/world/media-agenda-china-buys-newsrooms-influence-in-africa/article14269323/>.

Zafar, Ali. "The Growing Relationship between China and SSA: Macroeconomic, Trade Investment and Aid Links." *World Bank Research Observer* 22.1 (2007):103–130.

Zhao, Shelly. “The China-Angola Partnership: A Case Study Of China’s Oil Relations in Africa.” *China Briefing* 25 May 2011. 11 August 2013. <http://www.china-briefing.com/news/2011/05/25/the-china-angola-partnership-a-case-study-of-chinas-oil-relationships-with-african-nations.html>.

Zhejiang, Zhang. “China’s Globalisation and Its Policies: Focusing on Sino-American Relations.” *Journal of Rotsumeikan Social Sciences and Humanities* (2009): 85–112.

“Zhou Enlai Announces Eight Principles.” *China Daily* 13 August 2010. 11 May 2011. <http://www.chinadaily.com.cn/china/2010-08/13/content_11149131.htm>.

“ZTE Lands Angola Network Deal.” *Shenzhen Daily* 28 July 2005. 15 August 2013. <http://www.china.org.cn/english/BAT/136508.htm>.

“ZTE to deploy its FIrst Commercial African WiMAX Network.” *Total Telecom* 14 October 2005. 15 August 2013. <http://www.totaltele.com/view.aspx?ID=441981>.

Zweig, David and Bi Jianhai. “China’s Global Hunt for Energy.” *Foreign Affairs*. 2005.

“第一夫人着装大气受赞誉例外就彭丽媛服饰发公告.” *Guhantai*（古汉台）30 March 2013. 21 June 2013. <http://news.guhantai.com/2013/0330/222106.shtml>.

“以无私援助　求共同发展——新中国六十年援外工作纪实.” *China Daily (中国日报)* 13 August 2010. 11 May 2011. <http://www.chinadaily.com.cn/dfpd/2010-08/13/content_11147495.htm>.

Appendices

Appendix 1: China's African Policy

January 2006

Foreword

The first few years of the new century witness a continuation of complex and profound changes in the international situation and further advance of globalization. Peace and development remain the main themes of our times. Safeguarding peace, promoting development and enhancing cooperation, which are the common desire of all peoples, represent the irresistible historical trend. On the other hand, destabilizing factors and uncertainties in the international situation are on the rise. Security issues of various kinds are interwoven. Peace remains evasive and development more pressing.

China, the largest developing country in the world, follows the path of peaceful development and pursues an independent foreign policy of peace. China stands ready to develop friendly relations and cooperation with all countries on the basis of the Five Principles of Peaceful Coexistence so as to contribute to peace, stability and common prosperity around the world.

The African continent, which encompasses the largest number of developing countries, is an important force for world peace and development. China-Africa traditional friendly relations face fresh opportunities under the new circumstances. With this African Policy Paper, the Chinese Government wishes to present to the world the objectives of China's policy toward Africa and the measures to achieve them, and its proposals for cooperation in various fields in the coming years, with a view of promoting the steady growth of China-Africa relations in the long term and bringing the mutually-beneficial cooperation to a new stage.

Part I: Africa's Position and Role

Africa has a long history, vast expanse of land, rich natural resources and huge potential for development. After long years of struggle, the African people freed themselves from colonial rule, wiped out apartheid, won independence and emancipation, thus making significant contribution to the progress of civilization.

Following their independence, countries in Africa have been conscientiously exploring a road to development suited to their national conditions and seeking peace, stability and development by joint efforts. Thanks to the concerted efforts of African countries and the Organization of African Unity (OAU)/the African Union (AU), the political situation in Africa has been stable on the whole, regional conflicts are being gradually resolved and economy has been growing for years. The New Partnership for Africa's Development (NEPAD) has drawn up an encouraging picture of African rejuvenation and development. African countries have actively participated in the South-South cooperation and worked for the North-South dialogue. They are playing an increasingly important role in international affairs.

Africa still faces many challenges on its road of development. However, with the persistent efforts of African countries and the continuous support of the international community, Africa will surely surmount difficulties and achieve rejuvenation in the new century.

Part II: China's Relations with Africa

China-Africa friendship is embedded in the long history of interchange. Sharing similar historical experience, China and Africa have all along sympathized with and supported each other in the struggle for national liberation and forged a profound friendship.

The founding of the People's Republic of China and the independence of African countries ushered in a new era in China-Africa relations. For over half a century, the two sides have enjoyed close political ties and frequent exchanges of high-level visits and people-to-people contacts. Bilateral trade and economic cooperation have grown rapidly; cooperation in other fields has yielded good results; and consultation and coordination in international affairs have been intensified. China has provided assistance to the best of its ability to African countries, while African countries have also rendered strong support to China on many occasions.

Sincerity, equality and mutual benefit, solidarity and common development - these are the principles guiding China-Africa exchanges and cooperation and the driving force to lasting China-Africa relations.

Part III: China's African Policy

Enhancing solidarity and cooperation with African countries has always been an important component of China's independent foreign policy of peace. China will unswervingly carry forward the tradition of China-Africa friendship. Proceeding from the fundamental interests of both the Chinese and African peoples, China will establish and develop a new type of strategic partnership with Africa which features political equality and mutual trust, economic win-win cooperation and cultural exchange. The general principles and objectives of China's African policy are as follows:

- Sincerity, friendship and equality. China adheres to the Five Principles of Peaceful Coexistence, respects African countries' independent choice of the road of development and supports African countries' efforts to grow stronger through unity.
- Mutual benefit, reciprocity and common prosperity. China supports African countries' endeavor for economic development and nation building, carries out cooperation in various forms in the economic and social development, and promotes common prosperity of China and Africa.
- Mutual support and close coordination. China will strengthen cooperation with Africa in the United Nations and other multilateral systems by supporting each other's just demand and reasonable propositions and continue to appeal to the international community to give more attention to questions concerning peace and development in Africa.
- Learning from each other and seeking common development. China and Africa will learn from and draw upon each other's experience in governance and development, strengthen exchanges and cooperation in education, science, culture and health. Supporting African countries' efforts to enhance capacity building, China will work together with Africa in the exploration of the road of sustainable development.

The one-China principle is the political foundation for the establishment and development of China's relations with African countries and regional organizations. The Chinese Government appreciates the fact that the overwhelming majority of African countries abide by the one-China principle, refuse to have official relations and contacts with Taiwan and support China's great cause of reunification. China stands ready to establish and develop state-to-state relations with countries that have not yet established diplomatic ties with China on the basis of the one-China principle.

Part IV: Enhancing All-round Cooperation between China and Africa

1. The political field

(1) High-level visits
China will maintain the momentum of mutual visits and dialogues between Chinese and African leaders, with a view of facilitating communication, deepening friendship and promoting mutual understanding and trust.

(2) Exchanges between legislative bodies
China favors increased multi-level and multi-channel friendly exchanges on the basis of mutual respect between China's National People's Congress (NPC) and parliaments of African countries and the Pan-African Parliament of the AU, for the purpose of deepening understanding and cooperation.

(3) Exchanges between political parties
The Communist Party of China (CPC) develops exchanges of various forms with friendly political parties and organizations of African countries on the basis of the principles of independence, equality, mutual respect and non-interference in each other's internal affairs. The purpose of such exchanges is to increase understanding and friendship and seek trust and cooperation.

(4) Consultation mechanisms
Mechanisms such as national bilateral committees between China and African countries, political consultation between foreign ministries, joint (mixed) committees on trade and economic cooperation and mixed committees on science and technology should be established and improved, so as to institutionalize dialogue and consultation in a flexible and pragmatic manner.

(5) Cooperation in international affairs
China will continue to strengthen solidarity and cooperation with African countries in the international arena, conduct regular exchange of views, coordinate positions on major international and regional issues and stand for mutual support on major issues concerning state sovereignty, territorial integrity, national dignity and human rights. China supports African nations'

desire to be an equal partner in international affairs. China is devoted, as are African nations, to making the United Nations play a greater role, defending the purposes and principles of the UN Charter, establishing a new international political and economic order featuring justice, rationality, equality and mutual benefit, promoting more democratic international relationship and rule of law in international affairs and safeguarding the legitimate rights and interests of developing countries.

(6) Exchanges between local governments
China's Central Government attaches importance to the exchanges between local governments of China and African countries, vigorously supports twin province/state and twin city relationship aimed at facilitating bilateral exchanges and cooperation in local development and administration.

2. The economic field

(1) Trade
The Chinese Government will adopt more effective measures to facilitate African commodities' access to Chinese market and fulfill its promise to grant duty-free treatment to some goods from the least developed African countries, with a view of expanding and balancing bilateral trade and optimizing trade structure. It intends to settle trade disputes and frictions properly through bilateral or multilateral friendly consultation, mutual understanding and mutual accommodation. Efforts will be made to encourage business communities on both sides to set up China-Africa Joint Chamber of Commerce and Industry. When conditions are ripe, China is willing to negotiate Free Trade Agreement (FTA) with African countries and African regional organizations.

(2) Investment
The Chinese Government encourages and supports Chinese enterprises' investment and business in Africa, and will continue to provide preferential loans and buyer credits to this end. The Chinese Government is ready to explore new channels and new ways for promoting investment cooperation with African countries, and will continue to formulate and improve relevant policies, provide guidance and service and offer convenience. African countries are welcome to make investment in China. The Chinese Government

will continue to negotiate, conclude and implement the Agreement on Bilateral Facilitation and Protection of Investment and the Agreement on Avoidance of Double Taxation with African Countries. The two sides should work together to create a favorable environment for investment and cooperation and protect the legitimate rights and interests of investors from both sides.

(3) Financial cooperation
To further develop China-Africa cooperation in the area of finance, the Chinese Government will support the effort of Chinese financial institutions to increase exchanges and cooperation with their counterparts in African countries as well as regional financial institutions in Africa.

(4) Agricultural cooperation
China intends to further promote its agricultural cooperation and exchanges with African nations at various levels, through multiple channels and in various forms. Focus will be laid on the cooperation in land development, agricultural plantation, breeding technologies, food security, agricultural machinery and the processing of agricultural and side-line products. China will intensify cooperation in agricultural technology, organize training courses of practical agricultural technologies, carry out experimental and demonstrative agricultural technology projects in Africa and speed up the formulation of China-Africa Agricultural Cooperation Program.

(5) Infrastructure
The Chinese Government will step up China-Africa cooperation in transportation, telecommunications, water conservancy, electricity and other types of infrastructure. It will vigorously encourage Chinese enterprises to participate in the building of infrastructure in African countries, scale up their contracts, and gradually establish multilateral and bilateral mechanisms on contractual projects. Efforts will be made to strengthen technology and management cooperation, focusing on the capacity-building of African nations.

(6) Resources cooperation
The Chinese Government facilitates information sharing and cooperation with Africa in resources areas. It encourages and supports competent Chinese enterprises to cooperate with African nations in various ways on the basis of the principle of mutual benefit and common development,

to develop and exploit rationally their resources, with a view of helping African countries to translate their advantages in resources to competitive strength, and realize sustainable development in their own countries and the continent as a whole.

(7) Tourism cooperation
China will implement the program of Chinese citizens' group tour to some African nations and, grant more African countries, as they wish and as far as feasible, Approved Destination Status for out-bound Chinese tourist groups. China welcomes citizens from African nations for a tour of the country.

(8) Debt reduction and relief
China is ready to continue friendly consultation with some African countries to seek solution to, or reduction of, the debts they owe to China. It will urge the international community, developed countries in particular, to take more substantial action on the issue of debt reduction and relief for African nations.

(9) Economic assistance
In light of its own financial capacity and economic situation, China will do its best to provide and gradually increase assistance to African nations with no political strings attached.

(10) Multilateral cooperation
China is ready to enhance consultation and coordination with Africa within multilateral trade systems and financial institutions and work together to urge the United Nations and other international organizations to pay more attention to the question of economic development, promote South-South cooperation, push forward the establishment of a just and rational multilateral trade system and make the voices of developing countries heard in the decision-making of international financial affairs. It will step up cooperation with other countries and international organizations to support the development of Africa and help realize Millennium Development Goals in Africa.

3. Education, science, culture, health and social aspects

(1) Cooperation in human resources development and education
The Chinese Government will give full play to the role of its "African Human Resources Development Foundation" in training African personnel. It will

identify priority areas, expand areas of cooperation and provide more input according to the needs of African countries so as to achieve greater results.

Exchange of students between China and Africa will continue. China will increase the number of government scholarships as it sees fit, continue to send teachers to help African countries in Chinese language teaching and carry out educational assistance project to help develop Africa's weak disciplines. It intends to strengthen cooperation in such fields as vocational education and distance learning while encouraging exchanges and cooperation between educational and academic institutions of both sides.

(2) Science and technology cooperation

Following the principles of mutual respect, complementarity and sharing benefits, China will promote its cooperation with Africa in the fields of applied research, technological development and transfer, speed up scientific and technological cooperation in the fields of common interest, such as bio-agriculture, solar energy utilization, geological survey, mining and the R&D of new medicines. It will continue its training programs in applied technologies for African countries, carry out demonstration programs of technical assistance, and actively help disseminate and utilize Chinese scientific and technological achievements and advanced technologies applicable in Africa.

(3) Cultural exchanges

China will implement agreements of cultural cooperation and relevant implementation plans reached with African countries, maintain regular contacts with their cultural departments and increase exchanges of artists and athletes. It will guide and promote cultural exchanges in diverse forms between people's organizations and institutions in line with bilateral cultural exchange programs and market demand.

(4) Medical and health cooperation

China is ready to enhance medical personnel and information exchanges with Africa. It will continue to send medical teams and provide medicines and medical materials to African countries, and help them establish and improve medical facilities and train medical personnel. China will increase its exchanges and cooperation with African countries in the prevention and treatment of infectious diseases including HIV/AIDS and malaria and other diseases, research and application of traditional medicine and experience concerning mechanism for public health emergencies.

(5) Media cooperation
China wishes to encourage multi-tiered and multi-formed exchanges and cooperation between the media on both sides, so as to enhance mutual understanding and enable objective and balanced media coverage of each other. It will facilitate the communication and contacts between relevant government departments for the purpose of sharing experiences on ways to handle the relations with media both domestic and foreign, and guiding and facilitating media exchanges.

(6) Administrative cooperation
China will carry out exchanges and cooperation with African countries in civil service system building, public administration reform and training of government personnel. The two sides may study the feasibility of setting up a mechanism for personnel and administrative cooperation.

(7) Consular cooperation
China will hold regular/irregular consular consultations with African countries during which the two sides may have amicable discussions on urgent problems or questions of common interest in bilateral or multilateral consular relations in order to improve understanding and expand cooperation. The Chinese side will work with Africa to facilitate personnel flow and ensure the safety of their nationals.

(8) People-to-people exchanges
China will encourage and facilitate the exchanges between people's organizations of China and Africa, especially the youth and women, with a view of increasing the understanding, trust and cooperation of people on both sides. It will encourage and guide Chinese volunteers to serve in African countries.

(9) Environmental cooperation
China will actively promote China-Africa cooperation in climate change, water resources conservation, anti-desertification, bio-diversity and other areas of environmental protection by facilitating technological exchanges.

(10) Disaster reduction, relief and humanitarian assistance
China will actively carry out personnel exchange, training and technological cooperation in the fields of disaster reduction and relief. It will respond quickly to African countries' request for urgent humanitarian aid, encourage and support exchanges and cooperation between the Red Cross Society

of China and other NGOs on the one side and their African counterparts on the other side.

4. Peace and security

(1) Military cooperation
China will promote high-level military exchanges between the two sides and actively carry out military-related technological exchanges and cooperation. It will continue to help train African military personnel and support defense and army building of African countries for their own security.

(2) Conflict settlement and peacekeeping operations
China supports the positive efforts by the AU and other African regional organizations and African countries concerned to settle regional conflicts and will provide assistance within our own capacity. It will urge the UN Security Council to pay attention to and help resolve regional conflicts in Africa. It will continue its support to and participation in UN peacekeeping operations in Africa.

(3) Judicial and police cooperation
China is prepared to promote the exchanges and cooperation between Chinese and African judicial and law enforcement departments. The two sides may learn from each other in legal system building and judicial reform so as to be better able to prevent, investigate and crack down on crimes. China will work together with African countries to combat transnational organized crimes and corruption, and intensify cooperation on matters concerning judicial assistance, extradition and repatriation of criminal suspects.

China will cooperate closely with immigration departments of African countries in tackling the problem of illegal migration, improve exchange of immigration control information and set up an unimpeded and efficient channel for intelligence and information exchange.

(4) Non-traditional security areas
In order to enhance the ability of both sides to address non-traditional security threats, it is necessary to increase intelligence exchange, explore more effective ways and means for closer cooperation in combating terrorism, small arms smuggling, drug trafficking, transnational economic crimes, etc.

Part V: Forum on China-Africa Cooperation and Its Follow-up Actions

Launched in 2000, the Forum on China-Africa Cooperation has become an effective mechanism for the collective dialogue and multilateral cooperation between China and Africa and put in place an important framework and platform for a new type of China-Africa partnership featuring long-term stability, equality and mutual benefit.

China attaches importance to the positive role of the Forum on China-Africa Cooperation in strengthening political consultation and pragmatic cooperation between China and Africa, and stands ready to work with African countries to conscientiously implement the Beijing Declaration of the Forum on China-Africa Cooperation, the Program for China-Africa Cooperation in Economic and Social Development and the Forum on China-Africa Cooperation-Addis Ababa Action Plan (2004–2006) and its follow-up action plans. China will work with African countries within the framework of the Forum to explore new ways to enhance mutual political trust, promote the comprehensive development of pragmatic cooperation, further improve the mechanism of the forum, and try to find the best way for furthering cooperation between the Forum and the NEPAD.

Part VI: China's Relations with African Regional Organizations

China appreciates the significant role of the AU in safeguarding peace and stability in the region and promoting African solidarity and development. China values its friendly cooperation with the AU in all fields, supports its positive role in regional and international affairs and stands ready to provide the AU assistance to the best of its capacity.

China appreciates and supports the positive role of Africa's sub-regional organizations in promoting political stability, economic development and integration in their own regions and stands ready to enhance its amicable cooperation with those organizations.

Appendix 2: Chinese Footprints in Angola

Menounge Railway Station. Photo taken by Anton van Schalkwyk

Kuito Railway Station. Photo taken by Anton van Schalkwyk

Kilamba Kiaxi

China International Fund (CIF) HQ in Luanda (Luanda One Building). Photo taken by Sam Seyffert

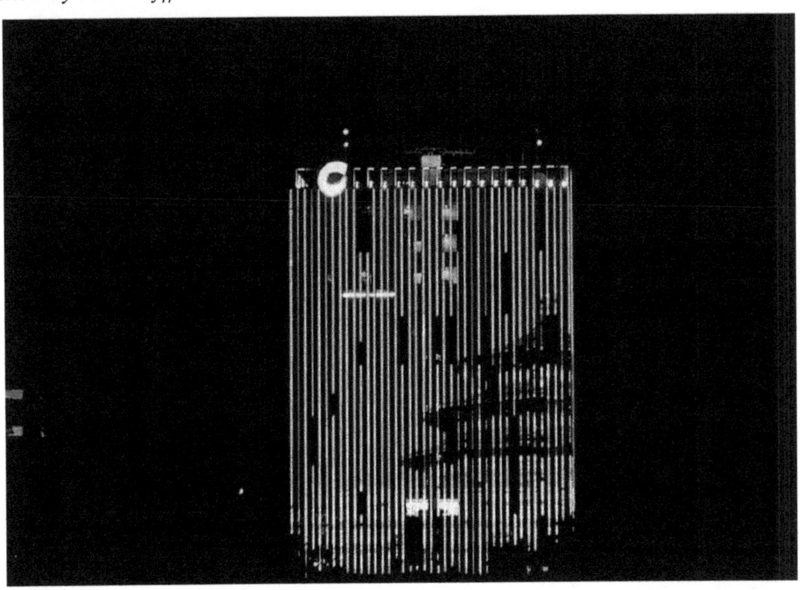

A Rail Crossing Warning Sign in Angola Written Both in Chinese and Portuguese Languages. Photo taken by Jose de Palma

Appendix 3: Map of Angola

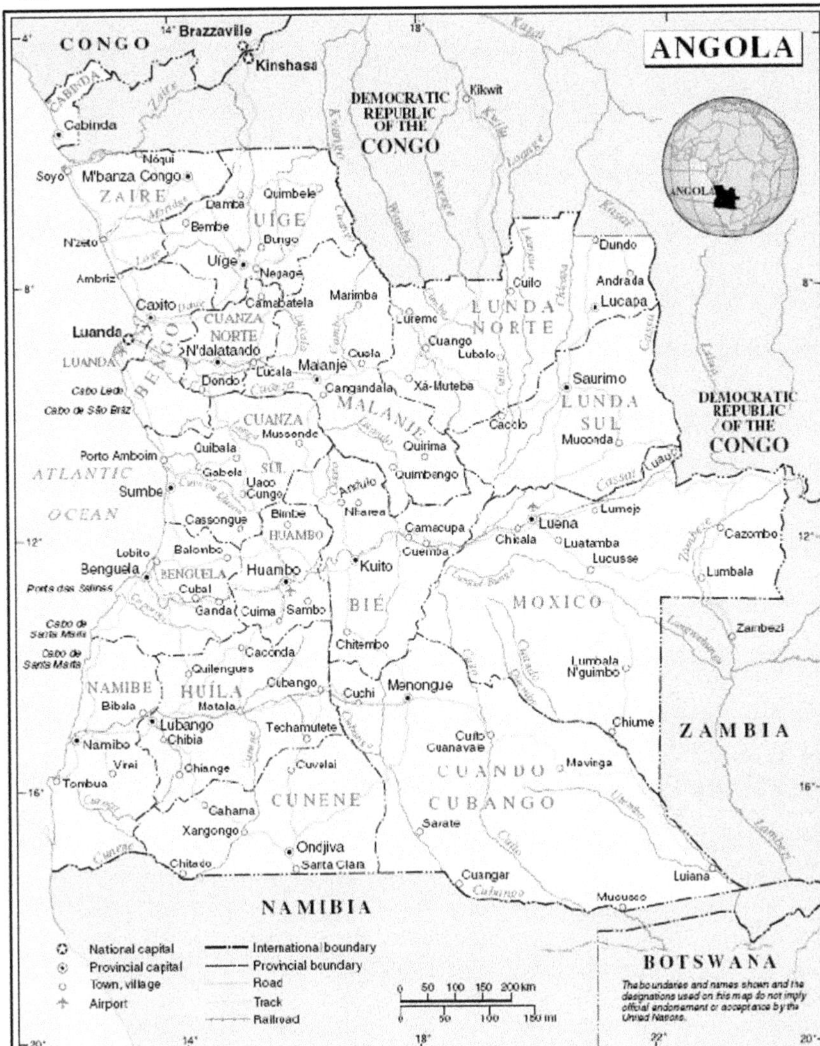

Map No. 3727 Rev. 5 UNITED NATIONS
January 2004

Department of Peacekeeping Operations
Cartographic Section

www.ingramcontent.com/pod-product-compliance
Ingram Content Group UK Ltd.
Pitfield, Milton Keynes, MK11 3LW, UK
UKHW021842100926
8556IPUK00019B/1009

9 783631 670354